COLOUR PREJUDICE

COLOUR PREJUDICE

WITH PARTICULAR REFERENCE
TO THE RELATIONSHIP
BETWEEN WHITES
AND NEGROES

By

SIR ALAN BURNS

G.C.M.G.,

*Formerly Governor and Commander-in-Chief
of the Gold Coast*

Magale Library
Southern Arkansas University
Magnolia, Arkansas

NEGRO UNIVERSITIES PRESS
WESTPORT, CONNECTICUT

Copyright 1948

Originally published in 1948
by George Allen & Unwin Ltd., London

Reprinted with the permission
of George Allen & Unwin Ltd.

Reprinted in 1971 by Negro Universities Press
Division of Greenwood Press, Inc.
Westport, Connecticut

Library of Congress Catalogue Card Number 70-155383

ISBN 0-8371-6076-6

Printed in the United States of America

"It is not intended to incite resentment and stimulate animosities. . . . If in the process the sensibilities of some may be wounded, it must be laid, not to intent, but to that unavoidable consequence that sometimes accompanies the revelation of unpleasant truths."
What the Negro Thinks
by R. R. Moton, p. vi.

"Those who have a real faith need not be afraid to look facts in the face"
Christianity and the Race Problem,
by J. H. Oldham, p. 66.

"Chi K'ang asked Confucius how to rule. Confucius answered: To rule is to set straight. If ye give an upright lead, Sir, who will dare walk crooked?"
The Sayings of Confucius,
trans. by L. A. Lyall, 2nd ed., p. 55.

"There is no difference in kind between man and man . . . in fact, there is no human being of any race who, if he finds a guide, cannot attain to virtue."
Cicero, *De Legibus*, I, 10.

CORRIGENDA

Page 49. Line 3. The reference is to the second note on page 48.

Page 68. Note 1. For "page 7" *read* "page 12".

Contents

INTRODUCTION   *Page* 9

I. The Existence and Growth of Colour Prejudice   15

II. The Attitude of Various Peoples to Racial and Colour Differences   28

III. Negro Resentment of Colour Prejudice   38

IV. Political and Legal Discrimination Against Negroes   46

V. Social Discrimination Against Negroes   60

VI. Alleged Inferiority of the Negro   75

VII. Alleged Shortcomings of the Negro   86

VIII. Physical and Mental Differences between the Races   97

IX. Physical Repulsion between Races   108

X. Miscegenation   116

XI. The Effect of Environment and History on the Negro Race   127

XII. Lack of Unity and Inferiority Complex Among Negroes   137

XIII. Conclusion   145

Index to Authors, Persons, and Publications referred to   152

General Index   156

INTRODUCTION

THERE is a popular belief among the British that their vast colonial empire is kept intact by the British genius for governing inferior races. Errors of judgment admittedly occur from time to time in particular cases, but it is generally felt that the British system of colonial administration is the best in the world, and that the coloured inhabitants of our numerous dependencies appreciate the blessings of our rule and would be reluctant to exchange it for any other, or even for independence.

To a certain extent this belief is justified. The Negro inhabitants of the British West Indies, for instance, are among the most loyal subjects of the Crown, and would passionately resent any action which would exclude them from the Empire. I believe that the inhabitants of British West Africa are as loyal.

Though I am admittedly prejudiced in the matter, I believe also that, with all its defects, British colonial administration is better than that of any other Power for, and more acceptable to, a large proportion of the inhabitants of our tropical dependencies,[1] namely, the more primitive peoples and those, chiefly of the Muslim faith, who have retained their own culture to the exclusion of our own.[2] There is, however, a considerable minority, increasing each year in numbers and importance, who, although they would probably wish to remain within the British Empire, are resentful of British colonial government. This minority includes most of the coloured inhabitants of the West Indies, and Africans who, for one reason or another, have become divorced from their native culture, who have received an English education of some kind, and who aspire to the privileges of the Englishman and the practical realisation of that equality which they theoretically enjoy as British subjects.

[1] An American writer says that "it is under the Englishman that I think the black man has the best chance to progress, and will receive the fairest-minded treatment while he is doing it." *Behind God's Back* (1940), by Negley Farson, p. 435.

[2] Lord Cromer has written in this connection: "My own experience certainly leads me to the conclusion that the British generally, though they succeed less well when once the full tide of education has set in, possess in a very high degree the power of acquiring the sympathy and confidence of any primitive races with which they are brought in contact." *Ancient and Modern Imperialism* (1910), p. 75.

It is often stated that, in colonial administration, while the British official is at his best with races still organised on a tribal basis,[1] he cannot compare with his French colleague in dealing with more advanced and educated coloured peoples. It would not be strange if this were so, for the Frenchman excels the Englishman in logic. It is not, for instance, logical to give the African an English education and then for some Englishmen to give the impression that they resent the existence of 'educated natives'; to teach the African the superiority of English law over native custom and then to condemn him when he clamours for more of it; to tell him that all men are equal before the law and then to deny him the equality which he claims. To the class of educated African to which I am referring, the French system should appear preferable to ours,[2] yet I do not believe that any British West Africans would wish to come under the French flag.

Puzzled by the curious failure of the educated Negro to appreciate fully the advantages of British rule, some have been led to regard this failure as evidence of the unfortunate results of education, or of an inexplicable perversity. Moreover, the comparatively small number of this class in Africa has tended to a disregard or neglect of its discontents, and to a lack of study of the causes of these discontents. The energies of the Colonial Service have, therefore, been directed rather towards the more responsive elements in the population, which include the majority of the inhabitants of British

[1] "As for the dealings of British officials with native populations, one generalisation may fairly be made. They run more smoothly, and show more of friendliness and mutual confidence, when they touch the tribal people than when they touch the African intelligentsia." *Empire or Democracy* (1939), by Leonard Barnes, p. 97.

[2] The different systems of the Colonial Powers were summarised by Lord Lugard in a paper read to the Royal Empire Society: *Some Colonial Problems of Today*; see *United Empire* for December, 1936, p. 666. Speaking of British rule in India, the French statesman, Clemenceau, has said: "Your English officers are rough with the Indians; they do not mingle with them at all; but they defer to their political opinions. That is the wrong way round. Frenchmen would be much more intimate but we should not allow them to dispute our principles of Government." See *Great Contemporaries* (1937), by Winston S. Churchill, p. 314. Lord Hailey points out that although the French are less tolerant of criticism from the Press or in speeches at public meetings their attitude is "less provocative than some others of a sense of social inferiority on the part of the subject race." *An African Survey* (1938), p. 254. See also references to the differences between British and French officials in *Africans learn to be French* (1937), by W. Bryant Mumford (in consultation with G. St. J. Orde-Browne), p. 68; and *The Atlantic and Emancipation* (1937), by H. A. Wyndham, p. xiii. See also page 29 below.

INTRODUCTION

Africa. Stimulated by the teaching of Lord Lugard and Sir Donald Cameron,[1] a very great interest has been shown in the theory and practice of 'Indirect Administration,' and the problems of this form of government have been carefully examined.[2] It is undoubtedly an admirable form of government for those to whom it can be applied,[3] but it is obviously impossible to apply it to the class of educated Negroes to which I am referring.[4] As I have said, this class is a growing one, and its needs and aspirations must be studied. It is admittedly a more difficult class to govern than that to which 'indirect' rule can be applied, but it cannot be airily dismissed from consideration as no more than a 'noisy minority.' The educated West Indian and the educated African (and, for that matter, the Negro in the United States) are faced with problems which differ superficially, but are in fact identical. The one problem at the bottom of all their troubles, and the one for which they passionately seek a solution, is how they are to obtain from the white world that recognition of social and political equality which has, up to now, been denied them. The object of this book is to suggest how a beginning can be made towards the granting of that recognition.

It is not an easy matter to overcome colour prejudice. Only those who have never lived in countries where people of different colours mingle can overlook the difficulties, and the unfortunate effects, of colour prejudice. This prejudice is the cause of many administrative difficulties. It interferes with economic, political

[1] I had the privilege of serving on the personal staff of both of these distinguished administrators.
[2] The student is referred to Lord Lugard's *The Dual Mandate in British Tropical Africa* (1922), and Sir Donald Cameron's memorandum on *The Principles of Native Administration and their Application* (1934). See also *My Tanganyika Service and Some Nigeria* (1939), by Sir Donald Cameron, and *Native Administration in Nigeria* (1937), by Miss Margery Perham.
[3] Mr. R. R. Oakley, formerly a District Officer in Nigeria, has pointed out in *Treks and Palavers* (1938), p. 41: "This is the great advantage of 'Indirect Rule,' that it does not lower a subject-race's self-respect. The two races travel together on parallel lines; the more advanced fostering and encouraging the more backward, but allowing it to retain its dignity and all that is best in its own civilisation." Some of the possible dangers of 'Indirect Administration' are, however, suggested in *Nigeria* (1936), by W. R. Crocker, p. 215 *et seq*.
[4] Lord Cromer has pointed out that "the country over which the breath of the West, heavily charged with scientific thought, has once passed, and has, in passing, left an enduring mark, can never be the same as it was before." *Ancient and Modern Imperialism* (1910), p. 120.

and even educational advance in the tropical colonies. It is present, even when not consciously felt, in the relations of white traders, teachers, missionaries and officials, to the coloured inhabitants, and there is a reaction on the part of the coloured peoples which obstructs policies intended for their benefit.[1] It may be impossible to eradicate colour prejudice altogether, but it should be easy, given sufficient good-will, to remove some of its more unpleasant manifestations, and so lessen its effect, by no more than the avoidance of discourtesy.

Although colour prejudice exists in all quarters of the globe, my personal experience has been limited to British colonies in West Africa and the West Indies, where the problem is confined mainly to the relationship between whites and Negroes, and it is this aspect of the question that I have dealt with in this book.[2] When I first contemplated writing it I was stationed in Nigeria, and there I had happily reached such a degree of mutual understanding with some of my African friends that we could discuss frankly the difficult and delicate questions of race and colour. One of the most distinguished Africans I have known, the late Dr. Henry Carr, had agreed to collaborate with me in the work, but my transfer to British Honduras made this arrangement impossible, and, by so doing, greatly reduced the value of the book. I was fortunate in having the opportunity, in 1942, of letting Dr. Carr read the manuscript and made several amendments on his suggestion.

There is one important point that must not be overlooked in dealing with the subject of colour prejudice, or, indeed, of other prejudices. In such matters a state of mind or a firm belief in something that is not true is just as real and important as a fact itself. If one man thinks that another is inferior to him the result of such thought is scarcely affected by its possible absurdity. I do not believe that the Negro is inherently inferior to the white man (although to-day he is in fact inferior in many respects) but it seems to me

---

[1] In his *Warning from the West Indies* (1936), p. 46, Professor W. M. Macmillan says that "the efforts of modern officials to help . . . and develop the country have to face unreasoning suspicion that their promoters are no more disinterested than earlier Governments in the days of slave-owning."

[2] If most of the examples of racial prejudice, and most of the quotations, in this book refer to the United States and the Union of South Africa, this is because comparatively little is written in the colonies on this subject.

INTRODUCTION

that the point is of little practical importance at the moment; what is more important is the fact that many people believe he is inherently inferior, and that, because of this, he may be treated with a lack of political consideration and a disregard for the elementary principles of courtesy. My personal belief, or the belief of any other individual, is in itself of little consequence. It is the cumulative effect of such beliefs, *and the way in which they have been expressed*, that has developed colour prejudice to its present point. For this reason I have considered it desirable to quote freely from many different authors, not generally available to the ordinary reader, in order that this reader may see for himself what has been said, and is still being said, on this important subject.[1] I have quoted those who consider that the Negro is an inferior type of humanity (and some who would deny that he is even human) in order to show how thoughtlessly cruel such writers can be, and I have quoted also some of the bitter and intemperate remarks drawn from Negroes by this very cruelty. With more satisfaction, I have quoted the weighty and carefully chosen words of those who deplore colour prejudice, while recognising its existence, who realise that it can do no good to dwell on the unhappy past, and prefer to seek some way of improving the present and the future.

There is a tendency in our tropical dependencies to classify all white men as negrophobe or negrophile. I see no necessity to be either. I like some Negroes and dislike other Negroes—as I like some white men and dislike others. Never have I consciously liked or disliked a man on account of the colour of his skin, and despite assertions to the contrary, I believe that there are large numbers of other white men in the Colonies who are ready to judge a Negro by his conduct rather than by his colour. Unfortunately, under existing conditions the Negro will not give any white man credit for this. Any action or decision unfavourable to a Negro is immediately attributed to a malignant hostility to the Negro race, and a determination to keep it down; the merits of the case are of no consequence. This attitude will continue as long as colour prejudice lasts.

I have endeavoured to write frankly on a problem that is both difficult and delicate. If in doing so I wound the susceptibilities of others, I can only express regret for what I must ask them to believe

[1] The date of publication of each book quoted has been given.

is unintentional. It is, in my opinion, better that the difficulties should be clearly seen and realised, with a view to their removal, than that they should be allowed to fester in private and be ignored in public, as they so often are by all but the most bitter speakers and writers on the subject of colour prejudice.[1]

ALAN BURNS.

[1] An important recent publication of the United States Government Printing Office, *The Report of the President's Committee on Civil Rights* (1947), confirms much that is written in this book of the treatment of Negroes in America, especially as regards lynching, segregation and the denial of the suffrage.

Chapter I

THE EXISTENCE AND GROWTH OF COLOUR PREJUDICE

THAT race and colour prejudice[1] exist to-day is not disputed, and, unhappily, is indisputable. An intense nationalism has grown up during the last hundred years, and the horrors of war, and the anxieties of armed peace, have done nothing to check its growth. Side by side with the rise of nationalism a worse evil has increased, the evil of race prejudice. This fact is appreciated by men of every shade of thought, and a Study Group of Members of the Royal Institute of International Affairs has expressed the opinion that "the discontent of native populations, exhibited from time to time in sporadic revolt, is undoubtedly often due to the handling of the colour question, and no satisfactory solution of the colonial problem can be reached without its adjustment."[2]

Dr. DuBois, a prominent Negro leader in the United States, says that "the problem of the twentieth century is the problem of the colour line—the relation of the darker to the lighter races of men in Asia and Africa, in America and in the islands of the sea."[3] Mr. Oldham, Secretary of the International Missionary Council from 1921-38, considers that racial prejudice "is a sinister fact in the life of the world today."[4] Sir Reginald Coupland, Beit Professor of Colonial History at Oxford, points out that "the Colour Problem is most urgent and most critical in Asia. It is most difficult and morally most dangerous in Africa."[5]

---

[1] Racial prejudice and colour prejudice are not the same, but for the purpose of this book there is no need to distinguish between them.
[2] *The Colonial Problem*, A Report by a Study Group of Members of the Royal Institute of International Affairs, p. 126.
[3] *The Souls of Black Folk* (1903), by W. E. B. DuBois, 2nd ed., p. 13.
[4] *Christianity and the Race Problem* (1924), by J. H. Oldham, 7th ed., p. 30.
[5] *The Empire in These Days* (1935), by R. Coupland, p. 21.

A number of other writers[1] have stressed the importance and urgency of the problem, and Mr. Noel-Baker, a Minister in the Labour Government, has shown that it is one in respect of which the citizens of the British Empire have a special and a grave responsibility.[2]

What exactly is meant by race and colour prejudice? It is nothing more than the unreasoning hatred of one race for another, the contempt of the stronger and richer peoples for those whom they consider inferior to themselves, and the bitter resentment of those who are kept in subjection and are so frequently insulted. As colour is the most obvious outward manifestation of race it has been made the criterion by which men are judged, irrespective of their social or educational attainments. The light-skinned races have come to despise all those of a darker colour, and the dark-skinned peoples will no longer accept without protest the inferior position to which they have been relegated.

It is a mistake to think that the intense race and colour prejudice which now exists is a phenomenon which followed the war of 1914–18; prejudice had been growing steadily for years, and, writing in 1912, Sir John Harris, Secretary to the Anti-Slavery and Aborigines Protection Society, referred to the growth of race prejudice in British West Africa, in spite of the increase of commerce and the spread of Christian thought.[3] There is no doubt, however, that prejudice increased considerably after the first world war, especially in those countries where the white and coloured races were in

[1] See *Africa and Some World Problems* (1929), by Field-Marshal J. C. Smuts, Prime Minister of South Africa, pp. 29–30; *The Clash of Colour* (1924), by B. Matthews, Professor of Christian World-Relations in the University of Boston, p. 5; *The Duty of Empire* (1935), by Leonard Barnes, pp. 142, 305; *The Clash of Culture and the Contact of Races* (1927), by G. H. Lane-Fox Pitt-Rivers, Honorary General Secretary of the International Union for the Scientific Investigation of Population Problems, p. 25.

[2] *The Problem of Colour in Relation to the Idea of Equality* (Supplement to vol. 1, no. 2, of the *Journal of Philosophical Studies*), p. 3. Mr. Noel-Baker points out that "in many parts of the Empire there are race and colour problems, not only of great and increasing importance, but in some cases of tragic significance for the future welfare of the peoples concerned. . . . No one can doubt that in the last fifty years the contact which has taken place has led to the growth of dangerous dogmas, which are not founded on fact, but which are as potent in political and social relationship as if they were the epitome of truth."

[3] *Dawn in Darkest Africa* (1912), by J. H. Harris, p. 122.

THE EXISTENCE AND GROWTH OF COLOUR PREJUDICE

economic or social rivalry.[1] Professor Gregory considers that "the progress of humanity is embarrassed by the rising tide of colour prejudice,"[2] and even in England the treatment of coloured persons had deteriorated: "Indians and Africans who visit this country report with striking unanimity the growing frequency with which they are subject to insults and indignities by boorish 'Nordic' self-consciousness."[3]

It is probable that race and colour prejudice has always existed where races have been brought into contact on a considerable scale through wars of conquest or in economic rivalry, although the prejudice may have been hidden by religious and other feelings. It is not unnatural that the conquerors should despise the conquered race, as the Normans despised the English after the Battle of Hastings, and that they should attribute their victory to innate superiority. Especially when the conquered people practised a different religion would they be looked down upon by those whose God had given them victory.[4]

Professor Toynbee, Director of Studies in the Royal Institute of International Affairs, maintains, however, that our modern Western race-feeling did not come into existence until the last quarter of the

[1] It is said, for instance, that prejudice has increased in the northern United States owing to the large numbers of Negroes who have moved north. See *America Comes of Age* (1927), by A. Siegfried, p. 104.

[2] *The Menace of Colour* (1925), by J. S. Gregory, 2nd ed., preface.

[3] *The Duty of Empire* (1935), by Leonard Barnes, p. 307. An African lady is also quoted as comparing present conditions in England with those existing in Victorian days when she and her sisters were at school there. "We were the only Africans," she says, "but we never knew we were black till we looked in the glass. There was not the slightest difference made in any shape or form between the other girls and ourselves. If anything we were rather more favoured, because we were strangers in a strange land." Letter from Adelaide Caseley-Hayford, contained in *Negro Anthology* (1934) (edited by Nancy Cunard), p. 763. The increase of prejudice in England is probably due to the increasing number of Africans who visit this country. While I deplore this increase of prejudice, I agree with Sir Bernard Bourdillon that "the enthusiast . . . must not go to the other extreme. To treat every man and woman with a coloured skin as if they were Royalty is just as foolish as to treat them as if they were inferiors, and has the most unfortunate reactions when they go back to their own country." See *The Future of the Colonial Empire* (1945), p. 82.

[4] A typical case was that of the Spaniards in Peru. Before the massacre which occurred when the Inca Atahuallpa was seized, Pizarro assured his men that God was on their side, and thanksgivings were afterwards offered up to Heaven "which had shown itself thus favourable to the Christian throughout this mighty enterprise." *The History of the Conquest of Peru*, by W. H. Prescott (Complete Works), pp. 360, 455.

fifteenth century. Before that time, he says, "instead of dividing mankind, as we do, into White people and Coloured people, our forefathers divided it into Christians and Heathens; and we are bound to confess that their dichotomy was better than ours . . . because a human being's religion is a vastly more important and significant factor in his life than the colour of his skin (and) . . . because the gulf between religions, unlike the gulf between races, is not impassable."[1]

Other authorities have maintained that there is no direct evidence of any racial hostility or antipathy, based on a difference of colour, until comparatively modern times.

Lord Cromer did not think that there was "any distinct indication that colour antipathy existed to any marked extent in the ancient world" and conjectured that "antipathy based on differences of colour is a plant of comparatively recent growth."[2] Lord Bryce was more definite in his conclusion that there was very little self-conscious racial feeling in any country until the days of the French Revolution.[3] He points out that we hear little of any repugnance in the Roman Empire to the dark-skinned Africans,[4] but admits that evidence of racial feeling can be found among the Greeks and Phoenicians.[5] Again, although he maintains that the national sentiment of Israel was religious rather than racial,[6] he notes that the Israelites were willing to intermarry with Amorites, Hittites and Jebusites, and to adopt their gods.[7] In this connection it is interesting to recall that Moses incurred the displeasure of his

[1] *A Study of History* (1935), by Arnold J. Toynbee, vol. 1, pp. 223–4. When the Dutch first settled in South Africa "the line of distinction between groups was less affected by differences of race or colour of skin than by differences of religion . . . a non-European at the Cape, once he had been baptised, was immediately accepted as a member of the Christian community and, as such, was entitled to his freedom, if a slave. . . . The only bar to intermarriage was one of religion." *Race Attitudes in South Africa* (1937), by I. D. MacCrone, pp. 41 and 8.

[2] *Ancient and Modern Imperialism* (1910), by the Earl of Cromer, pp. 140–1. Lord Cromer suggests that the difference between the attitude of the ancients and the moderns may be due to the fact that the former doomed all conquered peoples to slavery while the latter enslaved only the coloured races.

[3] *Race Sentiment as a Factor in History* (Creighton Lecture, 1915), by James Bryce, pp. 25–6.

[4] *Relations of the Advanced and the Backward Races of Mankind* (Romanes Lecture, 1902), by James Bryce, p. 18.

[5] *Race Sentiment as a Factor in History* (1915), by James Bryce, p. 25.

[6] *Ibid.*, p. 10.   [7] *Ibid.*, p. 10.

brother and sister on account of a *mésalliance* with an Ethiopian woman,[1] and the fifth and sixth verses of the first chapter of the Song of Solomon read very much like an apology.

It is probable also that the caste system of India, the exact origin of which is obscure, was founded on a diversity of race and perhaps of colour, and there seems to be no doubt that the depressed classes are remnants of conquered peoples.[2] Many writers maintain that caste is due to the determination of Aryan conquerors to keep their white blood pure,[3] and it is important to note that the word used for caste is the Sanscrit word *varna*, which means 'colour.' As a colour-line, however, caste seems to have worked very imperfectly,[4] and the system has survived long after the diversity of race and colour which first evoked it has been obliterated.[5] The tendency in Hindu society for castes to become coincident with occupations is worthy of note,[6] as is the fact that similar conditions existed in Peru under the rule of the Incas, occupations and offices descending from father to son.[7]

It is related in the *Mahabharata* that "when the Creator made men and divided them into four colours, then he assigned to each the conduct that should be proper to him."[8] This is a similar idea to that conveyed in *Genesis*, "cursed be Canaan; a servant of servants shall he be unto his brethren,"[9] and this text has been

[1] Numbers xii. 1.
[2] *Encyclopaedia Britannica*, 14th ed., vol. 4, p. 978.
[3] See, for example, *The Living India, Its Romance and Realities* (1934), by Lt.-General Sir George MacMunn, p. 49. For the opposite view see *Hindu Customs and their Origins* (1937), by S. Rice.
[4] *Clashing Tides of Colour* (1935), by Lothrop Stoddard, p. 285.
[5] *A Study of History* (1935), by Arnold J. Toynbee, vol. 1, p. 243.
[6] Ibid., vol. 2, p. 217.
[7] *The History of the Conquest of Peru*, by W. H. Prescott (Complete Works), p. 141.
[8] Article by Mr. J. H. Driberg in *The Spectator* of June 11, 1931.
[9] Gen. x, 25. In 1852 there was published a curious book by an American clergyman in which an attempt is made to prove that Noah's curse of Ham fully justified slavery. *A Bible Defence of Slavery* by the Reverend Josiah Priest, p. 91 *et seq*. See also the famous "cornerstone" speech of A. H. Stevens, at Savannah, Georgia, on March 21, 1861, ". . . the negro by nature or by the curse against Canaan, is fitted for that condition which he occupies in our system. . . . It is indeed, in conformity with the Creator. It is not for us to enquire into the wisdom of His ordinances or to question them. For His own purposes He has made one race to differ from another as He has made 'one star to differ from another in glory.'" *The Rebellion Record* (1861), edited by Frank Moore, vol. 1, p. 46.

skilfully used to justify and enforce by the aid of religion what could not be maintained by the use of the civil law alone.¹

Many analogies might be drawn between the caste system of India and the inter-racial distinctions now existing in, say, the United States of America, both resting on a theory of unchangeable social status.² In India the most important aspect of caste is the restriction on marriage which it imposes, and the neglect of caste distinctions in this matter is unheard of:³ in many of the United States the marriage of white and coloured persons is prohibited by law. Again, to a Hindu his caste is the determining factor in his life, and the opportunity of the census of 1921 "was therefore seized by all but the highest castes to press for recognition of social claims and to secure, if possible, a step upwards in the social ladder":⁴ the efforts of some of the lighter-skinned coloured persons in the United States to 'pass' into the white race are referred to in later chapters.⁵

In the circumstances, it is difficult to maintain that colour prejudice is a modern phenomenon, and did not exist in the ancient world. That there is little record of it is due probably to the comparatively few coloured persons who made their way into Europe:⁶ there is little colour prejudice even to-day in those countries where a coloured person is seldom seen. There is no doubt, however, that race and colour prejudice increased considerably soon after the discovery of America and of the sea route to India round the Cape of Good Hope. Economic reasons, and the growing spirit of nationalism, made this inevitable, and the superiority of the white races over all others was soon accepted as a matter of course.

¹ It is inconsistent to condemn the caste system of India, which is at least sanctioned by the religion of those who apply it, while our own religion is contrary to the spirit of the colour bar which is maintained by so many Christians. See *The Colour Bar* (1937), by Peter Nielsen, p. 117. It has been suggested that the British courts in India, "inspired by principles drawn from an alien civilisation," have made caste restrictions more rigid. "Caste and marriage, for instance, which under Indian law were continually undergoing adaptation and development, have become hardened and stereotyped under the decisions of the new courts." Essay by S. H. Swinny on "The Humanitarianism of the Eighteenth Century and its Results," in *Western Races and the World* (1922) (edited by F. S. Marvin), p. 137.
² See *The Anatomy of African Misery* (1927), by Lord Olivier, p. 135; and *The Menace of Colour* (1925), by J. W. Gregory, 2nd ed., preface.
³ *Report on the Census of India, 1921*, vol. I, p. 232.
⁴ *Ibid.*, p. 223. ⁵ See page 122.
⁶ See *Race Sentiment as a Factor in History* (1915), by Lord Bryce, p. 14.

THE EXISTENCE AND GROWTH OF COLOUR PREJUDICE

For the belief of the white men in their own superiority there was much material justification. They had held the gates of Christendom against Mongol and Turk and Moor, and had preserved in some measure the remains of Roman civilisation and order. They had crossed uncharted seas and Europe was growing rich with the spoils of other lands. A Spanish force of less than 600 men, under Cortez, had seized the empire of Mexico; Pizarro, with a still smaller force, had conquered Peru. Everywhere that the white races met those of darker hue they proved themselves invincible.

Following the discovery of America and the West Indies, moreover, the African slave trade came into being, and there can be no doubt that this trade developed enormously the white man's pride and his contempt for the Negro.[1] The slaves themselves were ignorant savages and their heathen customs were despised by the Christian people who bought them like cattle and transported them across the ocean, under unspeakable conditions, to a life of endless servitude. The chiefs who sold the slaves were brutalised by the trade itself and by the liquor which financed it, while European contemporaries ignored their own responsibilities for Negro degradation, and saw only the evil effects of slavery on a primitive race. The white races did not introduce slavery,[2] which had existed in Africa from immemorial times, but they contributed to the system their genius for organisation and multiplied its evils.

When doubts as to the justice of the slave trade began to disturb the Christian conscience, the existing contempt for the Negro was, no doubt, deliberately fostered by the advocates of slavery. Bosman, an early visitor to West Africa, writing at the beginning of the eighteenth century, says that "The Negroes are all without exception crafty, Villainous and Fraudulent . . . and it would be very surprising if upon a scrutiny into their Lives we should find any of them whose perverse Nature would not break out sometimes; for they seem to be born and bred Villains."[3] It was apparently not difficult to find excuses for Negro slavery. The Bible proclaimed the curse of Canaan, and the Reverend Thomas Thompsont after years of devoted missionary work on the Gold Coast, felt

[1] See *Ancient and Modern Imperialism* (1910), by the Earl of Cromer, p. 142.
[2] This is a point that must be emphasised as it is too often overlooked.
[3] *A New and Accurate Description of the Coast of Guinea*, by William Bosman (1705), p. 117.

justified in publishing, in 1772, a pamphlet entitled *The African Trade for Negro Slaves shown to be consistent with the principles of Humanity and with the Laws of Revealed Religion*.[1]

The Spaniards are said to have excused their ill-treatment of the natives of America and the West Indies on the ground that they were not the descendants of Adam and Eve,[2] and as it was possible, so late as the year 1900, for an American author to argue that the Negro, not being human, could have no soul, and that "all scientific investigation of the subject proves the Negro to be an ape,"[3] it is not surprising to find that, in the early days of slavery, fantastic theories were advanced to justify the enslavement of the blacks. It was maintained that whites and blacks were of different species, and, in spite of the large number of living witnesses to the contrary, it was held that the two races could not successfully interbreed, the alleged sterility[4] of the offspring, the 'Mulatto,'[5]

[1] See also *A Bible Defence of Slavery*, by the Reverend Josiah Priest, published in America in 1852. A list is given in a footnote on page 423 of *The Fall of the Planter Class in the British Caribbean, 1763–1833* (1929), by L. J. Ragatz, of pamphlets, etc., published by clerical advocates of the continuance of slavery. The Society for the Propagation of the Gospel, as trustees for sugar estates in Barbados which formed part of the endowment of Codrington College in that island, were slave owners, and did not emancipate their slaves until 1834.

[2] *We Europeans* (1935), by Julian S. Huxley and A. C. Haddon, p. 46.

[3] *The Negro a Beast or in the Image of God?* (1900), by C. Carroll, p. 87. One of the chapters of this remarkable work is headed "Convincing Biblical and Scientific evidence that the Negro is not of the human family." Even Herr Hitler did not go as far as this as he considered the Negro to be only a "half-ape." *Mein Kampf* (trans., published by Reynal and Hitchcock, New York, 1939), p. 640. Mr. Carroll was also the author of a yet more remarkable book, *The Tempter of Eve* (1902), which declared that "all the circumstances indicate that the beast of the field which tempted Eve was a *negress*, who served Eve in the capacity of a maid servant"; p. 402. See also note 4 on page 63.

[4] It has been suggested that an explanation of the alleged sterility of the Mulatto lies in the fact that the lighter coloured tend to 'pass over' to the white race and to be assimilated therein, their children being counted as white. See page 122.

[5] The Mulatto (through the Spanish and Portuguese *mulato*, diminutive of *mulo*, from the latin *mulus*, a mule, used as denoting a hybrid origin) is a person one of whose parents is of the white race and the other a Negro. The first use of the word in English, as recorded by the Oxford Dictionary, was in 1595, when the word was spelt 'Mulatow.' The word is now often, but incorrectly, used to describe any light-coloured person with Negro blood, although there are words to describe most of the degrees of crossing between whites and blacks. Thus the 'Quadroon' is the offspring of a white and a Mulatto and the 'Octoroon' the offspring of a Quadroon and a white; other words are 'Mustee,' 'Terceron' and 'Quintroon.' The 'Sambo' is the offspring of Negro and Mulatto, while the 'Mestizo' is the child of white and Indian.

being regarded as conclusive proof of the specific distinctness of black and white.[1] Although the alleged proof had long been discredited, Darwin thought it necessary, as late as the second half of the nineteenth century, to examine carefully the evidence for and against the identity of species, including the question of the fertility of intercrossed races. He was not satisfied that the mutual fertility of all races had been fully proved,[2] but concluded that "those naturalists who admit the principle of evolution . . . will feel no doubt that all the races of man are descended from a single primitive stock."[3]

The industrial revolution of the nineteenth century enriched Europe and the United States of America, and the white races increased enormously in numbers and wealth. It was in the middle of this economic white renascence that Darwin and other naturalists propounded the theory of organic evolution and the survival of the fittest, and that Mendel stressed the immense importance of heredity.[4] The doctrine of 'the survival of the fittest' was warmly accepted by the people of European stock who saw no reason to doubt that they were the fittest of all. As Graham Wallas has said: "Before Darwin wrote it had been possible for philanthropists to think of the non-white races as 'men and brothers' who, after a short process of education, would become in all respects except colour identical with themselves. Darwin made it clear that the difficulty could not be so glossed over, racial variations were shown to be unaffected by education, to have existed for millions of years, and to be tending perhaps towards divergence rather than assimilation."[5]

At the same time everything possible was being done to stimulate racial pride among the nations of Europe. National virtues and achievements were extolled to stimulate the vanity of the white races, and to justify the policy of expansion and aggression at the expense of 'inferior' peoples. Even before Darwin had published *The Origin of Species* a book had appeared which has exercised a profound effect on European thought. The author of *Essai sur*

---

[1] *Sex and Sex Worship (Phallic Worship)* (1919), by O. A. Wall, p. 34.
[2] *The Descent of Man* (1871), by C. Darwin, 2nd ed., pp. 264–8.
[3] *Ibid.*, p. 273.
[4] Darwin's *Origin of Species* was published in 1859, and the Austrian Abbot, G. C. Mendel, published in 1865 the results of his researches into the laws of heredity.
[5] *Human Nature in Politics* (1920). by Graham Wallas, 3rd ed., pp. 287–8.

COLOUR PREJUDICE

l'inegalité des races humaines[1] was Joseph Arthur, Comte de Gobineau, who may be regarded as the true founder of the 'Nordic School.' He propounded "the doctrine that the different races of mankind are innately unequal in talent, worth and ability to absorb and create culture, and change their innate character only through crossing with alien strains. The genius of a race depends but little on conditions of climate,[2] surroundings and period; it is therefore absurd to maintain that all men are capable of an equal degree of perfection. Only the white races are creative of culture."[3] Other writers took up the strain,[4] and it was not long before differences were found among the white races themselves. The three sub-species of the white race, the Nordics, the Alpines and the Mediterraneans, were held to vary in value among themselves, although all were worth far more than any of the coloured races; the Nordic was accepted (by writers of the Nordic School) as "far and away the most valuable type, standing, indeed, at the head of the whole human genus."[5] This 'Great Race,' as it is called by some writers,[6] coolly asserts its own superiority and maintains that its own existence and progress is essential to the future progress and civilisation of the world. This is held to justify the exploitation, and indeed the persecution, of the so-called inferior races, and the result has been seen in recent years, without going outside of Europe, in the 'Aryan' obsession of Nazi Germany with its inevitable persecution of 'inferior' races.[7]

[1] The first volume was published in 1853; this volume has been translated into English by H. Holtz, under the title of *The Moral and Intellectual Diversity of Races* (1856); and by A. Collins, as *The Inequality of Human Races* (1915).

[2] This is perhaps a reply to the argument of the Abbé Du Bos, who in his *Réflections Critiques sur la Poësie et sur la Peinture*, published in 1719, attributed the distribution of genius to the effects of climate.

[3] *Encyclopaedia Britannica*, 14th ed., vol. 10, p. 459.

[4] The great musician, Wagner, supported de Gobineau's theory and helped greatly to make it popular. The English Germanophile, H. Stewart Chamberlain, who married Wagner's daughter, developed the theory further in his book, *The Foundations of the Nineteenth Century* (1899). More modern evangelists of the Nordic doctrine are the Americans Lothrop Stoddard and Madison Grant. An earlier American writer of influence was J. W. Burgess, author of *Political Science and Comparative Constitutional Law* (1890).

[5] *The Rising Tide of Colour against White World-Supremacy* (1920), by L. Stoddard, p. 162.

[6] See Madison Grant's *The Passing of the Great Race* (1917).

[7] Professor W. E. LeGros Clark, Professor of Anatomy at Oxford University, says that "in the early years of the Nazi movement the authorities promulgated the

THE EXISTENCE AND GROWTH OF COLOUR PREJUDICE

Fortified by the assurances of scientists that they were indeed superior to all others, the European races courageously took up 'the white man's burden,' the duty of imposing their culture and their religion on alien peoples. In the last quarter of the nineteenth century Africa was divided up among the European nations, and the ease with which vast territories were conquered and kept in subjection did nothing to lessen the pride of the white races. Generally speaking, European rule in Africa has conferred immense material benefits on the inhabitants. Slavery has been made illegal and slave-dealing has been almost entirely stamped out. The progress of disease has been checked, and education and religion have done much to raise the people in the scale of civilisation. The late Lord Olivier, a former Colonial Governor and a member of the Labour Party, who was no bigoted admirer of his own race, speaking generally of South Africa and Kenya, stated that he was far from thinking "that the majority of the natives in those parts of Africa . . . are altogether worse off than they probably would have been by this time had British power and colonisation never intervened there." He adds that Western civilisation is an enormously better thing than any African culture, and that "native Africans recognise this, are attracted by it, profit by it, and, under its stimulus, education and discipline, are advanced in the faculties of humanity."[1]

theory of the Nordic Race. When it was realised that the majority of Germans did not conform to this type, this theory was replaced by the still more unscientific conception of an Aryan Race. The fallacy of this lies in the fact that 'Aryan' is not a racial but a language term. Race is not necessarily synonymous with language, culture or nationality. *Oxford University Summer School on Colonial Administration* (1938) *Summary of Lectures and Discussions*, p. 65.

[1] *The Anatomy of African Misery* (1927), by Lord Olivier, pp. 65, 152. Other members of the Labour Party have been more explicit, as the following quotations will show:

"Labour holds that the control of large portions of the earth has got to be carried on for some time, in a greater or less degree, by those powers possessing superior technical qualifications. Many backward peoples are incapable of governing themselves in the near future." *Labour's Way with the Commonwealth* (1935) by George Lansbury (Chapter on the Colonies written by C. R. Buxton), pp. 96-7.

"Our ideal is self-government, democracy and socialism. We fully realise that this is a far distant ideal as regards many of these territories for which we are responsible. In these territories the people are in a condition which would make it impossible for them to take over the government of their country on modern lines, perhaps for many generations to come." *Ibid.*, p. 112.

"To belittle the credit side of imperialism's account is merely to mishandle the

The African is apt, however, to ignore the advantages he has received through European culture and government, and to remember only the injustices which he suffered in the past, and the discrimination of the present. He can see no reason, for instance, for our complacent satisfaction over the abolition of the overseas slave trade; it was, he considers, started by us, and if we later spent life and treasure in stamping it out we were doing no more than setting right a wrong which our fathers had perpetrated.[1]

For this and other reasons, the Negro is often accused of ingratitude to his benefactors, and, indeed, from our point of view, he is frequently ungrateful.[2] Allowances must, however, be made for the survival of the slave mentality,[3] and for a point of view which is essentially different from ours.[4] Moreover, paternal

facts ... men on the spot have put much honest effort into lightening the burdens, both natural and man-imposed, under which our subject peoples struggle. ... It behoves socialists and revolutionaries at large to remember that the day-to-day work of colonial administration is already to a large extent in the hands of men who are quite as anxious as themselves to promote genuine native welfare." *The Duty of Empire* (1935), by Leonard Barnes, p. 285.

A distinguished anthropologist has said: "Political control of Africa by the white man is necessary, and it will have to continue for a long time to come; without it the continent would soon be disorganised and sink back into its former static conditions." *Africa and Christianity* (1937), by D. Westermann, p. 43.

[1] In this connection see *The Negro in the Future* (1934), by H. A. Moody, p. 2, regarding the meetings in England to celebrate the centenary of emancipation.

[2] As an example, there is little appreciation of the extent to which the preaching of the Christian religion in Africa and the West Indies is supported by European and American sympathisers. The building of large cathedrals, churches and schools, and the maintenance of the clergy, would scarcely be possible without this help. Considerable sums are raised in England for the African missions, and in British Honduras, for instance, a very large proportion of the cost of maintaining the Roman Catholic churches and schools is defrayed by subscribers in the United States, the collections in the churches from the local Roman Catholics amounting to very little.

[3] The white owner preserved the lives and the health of his slaves as he preserved other valuable property, for his own sake, and the sick slave restored to health would have little cause for gratitude when the restoration of health involved the resumption of hard work.

[4] Professor Levy-Bruhl has quoted (in his book *Primitive Mentality* (1922), authorised translation by L. A. Clare, Chapter XIII, *passim*) numerous instances of the apparent ingratitude of 'primitives' in various parts of the world. The 'primitive' who is treated by a missionary doctor expects to be paid for subjecting himself to the strange treatment he receives; the 'primitive' whose life is saved by a white man demands presents from his rescuer and abuses him if he is so mean as to refuse them. Professor Levy-Bruhl maintains that this is not really ingratitude, nor is it peculiar conduct from the 'primitive's' point of view. Illness and accident are to him not natural events, but the result of some mystic manifestation of unseen powers from

THE EXISTENCE AND GROWTH OF COLOUR PREJUDICE

governments and missionaries have been known to give to primitive people what is considered good for them rather than what they want: the child who is told that rice-pudding is better for it than a sweet is seldom grateful for the pudding.[1]

which the primitive mind can see no escape, and, indeed, from which it would be almost blasphemous to think of escaping. The white man has interfered with the arrangements of destiny, but the 'primitive' still feels the imminence of impending doom, possibly a worse doom in revenge for his temporary escape, and perhaps the ostracism of his fellows who may now have to share with the doomed man the anger of the unseen powers. The white man, then, is not a benefactor, and so far from being thanked or rewarded for his kindness, is under an obligation to the one whose life he has saved. An impossible conception to us, but the obvious one to those whose material life is so closely interwoven with the spiritual.

In *My Life and Thought* (1933), by Albert Schweitzer (trans. by C. T. Campion), p. 167, we read that the Africans, when on the point of leaving the hospital cured, would demand presents from the doctor, because he had now become their friend.

The educated Negro of to-day is, of course, far from such a primitive concept, but who knows what traditional, and scarcely conscious instincts still remain with him as an inheritance from his forefathers, who only a few generations back, were 'primitives.'

[1] Most Africans clamour for more education for their children, but there are exceptions. The primitive African, whose children are being educated, loses the valuable services of those children in the fields; he sees no reason to be grateful for this, and has actually been known to demand monetary compensation for the loss of his children's services.

Chapter II

THE ATTITUDE OF VARIOUS PEOPLES TO RACIAL AND COLOUR DIFFERENCES

WE have seen in the previous chapter that colour prejudice does exist, and has probably always existed, that it has increased in intensity in recent years and, unfortunately, is still increasing. It is, indeed, not surprising, in view of historical events in the last few centuries, that the whites, in their dealings with the coloured races, and especially the Negroes, should have experienced a feeling of superiority, and that they should have taken little pains to conceal it. What is surprising, at first sight, is the varying intensity of the feeling of racial superiority among the white races, and even among the members of the same nation in different parts of the world. It is, perhaps, less surprising that women should be almost always more prejudiced than men in their attitude towards coloured persons,[1] and that the presence of the increasing number of white women who now accompany their husbands to tropical colonies, very desirable as it may be from one point of view, should tend to

---

[1] Mr. Oldham says that "it often happens that the attitude of women is one of the chief obstacles to good relations between races": *Christianity and the Race Problem* (1924), by J. H. Oldham (7th edition), p. 242. Sir Ronald Storrs, formerly Governor of Cyprus, has referred to the unfriendly attitude of Englishwomen in the Near East: see *Orientations* (1937), p. 93. Lord Lugard has pointed out the importance of overcoming colour prejudice in our tropical colonies, and how effective a lead could be given by European ladies in this matter: *The Times* of May 4, 1935. A French resident in Senegal, speaking regretfully of the days when whites mixed more freely with blacks, blamed the advent of the white woman for the different conditions now existing: "*la femme blanche,*" he said, "*est l'adversaire stupide et implacable de tout ce qui est indigène*"; *Noirs et Blancs* (1931), by J. Weulersse, p. 9. Countee Cullen, an American Negro, has written the following verse entitled "For a Lady I Know":

"She even thinks that up in Heaven
Her class lies late and snores,
While poor black cherubs rise at seven
To do celestial chores."

RACIAL AND COLOUR DIFFERENCES

create a barrier to friendly social intercourse between the races which did not previously exist.[1] It has even been suggested to me that a white woman's instinctive feeling against racial intercourse may be proof of the deep-seated, biological origin of racial prejudice.

Colour prejudice is particularly strong among the 'Nordic' peoples of north-west Europe, and less developed among southern Europeans. Lord Bryce says that "the aversion to colour reaches its maximum among the Teutons,"[2] and Mr. Oldham refers to the strong prejudice among the Anglo-Saxon peoples against interracial marriage.[3] The feeling exists only to a limited degree among the French, Italians,[4] Spaniards and Portuguese. Sir John Harris says that "in Portuguese colonies there is a pleasing absence of race prejudice; natives of equal social status are as freely admitted to Portuguese institutions as white men."[5] Professor Toynbee attributes the freedom from prejudice of the Spaniards and Portuguese, and their descendants in America, to the fact that these races have remained more or less in the medieval phase of our western civilisation, and still distinguish peoples by their religion rather than by their colour.[6] The French, he admits, are not medieval in their outlook, but on the other hand they treat the possession of French culture, rather than the race of the individual, as the true criterion of his status.[7] For this reason, in the French colonies, full

[1] "The British appear to be popular wherever they go until they come to settle with their wives. The mere fact that such an importation makes the home more pleasant than it was causes an exclusion, though an unavoidable one, of the outer world." *Baghdad Sketches* (1937), by Freya Stark, p. 87.
[2] *The Relations of the Advanced and the Backward Races of Mankind* (1902), by Lord Bryce, p. 19.
[3] *Christianity and the Race Problem* (1924), by J. H. Oldham, 7th ed., pp. 149-50.
[4] Fascism, of course, cultivated and encouraged colour prejudice. See page 30 below.
[5] *Dawn in Darkest Africa* (1912), by Sir John Harris, p. 169.
[6] *A Study of History* (1935), by Arnold J. Toynbee, vol. 1, p. 224.
[7] T. E. Lawrence has pointed out that the French, while they have just as good an opinion of themselves as the English, encourage their native subjects to imitate them; even if they could never attain the true level, yet their virtue would be greater as they approached it. The English, he says, look upon imitation as a parody: the French as a compliment. *Seven Pillars of Wisdom* (1935), p. 347. See also the *Report on his visit to West Africa during the year 1926*, by the Honourable W. G. A. Ormsby-Gore (now Lord Harlech), Cmd. 2744, p. 23: "The Englishman has naturally an instinctive dislike of 'assimilation.' We like to keep our life distinct from that of other races whether European or not. The more another people acquire our culture,

COLOUR PREJUDICE

citizenship has been freely given to Asiatics and Negroes, and there has been little discrimination against such men in civil and political life or in the army. The French undoubtedly have less objection to social intercourse and intermarriage with the coloured races than have, for example, the British, but nevertheless they are not altogether free from colour prejudice.[1]

Among the Italians colour prejudice was not particularly strong in the past, but the conquest of Abyssinia undoubtedly accentuated it, and it is significant that Italian legislation prescribed severe penalties for those Italians who entered into sexual relations with Abyssinian women.[2]

It is particularly interesting to compare the colour prejudice evinced by the Dutch in South Africa and the absence of such prejudice among their compatriots in the East Indies, who recognise an Eurasian as Dutch if the father was a Dutchman.[3]

In the British colony of Jamaica there is practically no colour bar,[4] while in the neighbouring colony of the Bahamas the feeling regarding colour is particularly strong.[5] Of British West Africa,

our outlook and our social habits, very often the wider becomes the gulf between us." An American writer says that "the Englishman believes . . . that his superiority is so innate that it cannot possibly be absorbed by people of other races." *The Native Problem in Africa* (1928), by R. L. Buell, vol. ii, p. 77.

[1] See *The Colonial Problem*, a Report by a Study Group of Members of the Royal Institute of International Affairs, p. 118. It has been cleverly said that the Negro's position in Paris "was rather like that of the fashionable *divorcé* in the nineteenth century; a person whom it was *chic* to be seen with in the right place, but whom one did not invite to the house." *Africa Dances* (1935), by G. Gorer, p. 7.

[2] See *The Times*, January 11, 1937; and *Ethiopia, an Empire in the Making* (1939), by F. Quaranta, p. 5.

[3] This may be attributed to the fact that the half-caste in South Africa is generally the child of an African woman, while the Eurasian is the child of an Asiatic woman, and the prejudice against Africans is generally greater than that against Asiatics.

[4] *Christianity and the Race Problem* (1924), by J. H. Oldham, 7th ed., p. 163; see also an article by Lord Olivier, a former Governor of Jamaica, in *The Spectator* of May 9, 1931.

[5] *The Duty of Empire* (1935), by Leonard Barnes, p. 124. Mr. Barnes draws attention to the fact that the two West Indian colonies in which the colour line is still relatively sharply drawn are Barbados and the Bahamas which alone retain the old representative Assemblies; Jamaica and the rest of the British West Indies are "Crown Colonies," and he adds that it was only with the establishment of Crown Colony government that the Negroes really began to taste the proper fruits of emancipation from slavery. A list of the reforms that were 'rapidly effected' when Crown Colony government was first instituted in Jamaica is given in *The Atlantic and Emancipation* (1937), by H. A. Wyndham, p. 122. Compare Adam Smith, in *The Wealth of Nations* (1776), Book IV, Chapter VII: "The law, so far as it gives some weak protection

RACIAL AND COLOUR DIFFERENCES

Mr. Oldham says that "while officially there is no colour bar and Africans are . . . invited to official functions, social intercourse between the races is practically limited to these, and the racial feeling which is so pronounced in other parts of the world where the two races are brought into contact with one another is not without its influence on the attitude of the white community."[1] My own view is that in the Gold Coast the relations between Europeans and Africans are better than in any other colony I have known, and I hope that some improvement has been effected in Nigeria by the Lagos Dining Club, of which I was one of the founders; this Club consists of an equal number of Africans and Europeans, and meets once a month to afford members an opportunity of dining and talking together.

The fact that the white man in his own country shows less colour prejudice than when he is living in the tropics is not remarkable, inasmuch as the problem is less insistent.[2] He sees fewer coloured people and his attitude is one of curiosity rather than disdain; there is no economic rivalry to provoke hostility[3] and no danger of the whites being overwhelmed by 'the rising tide of colour'; there is no anxiety over white 'prestige' in a country predominantly white. The position is changed when members of the white race represent but a fraction of the total population of a country, and feel the

to the slave against the violence of his master, is likely to be better executed in a colony where the Government is in a great measure arbitrary, than in one where it is altogether free . . . where the master is perhaps either a member of the colony Assembly, or the elector of such a member."

[1] *Christianity and the Race Problem* (1924), by J. H. Oldham, 7th ed., p. 164.

[2] The visitor to the tropics is in much the same position, yet Professor Macmillan says that "it is common experience that—owing to incredible trials and irritations and to material losses suffered from the mere carelessness of Africans—traders, planters, even administrators, arriving fresh from Europe full of good-will, may quite soon become harder and more negative in their attitude than old-established colonists." See *African Emergent* (1938), p. 136.

[3] When as the result of exceptional circumstances, economic rivalry does arise in 'white' countries, it is at once followed by violent colour prejudice and inter-racial disorder. The presence of large numbers of coloured seamen in British and French ports after the war of 1914–18 was bitterly resented by the white seamen, and led to rioting. The migration of Negroes from the South to Chicago, where they entered into competition with the whites, resulted in serious disorders in which many Negroes lost their lives. At a later date, the presence of several thousand coloured seamen in Cardiff and other British ports, and the existence of unemployment among seamen, led to an agitation to prevent the signing-on of coloured seamen on British ships. Later again, in 1944, there were serious racial riots in Detroit.

need for asserting themselves; it is because of this that, as an Indian writer has said, the Englishman east of Suez "becomes acutely conscious of his pigmentary aristocracy."[1] Allowances must also be made for the fact that a tropical climate has a marked and injurious effect on the mental as well as the physical health of white residents.[2] "There is no doubt that Europeans in the tropics are more irritable and in general more highly strung than in their native land. Clearly, in some fashion the nervous tone is injuriously affected by residence in tropical climates."[3] It is possible that the increase of colour prejudice in England, to which reference has been made above, is due not only to the larger number of Negroes who now visit the country, but also to the fact that the home-staying Englishman is influenced in his attitude by the increasing number of those of his own race who live and work in tropical countries, who know the coloured peoples even if they do not understand them, and face a problem from which the Englishman at home is happily free.[4]

It would, however, be a mistake to consider, as some consider, that colour prejudice and a contempt for other races are shortcomings peculiar to the whites.[5] "The yellow man thinks himself no less superior to the white man than the white man believes himself superior to the yellow."[6] The Japanese have colour prejudice very

[1] *Indian Pilgrimage* (1939), by Ranjee G. Shahani, p. 174.

[2] And possibly of the native residents also. See *Manson's Tropical Diseases* (11th ed., 1940), edited by P. H. Manson-Bahr, p. 605.

[3] *The Population Problem, A Study in Human Evolution* (1922), by A. M. Carr-Saunders, pp. 343-4. Mr. W. P. Pitkin, who considers that the humidity of the tropics is largely responsible for the mentality of its inhabitants, says that this "makes more comprehensible to the dweller of the earth's cool belts those amazing changes of personality which take place in the white man who goes to the damp tropics." *A Short Introduction to the History of Human Stupidity* (1935), p. 72.

[4] See *A Study of History* (1935), by A. J. Toynbee, vol. 1, p. 210.

[5] See *Christianity and the Race Problem* (1924), by J. H. Oldham, 7th ed., p. 41. An Indian writer has pointed out that the "conceit of the legendary destinies of nations is not confined to the West. There are Indians who believe that true spirituality has never appeared anywhere in the world save on the sacred soil of India. There are Chinese who imagine that they alone are civilised. Public men in Japan often use the language of the Shinto divine Hirata of a hundred years ago, that the Japanese are the descendants of the god, different in kind rather than degree from all other nations." *Eastern Religions and Western Thought* (1939), by Sir S. Radhakrishnan, p. 349.

[6] *Papers on Inter-racial Problems*, communicated to the First Universal Races Congress held at the University of London, 1911, edited by G. Spiller; article by A. Fouillèe, p. 25.

strongly,[1] and for more than two centuries, from 1641 to 1858, they treated with almost unbelievable contempt and severity the Dutch merchants who traded with them;[2] moreover, the comparatively hairless Japanese thoroughly despises the 'Hairy Ainu.'[3] "The Chinese look on themselves as the greatest nation in the world and on their civilisation as superior to all others."[4] They regard all 'Foreign Devils' as barbarians, and it is amusing to recollect that one of the avowed objects of the Chinese war of 1842 was "to compel the Chinese to abandon their attitude of superiority towards other civilised nations."[5] The Jew has no doubt that he belongs to a Chosen Race, and has a supreme contempt for the Gentile.[6] A Swiss lady married to a high-caste Hindu, and resident in India for many years, has written as follows: "I realised the Mohammedan feels superior to the Hindu, the Brahmin to the non-Brahmin; I realised the gulf between English and Hindu is not one jot greater than that between high-caste and low-caste or outcaste. Always this maddening undercurrent of colour-antagonism everywhere, active and superficial on the part of the whites, placid and deep on the part of the high-caste. . . . No people are more colour-conscious than high-caste Hindus. Fairness was the universally stressed and desired quality."[7] The Red Indian expresses his contempt for the white man by calling him a 'pale-face,' and the so-called 'white Indians' of Panama are said to be ostracised and despised by their fellow Indians.[8]

[1] *Christianity and the Race Problem* (1924), by J. H. Oldham, 7th ed., p. 66.
[2] *A Study of History* (1935), by A. J. Toynbee, vol. 2, pp. 232-3.
[3] *Ibid.*, vol. 1, p. 229.
[4] *Christianity and the Race Problem* (1924), by J. H. Oldham, 7th ed., pp. 66-7.
[5] *The Duty of Empire* (1935), by Leonard Barnes, p. 84.
[6] "An unmixed race of a first-rate organisation are the aristocracy of Nature. . . . No penal laws, no physical tortures, can effect that a superior race should be absorbed in an inferior or be destroyed by it." *Coningsby*, pp. 220, 250. There can be little doubt that the Earl of Beaconsfield, in writing this, was referring to the Jewish people as the superior race.
[7] *A Marriage to India* (1931), by Frieda Hauswirth (Mrs. Sarangadbar Das), pp. 12, 57. See also *Hindu Races and their Customs* (1937), by S. Rice, p. 38. An Indian writer, admitting that this is a fact, places the blame on the British, who, he says, taught the Indian to admire a fair skin; the result is that "a man with a light skin gives himself airs, and thinks that he is somehow superior to his darker brethren. The colour complex is all-powerful in India." *Indian Pilgrimage* (1939), by Ranjee G. Shahani, p. 304.
[8] See article by J. H. Driberg in *The Spectator* of June 11, 1931.

COLOUR PREJUDICE

T. E. Lawrence said that although the Arabs have little colour feeling against Africans, the Indians evoke their race dislike,[1] while Sir Ronald Storrs found that the Indians were inclined to despise the Egyptians.[2] An Indian writer says that "an Indian does not wish to be confounded with a Negro; indeed, to tell the truth, he dislikes the Negro as much as any Westerner."[3] Professor Toynbee points out that "the Primitive Arabs who were the ruling element in the Umayyad Caliphate called themselves 'the swarthy people,' with a connotation of racial superiority, and their Persian and Turkish subjects 'the ruddy people,' with a connotation of racial inferiority; that is to say, they drew the same distinction that we draw between blonds and brunets, but reversed the values which we assign to the two shades of white."[4] "One explanation of prejudice, then," says a coloured American writer, "is simply difference," and he points out that all foreigners are under suspicion in every country, that all people of a different religion are heathen, and all those of a different culture are savages.[5]

Christianity itself is held not to be free from discrimination based on colour prejudice. The white Christian missionary has "no true brotherhood to offer the Negro except at best those of teacher with taught, master with servant, grown man with child."[6] In Dakar "there is a club attached to the mission . . . but although the congregation is predominantly negro you can seldom find one in the club, nor would he be welcome if he came."[7] This is the reason why Africans, resenting white control even in the churches, have set up so many independent churches of their own; particularly in South Africa is this the case, the number of separate communions there being remarkable.[8] Major Moton, President of Tuskegee Institute, says that it is in business that the Negro gets more "honest consideration and a fairer deal than in any other of his contacts

[1] *Seven Pillars of Wisdom* (1935), by T. E. Lawrence, p. 157.
[2] *Orientations* (1937), by Sir Ronald Storrs, p. 157.
[3] *Indian Pilgrimage* (1939), by Ranjee G. Shahani, p. 173.
[4] *A Study of History* (1935), by A. J. Toynbee, vol. I, p. 226.
[5] *Brown America* (1932), by E. R. Embree, p. 199.
[6] *The Future of Islam* (1882), by Sir W. S. Blunt, p. 26. See also *Indian Pilgrimage* (1939), by Ranjee G. Shahani, p. 299.
[7] *Africa Dances* (1935), by G. Gorer, p. 77.
[8] *The Colour Problems of South Africa* (1934), by E. H. Brookes, p. 162. Lord Hailey says that there are now no less than 325 Bantu Separatist Churches in the Union: see *United Empire* of February 1937, p. 86.

with the white man, not even excepting religion."[1] Another Negro says that even the Government officials in Africa are better than the missionaries.[2]

It has been stated that in the matter of discrimination Islam has a better record than Christianity, that it has destroyed race-prejudice and national sentiments, abolished caste and ignored colour, and broken down all barriers between man and man. What is of more importance is that it broke down the barriers between men and women of different races,[3] the conquering Arabs mating freely with the women of all nations, and giving their own daughters in marriage to black Muslims.[4] This is true up to a point, but I am not altogether convinced that the fair-skinned Muslim does not despise his dark-skinned co-religionist for his colour. It is significant that towards the end of the sixteenth century admission to the Janissary Corps was made open to all free Muslims except Negroes[5], and T. E. Lawrence speaks of the Turks despising a black man on account of his colour.[6]

The Negroes themselves are no more free from colour and racial prejudice than those of other races.[7] Of one town in California it was said that the Negroes show much more openly than the whites a feeling of superiority to the Japanese.[8] The Negro 'Creole' of British Honduras despises the 'Black Carib'[9] who lives beside him.

[1] *What the Negro Thinks* (1929), by R. R. Moton, p. 38.
[2] *Negro Anthology* (1934), edited by Nancy Cunard: article on '*White-Manning*' in *West Africa*, by T. K. Utchay, p. 762.
[3] *Ethics and some Modern World Problems* (1924), by W. McDougall, p. 12.
[4] *A Study of History* (1935), by Arnold J. Toynbee, vol. 1, p. 226. For the alleged result of this miscegenation see p. 121 below.
[5] *A Study of History* (1935), by Arnold J. Toynbee, vol. 3, p. 45.
[6] *Seven Pillars of Wisdom* (1935), by T. E. Lawrence, p. 117.
[7] This is admitted in a very reasonable and broad-minded article by O. A. Alakija, in *The Nigerian Daily Times* of June 27, 1936.
[8] *Alien Americans* (1936), by B. Schrieke, p. 36.
[9] The true "red" Caribs came originally from the mainland of South America and the islands of the eastern Antilles. Escaped Negro slaves mixed their blood with that of these Caribs and the present "Black Caribs" are the results of this mixture; in colour, hair and general appearance they differ little from the Negro. This mixed race gave considerable trouble to the settlers in various islands, and particularly to those in St. Vincent, and towards the end of the eighteenth century they were deported *en masse* to one of the islands in the Bay of Honduras. Thence they moved northward into British Honduras where they are settled along the coast. They keep much to themselves and speak a language which few non-Caribs can understand; it includes many French words and the numerals, indeed, are almost entirely French. They bitterly resent the superior airs of the Negro inhabitants who, for their part, despise the Caribs.

The Yoruba[1] of Nigeria despises the neighbouring Jekri tribe.[2] On the other hand considerable resentment was caused among the Yorubas of Lagos by a speech made by an inhabitant of Sierra Leone, claiming for the people of Sierra Leone a superiority over the Lagosian.[3] In Uganda, the ruling families of many of the tribes belong to the Bahima group, which looks down on all others. In South Africa the coloured community raises against the Bantu exactly the same sort of barrier that the Europeans have raised against them.[4] In the United States and the West Indies there is among the Negroes themselves the same "peculiar inconsistency of a colour question . . . it is evidenced most plainly in marriage selection."[5] Dr. Harold Moody, President of the League of Coloured Peoples, says that "our educated coloured girls will not look at anyone darker than themselves no matter how cultured,"[6] and Major Moton points out that "even within the Negro race itself there are to be found among certain elements discriminations based on colour and sometimes on racial admixture."[7] "There is anti-Semitism among the Negroes of Harlem, one 'underprivileged' people set against another."[8] Finally, we have on record the statement of Ibn Batuta, the Arab traveller of the four-

[1] The Yoruba is an important tribe of about 4,000,000 persons inhabiting Lagos and the south-western provinces of Nigeria. "Without saying that the Yoruba are more intelligent, we can safely say that their intellect is more cultivated . . . they are certainly the leading people in West Africa." *The Yoruba-speaking peoples of the Slave Coast of West Africa* (1894), by Sir A. B. Ellis, pp. 32–3.

[2] My friend the late Dr. Henry Carr, once described to me the amount of hostile feeling that was provoked some years ago in Lagos by the marriage of a Yoruba and a Jekri. A writer in *The Nigerian Daily Times* of January 10, 1935, says that "many of us who on the platform or in the Press proclaim the glory and fame of Africa and predict for her a great future are not yet above petty tribal spirit and a 'superiority-complex' which persists in discriminating against other members of the race who do not come from exactly the same stock as ourselves or have perhaps through no faults of their own not attained as high a level of civilisation as ourselves."

[3] See article headed "Sierra Leone Councillor's Bunkum" in *The Nigerian Daily Times* of August 24, 1935.

[4] *The Colour Problems of South Africa* (1934), by E. H. Brookes, p. 33.

[5] *The Autobiography of an Ex-coloured Man*, by J. W. Johnson, 1927 edition, p. 154. See also *Voodoo Gods* (1939), by Zora Hurston, pp. 3, 94.

[6] *The Negro in the Future*, an address delivered by Dr. H. A. Moody at the Conference, 'The Negro in the World to-day,' held in the Memorial Hall, London, July 1934, p. 5.

[7] *What the Negro Thinks* (1929), by R. R. Moton, p. 184.

[8] *The American Problem* (1944), by D. W. Brogan, p. 105.

teenth century, that he regretted visiting the country of the Negroes because of their lack of manners *and their contempt for the whites.*[1]

As between the European peoples themselves who are all 'whites' there is a strong feeling in each nation of superiority over other nations, even those descended from the same original stock, and the citizens of the United States look with pity, not unmixed with scorn, on the effete nations of Europe from whose loins they sprang.

It is not easy to explain away the existence of race and colour prejudice, and the fact that men, humane and reasonably minded in their relations with others of their own race, lose all sense of proportion and decency when dealing with those of other races, and particularly when dealing with those whom they regard as members of an inferior race. The explanation may lie in the limitations of the human mind, which has not yet been able to grasp the full significance of the brotherhood of man. We are filled with sympathy and horror if we are the witnesses of an accident in which one man is killed, we are mildly distressed (though we do little enough about it) at the periodical summaries of deaths and accidents caused by motor traffic on the roads of Great Britain, but we are left almost unmoved by the tragedy of millions of deaths caused by flood or famine in far-distant China.

This chapter has not dealt with the reason, or reasons, for colour prejudice, except so far as it is due, in the case of the white races, to their economic and military superiority in the past, but merely with the important fact of its existence and its incidence. It is recognised as an evil by most reasonable men, though the adherents of the so-called Nordic school consider it to be necessary for the preservation of their own racial purity and for the very existence of the race itself. The following chapter will deal with the effect that the colour prejudice of the whites has had upon the coloured races of the world.

[1] *Selections from the Travels of Ibn Batuta, 1325-1354* (Broadway Travellers), p. 320.

Chapter III

NEGRO RESENTMENT OF COLOUR PREJUDICE

IT has often been carelessly assumed that the usual docility of the Negro is a sign of contentment: nothing could be further from the truth. An American Negro, Major Moton, says that many "have been misled by the Negro's silence on this subject to believe that he is not only complaisant but contented and even happy under existing conditions."[1] The fact is that "the psychology of the Negro is protective . . . (The Negro race) has long been subject to adversity: this has made the race cautious. It has had a long history of slavery, long before American slavery; this has made it secretive in the presence of manifestly preponderant power and general animosity. The race still survives, for it has learned the discretion that is the better part of valour."[2] The American Indian, in the West Indies and the northern half of the continent, fought desperately against white domination and has practically disappeared: the Negro submitted and survives.[3]

Times, however, have changed and still are changing fast. The Negro has discovered that the white man is not omnipotent, and, perhaps, that the white man's conscience is more tender than it was. The race consciousness of the Negro is increasing. He is feeling a greater pride in himself and a greater resentment at the slights, real and fancied, that are put upon him. He no longer accepts as an axiom that the white man is inherently superior to him and that the backward races of the world can never attain to the level of the races more advanced. While such a change of attitude was inevitable, and has probably been proceeding slowly for some time, the change has been enormously accelerated during the present century. The overthrow of Russia by Japan in the war

[1] *What the Negro Thinks* (1929), by Major R. R. Moton, President of Tuskegee Institute, p. vii.
[2] *Ibid.*, p. 64.
[3] *The Relations of the Advanced and the Backward Races of Mankind* (1902), by Lord Bryce, p. 13.

of 1904–1905 was acclaimed throughout the coloured world as a triumph for the coloured races, and the victories of Negro boxers, such as Jack Johnson and Joe Louis, over white men are hailed with a delight which is astonishing.[1]

A Dutch writer points out that "we seem to make it a point of presenting ourselves through our films, our morbid self-analysis, and our murderous criticisms, to millions of amazed spectators and readers in the East as a degenerate civilisation of criminals, adulterers, atheists and individualists. Every day innumerable film performances are given in the East which dishonour Western womanhood and create the impression that, while maintaining law and order in the colonial world, we are unable to do so in our own country."[2] There is no doubt that the passionate love-scenes of the cinema degrade white women in the eyes of the African as well.[3]

Moreover, the visit of thousands of coloured troops and workers to Europe during the two world wars did nothing to increase their respect for white men or women.[4] Negro troops fought against the Germans and Italians in various theatres of war and formed part of the Army of Occupation on the Rhine after the Armistice of 1918.[5] The lunacy of European wars, in which the white races have nearly succeeded in destroying their own civilisation, has lost them, possibly for ever, their scarcely questioned position of authority over the coloured world.

The invasion of Abyssinia by the Italians in 1935 provoked a remarkable demonstration of feeling among the coloured races.

---

[1] The Negro reveals the existence of his inferiority complex by the undue importance he attaches to inter-racial sporting contests, by his depression when a black man is beaten by a white, and by exuberance of rejoicing when the tables are turned. When Joe Louis was defeated by Max Schmeling in 1936 the gloom among the coloured inhabitants of British Honduras was worthy of a major national disaster. A few weeks later when Louis defeated Jack Sharkey, the event was celebrated with great rejoicings by the Negroes of New York; these rejoicings led to an affray in which one Negro was killed and four wounded. See *The Times* of August 20, 1936.

[2] *Colonial Policy* (1931), by A. D. A. DeKat Angelino (abridged trans, by G. J. Renier in collaboration with the author), vol. 1, p. 186.

[3] See *The Clash of Colour, A Study in the Problem of Race* (1924), by B. Mathews, p. 43.

[4] A German writer says that Indian soldiers "have been cured of their respect for the white race by an acquaintance with the white brothel." *England*, by W. Dibelius (trans. by M. A. Hamilton, 1930), p. 63.

[5] Herr Hitler blamed the Jews for this. See *Mein Kampf* (complete trans. of 1939), p. 448.

In some of the British West Indian colonies there was rioting caused by sympathy for the Abyssinians and the belief that the European Powers were secretly supporting Mussolini. There were demonstrations in Harlem and clashes between Italians and Negroes in Jersey City. In West Africa subscriptions were raised for Abyssinia and the sending of a contingent was seriously suggested. Egypt, Syria and Japan showed marked sympathy for Abyssinia, which became a symbol of the unity of colour, and the Ethiopian Emperor was regarded as a hero who was fighting the battle of the blacks against the tyranny of the white races.[1] It mattered little to the Negroes of the world that the Abyssinians were not themselves Negroes, and that, in fact, they rather despised the Negro. They were black and they were fighting a 'white' nation, and that was all that mattered.

The double-edged weapon of propaganda has also had some influence on the attitude of the coloured races to the whites. The principle of self-determination proclaimed as the policy of the Allies during the first world war raised great hopes among all the subject peoples, and led to the cries of "Africa for the Africans" and "Egypt for the Egyptians," to "Swaraj," and to the dream of "Pan-Arabia." Everyone was looking for a new and better world when peace should come at last, but at the Peace Conference of 1919 the victorious Allies refused even to accede to the request of the Japanese delegation that the Covenant of the League of Nations should include a declaration of racial equality! The Japanese representatives pointed out that during the war men of different races had fought side by side, had brought succour to the disabled, and saved the lives of their fellow-men without thought of racial differences, and that a common bond of sympathy had been established to an extent never before experienced. "The discussion was marked by breadth of thought, free and sympathetic exchange of opinion," but the proposal could not be accepted by the British delegates or by President Wilson.[2] This may partly explain the increase of feeling in Japan against Great Britain and the United States after 1919.

[1] "In the United States the Negroes are sensing their affinity with other colored peoples ... the idea of a colored alliance dominates Afroamerican literature." *Half-Caste* (1937), by C. Dover, p. 284.

[2] *My Diary at the Conference of Paris* (1924), by D. H. Miller, vol. v, pp. 372-4; vol. viii, pp. 277-80.

NEGRO RESENTMENT OF COLOUR PREJUDICE

To some of the Negro leaders it appears that only by force can they obtain the recognition of equality that they crave, equality before the law and in social life. Dr. DuBois has expressed the opinion that the Great War of 1914-18 would be "nothing to compare with the fight for freedom which black and brown and yellow men must and will make unless their oppression and humiliation and insult at the hands of the White World cease. The Dark World is going to submit to its present treatment just as long as it must and not one moment longer."[1] In this connection it is interesting to note that Dr. DuBois, for long one of the recognised leaders of Negro thought in the United States, was later severely criticised for being too moderate in his attitude towards the colour question.[2] Another Negro leader, the late Mr. Marcus Garvey,[3] is reported to have said that "the bloodiest of all wars is yet to come, when Europe will match its strength against Asia, and that will be the Negroes' opportunity to draw the sword for Africa's redemption."[4]

A white historian speaks of "a conflict of colour, more terribly primitive in its impulses, more inexorable, more destructive than any of its predecessors, the authentic Armageddon, stamping out in blood and ruin the last hope of civilisation . . . unthinkable as such a conflict may seem, it is idle to suppose it could not happen. It might well happen if the peoples of the West allowed themselves to be convinced by dogmatic biologists that the ultimate relations between the white and coloured races can only be a fight to the death for the survival of the fittest."[5]

It is true enough that no serious racial conflict could arise for some years, as the white races are to-day collectively stronger than

---

[1] *Darkwater* (1920), by Dr. W. E. B. DuBois, p. 49.
[2] See *The Crisis*, the official organ of the National Association for the Advancement of Coloured People, of August 1943.
[3] A native of Jamaica, President-General of the Universal Negro Improvement Association, and 'Provisional President of Africa.' He served a sentence of imprisonment in the United States for 'using the mails to defraud' in connection with his activities as head of the Black Star Steamship Line. It has been said that "to a quick perception of the abstract (Garvey) joins a complete lack of practical sense, a taste for everything fanciful, and the activities of a charlatan." *The Twilight of the White Races* (1926), by M. Muret (trans. by Mrs. Touzalin), p. 78.
[4] Quoted in *The Clash of Colour, A Study in the Problem of Race* (1924), by B. Mathews, p. 76.
[5] *The Empire in These Days* (1935), by R. Coupland, pp. 16-17.

any possible combination of the coloured races, but is there any reason to believe that this disparity of relative strength will endure indefinitely, or that the whites would present a united front to a yellow or black peril?

It is extremely difficult to estimate the numbers of the various races of the world. In *Whitaker's Almanack* for 1940[1] the figures were given as follows:—

Caucasian	725,000,000
Mongolian	680,000,000
Negro	210,000,000
Malayan	104,500,000
Semitic	100,000,000
Red Indian, etc.	30,000,000

Taking colour as the basis, Professor East estimated[2] that the numbers of the various races in 1916 were:—

Yellows	510,000,000
Whites	710,000,000
Browns	420,000,000
Blacks	110,000,000

while Dr. Stoddard estimated[3] that there were in 1914:—

Yellows	500,000,000
Whites	550,000,000
Browns	450,000,000
Blacks	150,000,000
Reds	40,000,000

Whichever figures are accepted, there appears to be no doubt that the white races are considerably outnumbered by the coloured, and it is important to remember that over 100,000,000 of the whites are resident in North America.

Dr. Stoddard maintains that the black race offers no real danger to the whites except as the tool of Pan-Islamism,[4] and it is suggested by Mr. Putnam Weale that the Negro should be Christianised to prevent him from becoming Islamised, and therefore militant. "If he is Christianised his destructive strength is stripped from him, much as was Samson's strength when his locks were cut. The part

---

[1] Page 226.   [2] *Mankind at the Cross-Roads* (1923), by E. M. East, pp. 111–2.
[3] *The Rising Tide of Color against White World-supremacy* (1920), by L. Stoddard, pp. 6–7.   [4] *Ibid.*, p. 240.

NEGRO RESENTMENT OF COLOUR PREJUDICE

the white man is politically called upon to play in Africa, is, then, the part of Delilah and no other."[1]

Everywhere throughout the world to-day may be seen the signs of coloured feeling, and, as a Bantu writer says, "the seething discontent so widespread seems to demand immediately careful and sympathetic study."[2] An American writer says of a Haitian 'patriot' that ninety per cent of his patriotism consists of hatred for the whites,[3] and there is no doubt that the political leader or newspaper editor in tropical colonies must be violently and abusingly anti-white if he is to secure a popular following.[4] He must see no faults in any black man (except in an 'Uncle Tom' or the 'white man's nigger')[5] and still less must he see any virtue in a white.

---

[1] *The Conflict of Colour* (1910), by B. L. Putnam Weale, p. 257.
[2] *The Bantu Past and Present* (1920), by S. M. Molema, p. 352.
[3] *Cannibal Cousins* (1935), by J. H. Craige, p. 61.
[4] See also page 141 below. The impudence of a Negro to a white man, especially one in authority, is always popular among the unthinking section of a race which suffers from an inferiority complex. See *Alien Americans* (1936), by B. Schrieke, p. 150. It is for this reason that the Negroes will so often choose as their leader and representative a man whose only qualification is his ability to abuse others, preferring such a man to a wise and moderate leader. They overlook the fact that vulgar abuse is not a good substitute for argument, and that bad manners will often spoil a good case. The Negro legislator in the colonies is as susceptible as politicians the world over to newspaper criticism, and the local Press does not hesitate to accuse the supporter of an unpopular measure of the betrayal of his people. There are few who have the moral courage or the strength of character to resist the temptation to gain a cheap local reputation by fierce denunciations of white officials and the Government. Another reason may lie in the form of government which relieves the popular leaders of the responsibilities of opposition, and in this connection it is interesting to quote Lord Durham's Report on Canada, written more than a hundred years ago. "The Colonial demagogue," he says, "bids high for popularity without the fear of future exposure. Hopelessly excluded from power, he expresses the wildest opinions, and appeals to the most mischievous passions of the people, without any apprehension of having his sincerity or prudence hereafter tested, by being placed in a position to carry his views into effect; and thus the prominent places in the ranks of opposition are occupied for the most part by men of strong passions, and merely declamatory powers, who think but little of reforming the abuses which serve them as topics for exciting discontent." See *Report and Despatches* of the Earl of Durham, Her Majesty's High Commissioner and Governor-General of British North America (1839), p. 58.
[5] The names applied by the Negroes themselves to those of their own race who are accused, often most unjustly, of being on the side of the white man and against their own people. See *Negro Anthology* (1934), edited by Nancy Cunard, p. 147. Compare this with the epithet 'nigger-lover,' applied so often to the white man in the Southern States of America who tries to treat the Negroes decently. As regards the treatment by Negroes of their own leaders, see pp. 137–140.

Any criticism of his own people is deemed to be 'treason to the race.' The arrogance of Japan which finally led to war, the racial riots in the United States, and the clamour of Negroes in the British West Indies and British Africa for greater political rights, are symptoms which cannot be ignored. Professor Pitt-Rivers points out that "a feature of considerable interest and importance in connexion with this world-wide unrest among subject races and their revolt against European tutelage lies in the fact that the movement is articulated and led to a marked degree by those members of subject races that have been most closely under the influence of our proselytising culture, and who have, in the process, assimilated most 'successfully' European education, European religion and European blood."[1]

Why should this be? Is it the unreasoning hatred of the 'underdog' for all above him, or is there something more? It is important to discover what the grievances of the coloured races really are and what it is that they want.

There is an obvious cause for grievance in the fact that the white races have seized for themselves control of the greater part of the habitable world. The economic advantages gained by the control of political power and the ownership of land have given an enormous advantage to the European races in the struggle for life.

A second grievance, which is almost a corollary to the first, is the existence in some countries of legal discrimination based on race and colour. The worst examples of this occur in the United States of America and in the Union of South Africa.

The third grievance, and in my opinion the one that rankles the most, is the social segregation of the coloured races, which is accompanied by deliberate slights and insults as well as by careless and unintentional rudeness. As one writer has put it ". . . this lies at the root of things—they desire passionately to be freed from the perpetual ostracism and degradation that labels them as though they were members of another and a lower, almost a sub-human species."[2]

The removal of the first of these grievances would scarcely be

---

[1] *The Clash of Culture and the Contact of Races* (1927), by G. H. Lane-Fox Pitt-Rivers, p. 28.
[2] *The Clash of Colour, A Study in the Problem of Race* (1924), by Basil Mathews, p. 72.

practical politics to-day. The removal of white political control from many tropical colonies, without long and careful preparation, would lead to chaos, and would not be acceptable to any but a small proportion of the coloured races, while the difficulty of restoring to their original owners those lands which have been alienated to white farmers is almost insuperable.

There is, however, no reason why legal discrimination based on race or colour should be allowed to remain. Such discrimination is hard to maintain and impossible to justify. It is contrary to Christian teaching, and, in the United States of America, it is contrary to the constitution. It leads to gross abuses and miscarriages of justice. It is argued that these discriminatory laws are necessary if the purity of the white race is to be preserved, and if white civilisation is to continue, but in spite of these laws the purity of the white race has not been preserved in the past, and a civilisation which denies justice to a large proportion of the world's population is scarcely worth preserving. There is no immediate prospect of these laws being repealed; time and public opinion will, however, have their effect.

As regards the third grievance no reasonable man can fail to sympathise with the coloured races. Apart from ethical considerations, it is unnecessary and unwise to insult, whether by accident or design, a number of human beings. The bad manners of a white man may hurt the feelings of a black, but are more degrading to the white. The most serious complaint of the coloured races against the whites, the most potent cause of world-bitterness to-day, the most probable cause of bloodshed in the future, could be removed without expense, without trouble, and in a very short space of time, if white men and women throughout the world would treat those of the coloured races with ordinary decency and civility. Wars of religion have ceased owing to increased religious toleration. Racial wars can only be prevented by a similar toleration in racial relationships. Most of the agitation for constitutional reform in British colonies, is, in its essence, racial rather than political.

Chapter IV

POLITICAL AND LEGAL DISCRIMINATION AGAINST NEGROES

AS stated in the preceding chapter, the first grievance of the coloured races lies in the fact that the white races have assumed political suzerainty of the greater part of the habitable lands of the world. In some cases they have been content with political and economic power only, as in West Africa; in other cases, as in Australia and North America, they have practically annihilated the aboriginal inhabitants and taken their country. In South and East Africa the better lands have been taken by the whites.

It is interesting to note that, after the discovery of America, Spanish and other jurists protested against the seizure of lands belonging to the aborigines, and that "extending over some three and a half centuries, there had been a persistent preponderance of juristic opinion in favour of the proposition that lands in the possession of any backward peoples who are politically organised ought not to be regarded as if they belonged to no one. . . . In comparatively modern times, (however) a different doctrine has been contended for and has numbered among its exponents some well-known authorities; a doctrine which denies that International Law recognises any rights in primitive peoples to the territory they inhabit, and, in its most advanced form, demands that such peoples shall have progressed so far in civilisation as to have become recognised as members of the Family of Nations before they can be allowed such rights."[1]

Whatever the opinion of contemporary jurists may have been, Queen Elizabeth was more modern in her ideas, as in 1578 she granted a charter to Sir Humphrey Gilbert "to inhabit and possess at his choice all remote and heathen lands not in the actual possession of any Christian prince." This calm disregard of the rights of

[1] *The Acquisition and Government of Backward Territory in International Law* (1926), by M. F. Lindley, p. 20.

non-Christians invites attention to the alleged remark of an African more than three hundred years later, to a European missionary: "when you came, Sir, you had the Bible and we the land: now we have the Bible and you the land." However that may be, Englishman and Spaniard alike seized all the land they could in the New World without consideration of the claims of those whom they found in possession.[1]

The same disregard of native rights was displayed by the European governments at the Berlin Conference of 1885, where each government asserted its 'claims' to a share in the African continent, completely ignoring the fact that no European nation had the right to assume sovereignty over the inhabitants of any part of Africa. Many of the treaties that were obtained from native rulers, while they may have been good as against the claims of other European Powers, conferred little or no moral right to territories which were admitted by the Conference to belong to the various nations. Lord Lugard expressed the opinion that these treaties were often misunderstood by the chiefs who signed them, owing to faulty interpretation; "the Sultan of Sokoto, for instance, regarded the subsidy promised to him by the Chartered Company[2] as tribute from a vassal."[3] "The Portuguese, in the Delegoa Bay arbitration, declared that what the British regarded as treaties of cession were considered by the chiefs to be merely lists of the merchandise which had been promised them."[4]

[1] Professor Toynbee has drawn attention to the difference between the treatment accorded to the aborigines by their Catholic and Protestant conquerors respectively. The Protestant English, he points out, whose religion was inspired by the ferocity of the Old Testament, did their best to exterminate the aborigines of Australia and of what are now the United States. The Catholic French lived in comparative peace with the Indians of Canada, while the Spaniards, after their first excesses in the West Indies, Mexico and Peru, mixed their blood freely with the native inhabitants and treated them as equals. *A Study of History* (1935), by Arnold J. Toynbee, vol. 1, p. 211. Although, as a Catholic myself, I find this suggestion gratifying, I feel bound to point out that the different treatment of the aborigines may have been due to race rather than to religion. As Professor Toynbee himself says, the tribes from which the English are largely descended were the only Barbarians who destroyed the inhabitants of the Roman Empire when they conquered it. *Ibid.*, p. 465.

[2] The Royal Niger Company, Chartered and Limited, made the first treaties with Sokoto and the neighbouring territories which are now included in the Protectorate of Nigeria.

[3] *The Dual Mandate in British Tropical Africa* (1922), by Lord Lugard, p. 15.

[4] *The Acquisition and Government of Backward Territory in International Law* (1926), by M. F. Lindley, p. 173.

It is pointless at this stage to discuss the rights and wrongs of the policy, or lack of policy, which gave the white races control of vast tracts of land throughout the world. They are there now for better or for worse, and it is not likely that their power will be shaken for many years to come. If they have deprived races of political independence they have given liberty to individuals. The 'tyranny' of European rule has replaced tyrannies less bearable, and even if good government is no real substitute for self-government,[1] there are not many of the subject peoples who would

[1] In view of the criticisms frequently directed at the failure to grant self-government to the colonies of European Powers, it is desirable to quote some writers who are certainly not hostile to African aspirations.

(a) "What so-called self-government means for primitive and semi-primitive people can be gathered from the fact that in the Black Republic of Liberia domestic slavery and what is far worse, the compulsory shipment of labourers to other countries, have continued to our own day. They were both abolished on October 1, 1930—on paper." *My Life and Thought* (1933), by Albert Schweitzer (trans. by C. T. Campion), p. 223.

(b) See also the reference by Sir John Simon to "the corrupt and inefficient oligarchy of Monrovia," in *Papers concerning Affairs in Liberia* (Cmd. 4614) (1934), p. 52.

(c) "The granting of self-government now or in the near future to any particular colony means handing over control of the central government from the British Colonial Office to a small minority of that Colony's people. ... For some considerable time responsible self-government in Africa must mean control of an uneducated majority by an educated minority." *Thoughts on African Citizenship* (1944), by T. R. Batten, Vice-Principal of Makerere College, Uganda, p. 59.

(d) "To advocate complete independence as a sure and speedy cure for all the ills of African life is a doctrinaire approach which feeds upon the fires of race prejudice. It lends itself to the idealism of the western democracies. It also lends itself to the uses of clever and unscrupulous Africans who would like to gain control for selfish advantage. This kind of democracy may be a cloak for exploitation. The doctrinaire agitators make most of the noise, and they get a following and help from well-meaning but ill-informed people." *Africa Advancing* (1945), by Jackson Davis, Thomas M. Campbell, and Margaret Wrong (two Americans, one of whom is coloured, and a Canadian), p. 83.

(e) As a matter of fact many Africans realise that the colonies are not yet ready for self-government. In *The African Morning Post*, of November 15, 1944, an Editor's note referring to a contributed article on the subject of self-government in the Gold Coast said "We do not think any rational person will fail to congratulate the writer of this article. Everything he says is perfectly true. This country is certainly not ripe for self-government yet." Again, at Lake Success on December 8, 1947, addressing the Trusteeship Council of the United Nations, the accredited representative of the Ewe people said: "We do not ask for self-government at the moment because we are incapable of governing ourselves just now, but in a few years' time we shall be capable of doing so." (The Ewe people inhabit the south-eastern part of the Gold Coast and the Trusteeship Territory of Togoland.)

[2] In this connection see *The Future of the Colonial Empire* (1945), by Sir Bernard Bourdillon, p. 28.

willingly change their present Government for the uncertainties of independence; the almost complete absence of white troops from tropical colonies affords, at least, some ground for this statement.[2] It is conceivable, also, that colonial peoples would find the native bureaucrat a harder taskmaster than the European official.[1] It has been said, with reference to a French colony, that no one could be more heartlessly brutal to the Negroes than the uniformed Negroes who represent the Government,[2] and the whole of the blame for this cannot rest on the white official. The cruelties that stained the independent Governments of Dahomey and Benin, and the tyrannies of Zulu and Matabele chiefs, were not due to any foreign influences. The native chiefs of Malaya and British Africa, through whom vast numbers are governed, appreciate the security of their present position as compared with the precarious past; it is true that the British administrator looks with disfavour on the time-honoured practices of slavery and extortion, but it must be comforting to feel that British authority is there as a protection against rivals and the dangers of assassination. The peasant cultivator, on the whole, realises the blessings of a settled Government, the protection of impartial officials and the greater opportunity afforded him to market his crops and to retain the profit for himself.

With all its imperfections, European government in Asia and in Africa has given to the native inhabitants of the tropics greater personal liberty and economic opportunity than they have ever enjoyed before. On the whole the justice they receive is of a high standard and incomparably better than that which was the lot of

[1] "Those of us who have long and intimate knowledge of Africans as the great majority of them are now, can have no doubt that the result (of the Europeans withdrawing from Africa and leaving the Africans to themselves) would be disastrous for them." *Colour Conflict: Race Relations in Africa* (1943), by G. W. Broomfield, General Secretary, Universities' Mission to Central Africa, p. 16.

[2] *Africa Dances* (1935), by G. Gorer, p. 122. Major Moton speaks of the "truculent air of some Negro porter (on the railways of the United States) who apparently finds great satisfaction in lording it over the members of his own race." *What the Negro Thinks* (1929), p. 84. As long ago as 1807 Bryan Edwards wrote that the Mulattoes in Jamaica "are accused of proving bad masters when invested with power; and their conduct towards their slaves is said to be, in a high degree, harsh and imperious. I suspect," he added, "there is some truth in this representation; for it is the general characteristic of human nature, that men whose authority is most likely to be disputed, are the most jealous of any infringement of it, and the most vigilant in its support." *The History, Civil and Commercial, of the British Colonies in the West Indies*, 4th ed., vol. 2, p. 25. See also *Journal of a Residence among the Negroes in the West Indies* (1845), by M. G. ("Monk") Lewis, p. 180.

their ancestors. The *Pax Britannica* and the ordered government of other European nations have brought security to peoples accustomed for centuries to every form of outrage and spoliation. The people of these countries have received immense material benefits, hospitals, schools, railways, roads and bridges, which have brought them improved health, comfort and prosperity.[1] Lastly, and they themselves would count it not the least, though government by an alien race was not its necessary accompaniment, they have received Christianity, which in Africa, at least, is professed by nearly the whole of that class which is the most bitter in its attitude towards the white race.

In those parts of the world where climatic conditions prevent permanent settlement by members of the white race, in tropical West Africa for example,[2] it would seem that the native population has, on balance, benefited by European rule, except so far as the third grievance referred to in the previous chapter is concerned.

In other countries the position has been complicated by the seizure of the land by members of the ruling race, and a definite grievance exists on a point which is very deeply felt. The coloured inhabitants of tropical countries are passionately attached to their ancestral lands. Practically throughout Africa the communal ownership of land was the basis of tribal economy. "The native conception appears to be that each head of a family is entitled to the enjoyment of sufficient land within the limits of the village or other community to which he belongs for the support of his household."[3] Mr. C. L. Temple, formerly a Lieutenant-Governor in Nigeria, held the view that "all those acts of native chiefs, which,

[1] A Dutch writer points out that "it is to Western authority, however limited its capacities in the past, that the autochthonous population in different parts of the world owes the beginning of a fuller consciousness which could never have been born under a primitive popular authority or under despotic princes." *Colonial Policy* (1931), by A. D. A. DeKat Angelino, vol. 1, p. 8. At the same time, we should remember the bitter disillusionment of the Gothic King of Italy, who "learnt by experience that not even the wisest or most humane of Princes, if he be an alien in race, in customs and religion, can ever win the hearts of the people." See *Rome in the Middle Ages* (1900), by F. Gregorovius (trans. by Mrs. G. W. Hamilton) vol. 1, p. 327.

[2] Mr. C. R. Buxton considers that the marked difference in the happiness and prosperity of the West African as compared with the coloured populations of East and South Africa is to be attributed to the land question. The West African, who retains the ownership of his land, belongs to a 'happy people' and shares in a 'prosperous peasant economy.' *The Manchester Guardian* of January 7, 1935.

[3] *Report of Northern Nigeria Lands Committee*, 1910 (Cmd. 5102).

POLITICAL AND LEGAL DISCRIMINATION AGAINST NEGROES

by means of treaties made with strangers, alienated the tribal lands, are . . . according to native law and custom, *ultra vires.*"[1]

If in West Africa a climate hostile to white settlement has saved his land for the native of the country, such has not been the case in Kenya and South Africa. As pointed out above, the difficulty of restoring to their original owners those lands which have been alienated to white farmers is almost insuperable. The settlers of Kenya, for instance, took up their lands with the consent, and indeed with the encouragement, of their Government, and, so long as the mistakes of the past are not repeated or aggravated in the future, there is reason in the argument that their interests should be respected. It is even possible that time will adjust the difficulty, as "no serious person to-day is yet convinced that the White settlers in Kenya Colony will prove able to bring up their children in the country, or that a native-bred generation of Whites, even if it is actually reared in the Kenya highlands by a *tour de force*, will display the physical and psychic stamina of its European-bred parents."[2] Meanwhile, however, we are faced in Kenya (as in South Africa) with a problem of the first magnitude, the problem of reconciling the equitable rights of the natives with the legal claims of the white settlers.[3]

The legal disabilities of which coloured peoples complain are, of course, the result of white domination. That these disabilities exist, based on colour and race distinctions, are well known, and

[1] *Native Races and their Rulers* (1918), by C. L. Temple, p. 140.

[2] *A Study of History* (1935), by A. J. Toynbee, vol. 2, p. 303. Lord Hailey, in *An African Survey* (1938), p. 1636, says that "it must remain open to question, until further knowledge has been gained, whether the more tropical portions of the 3,000-foot plateau are suited for the permanent residence of a European population." See also the argument that the white race cannot successfully colonise tropical Australia, in *Environment and Race* (1937), by G. Taylor, Chapter XXIV; and the very interesting publication of the American Geographical Society, *White Settlers in the Tropics* (1939), by A. Grenfell Price, particularly the conclusions reached on pages 83 and 102. For an Italian view of the possibility of white settlement in Abysinna, see *Ethiopia, An Empire in the Making* (1939), by F. Quaranta, p. 54.

[3] An interesting comparison has been drawn with British policy in Kenya and South Africa. "This is the old West Indian slave policy of the eighteenth century, with the difference and the aggravation that, instead of importing slaves into European-owned territory, it exports Europeans to native territory, from which it first ousts the native owners and to which it later recalls them in the capacity of wage-earners or 'labour-tenants' dependent on their white masters." *The Duty of Empire* (1935), by Leonard Barnes, p. 128.

COLOUR PREJUDICE

especially in South Africa,[1] and in the United States of America they are very real.[2] For instance, "marriage between white and coloured persons is illegal in all the southern and in twelve northern states (of the United States) ... A Negro who has married a white woman in a northern state and goes south is liable to imprisonment—in some states for ten years."[3] In their Declaration of Independence the founders of the United States of America stated: "We hold these truths to be self evident: That all men are created equal;[4] that they are endowed by their Creator with certain inalienable rights; that among these are life, liberty and the pursuit of happiness."[5] Yet in 1857 the Supreme Court of the United States laid down, in the case of Dred Scot[6] v. Sandford, that the

[1] Extra-marital miscegenation was made a criminal offence in South Africa by the Tielman Roos "Immorality" Act of 1926.

[2] On the other hand, in Liberia, no one can become a citizen and hold land unless he is of African descent. *The Atlantic and Emancipation* (1937), by H. A. Wyndham, p. 186.

[3] *The Menace of Colour* (1925), by J. W. Gregory, 2nd ed., p. 56.

[4] Lord Balfour, discussing the American Declaration of Independence at the Peace Conference of 1919, agreed that "it was true in a certain sense that all men of a particular nation were created equal, but not that a man in Central Africa was created equal to a European." *My Diary at the Conference of Paris* (1924), by D. H. Miller, vol. 1, p. 116. See also *Some Impressions of the United States* (1883), by E. A. Freeman, p. 144: "The Negro may be a man and a brother in some secondary sense; he is not a man and a brother in the same full sense in which every Western Aryan is a man and a brother. He cannot be assimilated; the laws of nature forbid it."

[5] In the 'cornerstone' speech by A. H. Stevens, at Savannah, Georgia, on March 21, 1861, reference was made to the prophecy of Jefferson that slavery was the rock on which the United States constitution would split, and to his idea that the enslavement of the African was wrong and that the institution of slavery would pass away. "These ideas," said the speaker, "were fundamentally wrong. They rested upon the assumption of the equality of races. This was an error. ... Our new Government (i.e. of the Southern States) is founded upon exactly the opposite ideas; its foundations were laid, its corner-stone rests, upon the great truth that the Negro is not equal to the white man; that slavery, subordination to the superior race, is his natural and moral condition. This, our new Government, is the first, in the history of the world, based upon this great physical, philosophical and moral truth." *The Rebellion Record* (1861), edited by Frank Moore, vol. 1, p. 45.

[6] Scot was a Negro slave, who was taken by his master from Missouri, a slave state, to Illinois, and then back to Missouri, where he claimed his freedom on the ground that his removal to the free state of Illinois had emancipated him. He was successful before the State Court of Missouri, but the judgment of this Court was reversed by the Supreme Court; in delivering the judgment of the Supreme Court the Chief Justice said: "Such persons had been regarded as unfit to associate with the white race, either in social or political relations, and so far inferior that they had no rights which the white man was bound to respect, and that the Negro might justly and lawfully be reduced to slavery for his benefit; that this opinion was, at that time, fixed and universal in the civilised portion of the white race, and was

references to the rights of men in the Declaration could not be interpreted as intended to apply to all human beings, and that the authors of the Declaration could not have meant to include among the people who were declaring their independence the members of the "enslaved African race." So for nearly one hundred years after the signing of this Declaration liberty was withheld from the Negro slaves of America, and the lives and happiness of American Negroes are too often to-day at the mercy of irresponsible white mobs. Again, in spite of the Fifteenth Amendment to the Constitution, which enacted that "the rights of citizens of the United States shall not be denied or abridged by the United States or by any State on account of race, colour, or previous condition of servitude," the experiment of Negro suffrage in America has been "silently and almost unanimously dropped."[1] Professor Gregory says that "the denial of the vote to the Negro (in the United States) has been attended by the serious drawback that it has handicapped the even administration of justice."[2] As evidence of this it is scarcely necessary to do more than refer to the notorious "Scottsboro" case, and the appalling record of lynchings in the Southern States.

From 1885 to 1926, inclusive, 4,250 persons were lynched in the United States, and of these 3,205 were Negroes.[3] From 1889 until the end of 1899 the average number of persons lynched each year was 187·5. From 1900 to the end of 1930, the average number of lynchings was under sixty-one a year, and the figures had actually dropped for the five years 1926 to 1930 to 17·6.[4] The position was improving steadily, and in 1941 only four persons were lynched,[5] but

---

regarded as an axiom in morals as well as politics, which no one thought of disputing, or supposed to be open to dispute." Quoted from *The Slave Power* (1863), by J. E. Cairnes, p. 250.

[1] *Human Nature in Politics* (1920), by Graham Wallas, 3rd ed., p. 7. For a description of the methods employed to prevent the Negroes from voting in the Southern States, see *Race, Class and Party* (1932), by P. Lewinson, *passim*. Another writer has said that "the principles of universal ethics . . . demand that the American Negro shall be given social and political equality; yet . . . the good sense of the southern white man still steadily forbids him to obey these precepts and impels him in a course of conduct inconsistent with his acknowledged ethical principles." *Ethics and some Modern World Problems* (1924), by W. McDougall, p. 38.

[2] *The Menace of Colour* (1925), by J. W. Gregory, 2nd ed., p. 48.

[3] *Encyclopaedia Britannica*, 14th ed., vol. 14, p. 526.

[4] *Culture in the South* (1934), edited by W. T. Couch. Article by H. C. Brearley on "The Pattern of Violence," pp. 679, 691–2.

[5] *An American Dilemma* (1944), by G. Myrdal, p. 561.

COLOUR PREJUDICE

since the end of the last war there has been a serious recrudescence of this crime. *The Times* of July 27, 1946, reported that two Negroes and their wives had been shot in Georgia by a band of twenty to thirty white men, while *The Economist* of October 5, 1946 stated that since V.J. Day there had been forty-one lynchings in the United States. Public opinion has been shocked by the acquittal by a white jury in South Carolina of a number of men who admitted in writing that they had been concerned in the lynching of a Negro,¹ and this case may well result in an improvement of the position, as the scandal is too flagrant to be overlooked.

It is true that white men as well as Negroes are sometimes lynched in the United States, but it was pointed out some years ago that lynching was practised against Negroes four times as frequently as against whites, or nearly forty times as frequently in proportion to population.² It is good to learn that lynching accompanied with torture is not typical,³ though of course it exists, and that it is wrong to assume that everyone in the South approves of such atrocities.⁴ On the other hand it is admitted that lynchings "have their defenders yet among southern Christians." In response to a question widely scattered among southerners regarding the stand the Church ought to take on race relationships, numerous replies indicated a disapproval of lynching "except in the case of rape."⁵

Lynch law would be bad enough if there could be any certainty that its victims were actually guilty of the crime for which they suffer, but there seems to be little doubt that in many cases suspicion

¹ See *The Economist* of May 31, 1947: "Of the thirty-one defendants in South Carolina's mass lynching trial at Greenville, twenty-six had signed statements admitting their participation in the murder of Willie Earle. The Governor of the State had demanded their conviction; the Federal Bureau of Investigation had been called in. The judge, who warned the jury to disregard any "so-called race issue" had maintained exceptionally high standards of court procedure. Again and again he halted the defending attorneys in their denunciations of "northern meddling" and in their appeals to race passions. Yet an all-white jury acquitted the defendants on each of ninety-six counts. The South was conscious that it, as well as the lynch mob, was on trial. The verdict has gone against Carolina justice, despite the best efforts of the State."

² *Race Relations, Adjustment of Whites and Negroes in the United States* (1934), by W. D. Weatherford and C. S. Johnson, p. 433.

³ *Culture in the South* (1934), edited by W. T. Couch. Article by H. C. Brearley on "The Pattern of Violence," p. 681.

⁴ *Ibid.* Article by W. T. Couch on "The Negro in the South," p. 461.

⁵ *Ibid.*, edited by W. T. Couch. Article by E. M. Poteat, Jr., on "Religion in the South," p. 258.

POLITICAL AND LEGAL DISCRIMINATION AGAINST NEGROES

alone, or the fevered imagination of a hysterical woman,[1] is sufficient to send a Negro to his death in those parts of the United States where race prejudice runs high. It has been suggested that the pride of race for which the Anglo-Saxon peoples are notorious has, in America, manifested itself in acute form in the lynching of Negroes.[2] In South Africa, on the other hand, lynching is entirely unknown.[3]

Other legal disabilities under which the Negroes suffer in the United States, such as segregation, will be referred to later. It is sufficient here to observe that in a country the Constitution of which is based on the principles of liberty and equality, the coloured man is, to a great extent, deprived of both, and Professor Brogan says that the South Carolina legislature was undoubtedly speaking for most Southerners when it went on record in 1944 as being against the "co-mingling of the races upon any basis of equality as un-American," and solemnly pledged its collective life to maintaining white supremacy "whatever the cost."[4]

In the proclamation of Queen Victoria annexing Natal in 1843, it was declared that "there shall not in the eye of the law be any distinction of persons or disqualification founded on mere distinction of colour, origin, language or creed, but that the protection of the law, in letter and in substance, shall be extended impartially to all alike."[5] On the other hand, in clause 9 of the Grondwet (Constitution) of the South African Republic of February 1858, it was laid down that "the people desire to permit no equality between coloured people and the white inhabitants, either in Church or State."[6] With the omission of the last five words, this statement was repeated in the Grondwet of 1889. There can be no

[1] Truth is often disguised as fiction, and the following quotation from an American novel probably interprets white sentiment in the Southern States not unfairly: " 'It won't do him no good,' said Henry. 'It's a white woman's word against a nigger's, ain't it? Maybe she ain't all she should be but she's white, an' she come from these parts, an' no black bastard from down-state kin tell her she lies an' git away with it.' " *Stars fell on Alabama* (1935), by C. Carmer, p. 75.
[2] *England* (1923), by W. Dibelius (translated in 1930 from the German by M. A. Hamilton), p. 97.
[3] *Race Attitudes in South Africa* (1937), by I. D. MacCrone, p. 283.
[4] *The American Problem* (1944), by D. W. Brogan, p. 117.
[5] *The Annals of Natal*, 1495 to 1845, vol. 2, p. 166.
[6] *Select Constitutional Documents illustrating South African History*, 1795–1910, edited by G. W. Eybers, p. 364.

question which document now inspires the Nationalist Party of South Africa in its attitude towards the coloured population. Sir Arthur Keith says that "Boer and Briton may differ in speech, habit, and outlook, but both agree that there is an impassable frontier between them and the native races of Africa and Asia. They do not even camouflage the racial barricade which they have erected."[1] It is interesting to note that Lord Milner, in his "Watch Tower"[2] speech of 1903, at Johannesburg, accepted the dictum of Cecil Rhodes that civilisation, not colour, should be the test of fitness for civic rights. He asserted the superiority of the white man, and doubted whether the black man would ever rise to the same level, but "if a black man, one in a thousand—perhaps it would be more correct to say one in a hundred thousand—raises himself to a white level of civilisation," then he should receive the same treatment as a white man.[3]

It has been estimated[4] that the percentages of the various races making up the population of South Africa are as follows:—

Europeans	21·9%
Bantus	67·8%
Coloured (of mixed blood)	7·9%
Asiatics	2·4%

In spite of their comparatively small numbers, the Europeans control the Government of the country, and Mr. Lansbury has remarked that "in Natal, where such discrimination is expressly forbidden by the foundation law of the Colony, the conditions have been so gerrymandered that only one native has the vote."[5]

---

[1] *Nationality and Race from an Anthropologist's Point of View* (1919), by Sir Arthur Keith, p. 17.

[2] "I am the man on the watch tower, and the man on the watch tower may see further," etc.

[3] *The Milner Papers* (1931), edited by C. Headlam, pp. 467-8.

[4] *The Problem of Colour in Relation to the Idea of Equality* (Supplement to vol. 1, no. 2, of the *Journal of Philosophical Studies*); paper by the Honourable H. A. Wyndham, p. 24.

[5] *Labour's Way with the Commonwealth* (1935), by George Lansbury, p. 26. It has been stated (see *South Africa Past and Present* (1900), by Violent R. Markham p. 241) that South Africa is the only instance of a country possessing representative institutions where the black population largely outnumbers the white. This is scarcely correct as the whites are outnumbered by the blacks in Barbados, Bermuda and the Bahamas, and all three Colonies possess representative, though not responsible Government. When I was a member of the Bahamas House of Assembly (from

POLITICAL AND LEGAL DISCRIMINATION AGAINST NEGROES

The effect of this control of the Government in South Africa by a minority has, of course, resulted in discriminatory legislation against the non-white population, for the benefit of the white inhabitants. In 1926 an amendment to the Mines and Works Act of 1911 gave the Government power to differentiate by regulation between different classes of labour, on the ground of race or colour alone. This 'Colour Bar Act,' as it is called, has been described as a huge psychological blunder;[1] it has resulted in the exclusion of the natives from the better-paid types of employment,[2] and there can be no doubt that it is responsible for the growth of anti-white prejudice, and the general embitterment of race relations throughout the Union.[3] Again, the Women's Enfranchisement Act of 1930 gave the franchise to European women only, thus adding to the white vote and the white control of government.

Various observers have referred, however, to an improved attitude on the part of the younger South Africans, both British and Dutch, towards the native question,[4] though even this suggested

---

1925 to 1928) approximately two-thirds of the members were white and one-third coloured; had the proportion been reversed the white population would still have been over-represented. This over-representation was undoubtedly due to the 'open' voting allowed in the Colony, and the abuses which inevitably resulted, the white members having successfully resisted, for many years, legislation designed to ensure a secret ballot. Only one other white member voted with me when I tried to have the question of a secret ballot referred to a Select Committee, with a view to the passing of the necessary legislation. Some years later the secret ballot was introduced for elections in New Providence, but 'open' voting was still the rule in the Out-Island constituencies until 1947. It should, however, be remembered that 'open' voting was not abolished in Great Britain until 1872, and that many people then disapproved of the ballot, holding that anonymous voting was "a sneaking practice, like anonymous letter writing." See *Great Britain and the Empire*, by J. A. Williamson, p. 140.

[1] *Western Civilisation and the Natives of South Africa* (1934), edited by I. Schapera; article by W. H. Hutt on "The Economic Position of the Bantu in South Africa," p. 233.

[2] "Since 1927 the Government has steadily pursued the policy of substituting Poor Whites for Blacks in the lower grades of labour on the Railways. It has been an expensive process and does not appear to have brought a solution of the Poor Whites problem appreciably nearer. The principle of the Colour Bar in industry, which received statutory recognition in 1926, is enforced, in actual practice, more by Trade Union action than by Government Regulations." *Native Policy in Southern Africa* (1934), by Ifor L. Evans, p. 67.

[3] *The Colour Problems of South Africa* (1934), by Edgar H. Brookes, p. 10.

[4] *The Protectorates of South Africa* (1935), by Margery Perham and Lionel Curtis, pp. 70–71; *Native Policy in Southern Africa* (1934), by Ifor L. Evans, p. 63.

COLOUR PREJUDICE

change of attitude has been indignantly denied.[1] Professor Brookes, Principal of Amanzimtoti Institute, Natal, speaks of the "rapid growth of liberal ideas among young South Africans"; more and more of them, he says, "are beginning to face the issues of their national life with honesty and courage . . . mere prejudice is becoming unfashionable."[2] Perhaps the most promising sign was the Conference at Fort Hare,[3] in the winter of 1930, summoned by the Student Christian Association of South Africa; at this Conference the white students, both English and Dutch, spontaneously suggested that there should be no discrimination against the Bantu students and joined them both at games and at meals. This, and recent remarks in the South African Press,[4] give hope for the future, but legislation passed within recent years has made the position of the coloured South African worse even than it was from the point of view of representation in the legislature.

My personal impression, formed admittedly after a very short visit to the Union at the end of 1943, is that Field-Marshal Smuts' Government was honestly trying to improve the position of the coloured inhabitants of the Union, but was handicapped in its efforts by the violent hostility of the Opposition to any measures designed towards this end, and the lukewarm interest of some of its own supporters.[5] There can be no doubt that the pro-German attitude of some of the Nationalist leaders was due to the belief that

[1] *The Protectorates of South Africa* (1935), by Margery Perham and Lionel Curtis, p. 94.
[2] *The Colour Problems of South Africa* (1934), by Edgar H. Brookes, pp. 2, 18.
[3] I was able to see for myself, and to admire, the good work that is being done for Africans at Fort Hare, Lovedale, and Healdtown. These three educational establishments are run by the Missions which have done so much for the natives of South Africa. Good work is also being done by several Agricultural Colleges run by the Government.
[4] *The Rand Daily Mail* of December 6, 1946, is quoted by *The Economist* (of December 28, 1946) as saying that "the time has come for the Union to do a little heart-searching about its native policy." See also the speech by Field-Marshal Smuts at Pretoria on December 20, 1946: "There is too much tendency in this country to look merely at a man's skin and judge him on that. The question to be seriously considered is whether we should not give a man of different colour, who is highly educated and has outstanding qualities of leadership, a chance. Why treat them all on the lowest level? If we are wise and fair we will study this aspect and decide whether a man of a different colour and who lives a European life should not be accorded a position higher than the lowest level of his own people." *The Times* of December 21, 1946.
[5] Through the courtesy of the Union Government I was able to visit and inspect

POLITICAL AND LEGAL DISCRIMINATION AGAINST NEGROES

a Nazi victory would leave them free to treat the coloured people of South Africa (and, incidentally, the British section of the population) as they think they should be treated. South Africa is a beautiful country, which is in a fair way to being ruined by racial strife, Dutch against British,[1] white against coloured, and one coloured race against another.[2]

The position of the Negro in Africa is well summed-up by Professor Brookes, "The century," he says, "which began in 1833 has seen a great advance in the position of the Black man. He was then in chains. He is, to-day, free in as far as legal bonds are concerned. But that does not mean to say that he is wholly emancipated. He remains in economic semi-slavery in many parts of Africa. He is still less than a freeman in the sphere of opportunity of service to the State. Restrictions, some legal, some extra-legal, hem him in. He is not yet free from the wretched fears of superstition. Poverty, disease and contempt are important factors in making him what he is."[3]

the work that is being done by the Native Affairs Department in the Ciskei and Transkei territories, and I was much impressed by the zeal and energy of the officers of that Department; if more money were placed at their disposal their efforts would be more successful. I was also able to see the excellent housing scheme for Natives at Port Elizabeth.

[1] But both those of Dutch and of British origin are most friendly and hospitable to visitors. I should like to take this opportunity of thanking all the kindly people I met in South Africa.

[2] The non-white people of South Africa include "Natives" (Bantus, Hottentots, etc.), "Coloured" (Mulattoes, etc.), Indians, and Malays.

[3] *The Colour Problems of South Africa* (1934), by Edgar H. Brookes, p. 176.

Chapter V

SOCIAL DISCRIMINATION AGAINST NEGROES

WE come now to the third grievance of coloured people, which in my opinion is the most important, not only because it is the one most bitterly felt but because it is also the one most easily removed.

It is not unnatural that the black man should be resentful of the white attitude of superiority. "At the bottom of his heart the Negro believes that he has capabilities of culture and character equal to that of any other race; he believes that his gifts and endowments are of equal worth to those of any other people; and even in the matter of the mingling of racial strains, however undesirable it might seem to be from a social point of view, he would never admit that his blood carries any taint of physiological, mental, or spiritual inferiority."[1] Believing this, he finds it difficult to accept complaisantly even a tacit assumption of white superiority, which, to be just, is the most that he has to complain of in his dealings with white men of decent breeding in most countries. But in some countries he has to complain of legal discrimination and in practically all countries he suffers from social disadvantages and the gross insults or offensive pleasantries of ill-bred or unthinking whites. The harm done, deliberately or carelessly, by one ill-mannered white man can undo years of patient work by others in the cause of inter-racial friendship.[2] It is true that the Negro is often

[1] *What the Negro Thinks* (1929), by R. R. Moton, p. 239.
[2] *Christianity and the Race Problem* (1924), by J. H. Oldham, 7th ed., p. 162. An Indian writer has suggested that it might be useful if every European arriving in India were given a tract entitled "What a Westerner ought to know," containing such hints as these:

"1. Indians criticise one another freely, even bitterly, but they hate to be criticised by a stranger.
"2. All Indians are not coolies or clerks; so do not speak to everyone in the same lofty manner. Above all avoid the word 'native' as you would the black plague. Talk naturally, as man to man. . . ."
See *Indian Pilgrimage* (1939), by Ranjee G. Shahani, p. 149.

SOCIAL DISCRIMINATION AGAINST NEGROES

over-sensitive, and too quick to see an insult where none is intended, but his past experience has caused him to be suspicious.[1]

Even in America, where the legal discrimination against the Negro and his political disfranchisement are more effective than elsewhere, it is the social restrictions and the personal insults that are the more bitterly resented.[2] It is difficult for one who has never visited the United States, or studied the literature on the subject, fully to appreciate the extent of these restrictions or the grossness of these insults. The exclusion of Negro passengers, of whatever class, from certain portions of railway trains and street cars and the provision of special 'Jim Crow' cars for Negroes are humiliating and not infrequently ridiculous. Special waiting rooms are provided for Negro travellers in railway stations, and it is generally found that they are inferior in all respects to the 'white' waiting rooms in the same stations. Special schools are provided for Negro children. From most 'white' hotels and restaurants black patrons are excluded,[3] either by a direct refusal of their custom or by round-about methods even more insulting.[4] It has been naïvely suggested by an American writer that there is nothing wrong with the principle of the 'Jim Crow' car, as the Negro is merely given a different place and not necessarily an inferior one to the white.[5]

The attitude of the reasonable American Negro to this matter is well stated by Major Moton: "Mere separation of the races . . .

[1] Lord Olivier says that the Africans "are excessively suspicious, and, out of an excess of caution and of generations of bitter experience, often give white men less credit than they really deserve for good will and good faith towards them." *The Anatomy of African Misery* (1927), by Lord Olivier, p. 190.

[2] Cf. *The Menace of Colour* (1925), by J. W. Gregory, 2nd ed., p. 51. See also *The Colour Problems of South Africa* (1934), by E. H. Brookes, p. 90: "The tacit assumption behind many of the attacks on the Cape Native franchise is that the Native is thirsting for power—power to rule Europeans. It is an utterly false picture. The African is striving not for power, but for dignity and recognition."

[3] If the revulsion from colour is the reason for exclusion it is strange that servants, who handle the plates and come into closer contact with white patrons than other patrons can possibly do, are not excluded also, but it is pointed out that "a maid's apron, a porter's cap, or a white child in the arms, will gain any Negro entrance to places closed to the most distinguished members of the race." *The Story of the American Negro*, by I. C. Brown, p. 115.

[4] Chinese and Japanese are not, as a rule, excluded from 'white' hotels and restaurants, but, in California especially, they are often prevented from using 'white' swimming pools or from joining in 'white' games. See *Alien Americans* (1936), by B. Schrieke, pp. 18, 39.

[5] *Problems of the Present South* (1904), by E. C. Murphy, p. 277.

is not always objectionable to Negroes and under certain circumstances may be preferable to both races; but its requirement in law and the assumption of superiority in station which it sooner or later inspires does and always will meet with an uncompromising protest from the Negro."[1] He points out that it is this policy of separation of the two races that has caused "the greatly heightened race consciousness within the Negro race as a whole which is noticeable on every hand . . . Without contact there cannot be knowledge; segregation[2] reduces the contacts, and so knowledge and understanding decrease. With decreasing knowledge comes increasing distrust and suspicion, and these in turn engender prejudice and even hatred. So a vicious circle is established."[3] A typical example of deliberate avoidance of contact was the refusal of the South African Government, some years ago, to allow the "Pathfinders," the local "coloured" equivalent of the Boy Scouts, to attend the International Jamboree in Hungary.[4]

It is the insult in this enforced separation in public conveyances and elsewhere, rather than the separation itself, that is resented. It is the discrimination against colour, rather than against the lack of culture and education, that appears so unfair, the preference for the company of a low-class white rather than that of a well-behaved and well-educated black man. Major Moton admits that the original discrimination against the Negro, at a time when few, if any, had attained to any degree of culture, was perhaps justified. "There

[1] *What the Negro Thinks* (1929), by R. R. Moton, p. 185. A West African says that "the fad of segregation in social gatherings and religious worship recently brought into prominence by the imprudent and impolitic among white people is not distasteful to the un-Europeanised African." Pastor M. Agbebi, of Lagos in *Papers on Inter-racial Problems* communicated to the First Universal Races Congress at the University of London, July 1911 (Edited by G. Spiller), p. 344.

[2] Segregation is used by Major Moton to include the separation of the races in public conveyances, schools, etc., as well as in residential areas. A South African writer says that "present day discussions about native policy revolve around the blessed word 'segregation'—political, economic, social, sexual." Article by R. F. A. Hoernlé on "Race Mixture and Native Policy in South Africa" in *Western Civilisation and the Natives of South Africa* (1934), edited by I. Schapera, p. 263. For a list of the many variations in the kind or form of segregation, see *American Caste and the Negro College* (1938), by Buell G. Gallagher, pp. 136–7.

[3] *What the Negro Thinks* (1929), by R. R. Moton, pp. 5, 44.

[4] Coloured boys were formerly not allowed to be Boy Scouts in South Africa. As a result of Lord Baden-Powell's visit to South Africa in 1936 coloured boys will be admitted, but their organisations will be distinct from those of the white Scouts. *The Times* of May 28, 1936.

SOCIAL DISCRIMINATION AGAINST NEGROES

was a time," he says "when Negroes were conspicious in public places because of bizarre effects in their dress and an unrestrained boisterousness, but that distinction, happily, has almost gone. One early apology for the 'Jim Crow' car was the unsightly appearance, bad manners, and rough conduct of the Negroes. . . . Negroes have changed."[1]

There is still an unfortunate tendency among the whites to group all Negroes in the same class,[2] and an American State Governor is quoted as having said that he was just as much opposed to Dr. Booker Washington[3] as a voter as to the "typical little coon . . . who blacks my shoes every morning. Neither is fit to perform the supreme functions of citizenship."[4] Such an assertion is significant as showing the absurdity[5] to which colour prejudice is bound to lead. There are different classes and different levels of culture among the black[6] as among the white races. No one would think of classing that delightful person, the cultured American, with his noisy and aggressive compatriots, and I hope that other nations do not judge Englishmen from the worst type of English tourist. It is difficult, therefore, to understand why a distinction cannot be drawn between the educated and well-mannered Negro gentleman and the Negro of a lower class.

In addition to the indirect insult involved in this social separation of the races, the Negro, especially in America, has to complain of insults more direct. It is true that many of the insults of which he complains are not intended as such, that many more are of so

---

[1] *What the Negro Thinks* (1929), by R. R. Moton, p. 36.
[2] Major Moton says that this tendency was expressed in a popular song, "All coons look alike to me"; see *What the Negro Thinks* (1929), p. 18. It is a fact that Europeans find it difficult to distinguish one black man from another when they first go to the tropics; the African finds it just as difficult to distinguish white faces.
[3] The distinguished Principal, at that time, of Tuskegee Institute.
[4] *The Aftermath of Slavery* (1905), by an ex-slave, W. A. Sinclair, p. 196. In the *News Letter* of the League of Coloured Peoples for October 1945, it is stated that, in discussing the question of the municipal franchise being given to Africans, the Mayor of Salisbury, Southern Rhodesia, said that "you might as well give the vote to baboons."
[5] An Englishwoman, writing in 1844, tells us that in Antigua a different bell was used to toll at the death of coloured people than was used when a white person died. *Antigua and the Antiguans*, vol. 2, p. 179.
[6] Sir Reginald St. Johnston, formerly Governor of the Leeward Islands, has had to point out that "there are distinct classes among the coloured people, a fact that is too little realised in England." *Strange Places and Strange Peoples* (1936), p. 279.

trifling a nature that they would not be noticed save by those on the look-out for insults, and that a complex of inferiority tends to magnify the careless word into deliberate and calculated discourtesy.

Such, for instance, is the objection of the African to being styled a 'native,' a word in which he sees an implied contempt;[1] a similar objection to the use of the word in India[2] resulted in the issue of an order forbidding its use by any official in referring to an inhabitant of the country.[3] The word is freely used in many countries to distinguish the locally-born white inhabitants from alien residents, and carries no suggestion of inferiority; as a matter of fact, in the West Indies both whites and blacks would speak of themselves as natives if born locally. At the same time it must be admitted that the present-day connotation of the word 'native,' and its equivalent in other European languages, carries with it the idea of inferiority. The Oxford Dictionary says that the word is applied disparagingly to local residents belonging to any place, and with a suggestion that these residents are not European, but members of a backward race.[4]

For very similar reasons the word 'Eurasian' has become unpopular among those to whom it used to be applied, and these people prefer now to be known as Anglo-Indians.[5] A Chinese gentleman objects to being called a 'Chink,' or even a 'Chinaman,' and I have no doubt that the southern European resents the use of the words 'Wop' and 'Dago.'[6] We can appreciate the point of view of these people better if we recollect that the white American servant refuses to be known as anything else than a 'help,' and if

---

[1] I believe, however, that the 'civilised' Liberian speaks of the aboriginal as a 'Native,' and that the distinction is officially recognised. In *The Soul of Nigeria* (1937), by I. O. Delano, himself a Yoruba, the author repeatedly speaks of 'natives,' with a small 'n'!

[2] For an indication of this see note 2 on page 60.

[3] See the Parliamentary Report in *The Times* of July 29, 1927.

[4] The use of the word in this sense dates back to the year 1800.

[5] The word 'Eurasian' was formerly used to indicate a person of mixed European and Asiatic, especially Indian, parentage. Such a person was, until about 1844, called an East Indian (*Oxford Dictionary*). The word 'Anglo-Indian' was formerly used of a person of pure European parentage, born or domiciled in India.

[6] In India the word *Feringhi* (= Frank), originally merely a geographical reference to the origin of the white man, is now used with offensive intent as a name for Europeans. On the other hand, the word *Giaour*, once used contemptuously by the Turks of Christians and other non-Muslims, is not now, as a rule, intended to be insulting. See *Encyclopaedia Britannica*, 14th ed.

we consider the reason for the extended use of the word 'gentleman' in England to-day.

There are a number of names, other than 'native,' used in speaking of Negroes to which they have more reason to object. Major Moton says that "the word 'nigger' as employed in the American vernacular embodies every shade of discrimination, from good-natured tolerance to despicable contempt. . . . The thrust at the Negro's self-respect conveyed in this term is always keenly resented by every class of Negroes."[1] It is true, he adds, "that certain elements of the race bandy this term lightly back and forth among themselves; but this does not confute the fact that all Negroes everywhere resent being called 'nigger' by any white person under any circumstances. And even when the term is used in badgering among themselves, it is intended to convey, good-naturedly, a certain contemptuous disregard for the other's estimate of himself."[2]

Considerable resentment was caused by the use of the word 'nigger' by the late Earl Baldwin in a speech in London, and a protest was made on the subject by the League of Coloured Peoples.[3] The careless use of the word is certainly unfortunate in view of the violent feelings that it can arouse.[4]

[1] *What the Negro Thinks* (1929), by R. R. Moton, p. 185.
[2] *Ibid.*, p. 186.
[3] Dr. Harold Moody, the President of the League, was reported as saying that the whole future relationship of the coloured people with the British people might hang on this matter. Earl Baldwin's words were "With luck we may hope to see the day when we shall be able to put a billy-cock hat on every nigger between Morocco and Capetown." See the *Manchester Guardian* of February 23, 1933, and the *Daily Express* of March 18, 1933.
[4] The following verses by Una M. Marson, of Jamaica, appeared in *The Keys*, the official organ of the League of Coloured Peoples, vol. 1, no. 1, p. 9:

> We will not be called 'Niggers'
> Since this was the favourite curse
> Of those who drove the Negroes
> To their death in days of slavery.
>
> In later years when singing Negroes
> Caused white men to laugh
> And show some interest in their art
> They talked of 'Nigger Minstrels'
> And patronised the Negro.
>
> 'Nigger' was raised then to a Burlesque Show
> And thus from Curse to Clown progressed.
> A coloured man was cause for merriment.

COLOUR PREJUDICE

Only slightly less offensive, says Major Moton, are the terms 'darky,' 'coon' and 'shine';[1] "but the limit of contumely is reached in the use of the word 'negress.' "[2] It is not easy to appreciate the reason for the strong resentment caused by the use of this word, as the word Negro is generally accepted, and 'Negress' is as suitable a word to express the feminine as 'duchess' or 'empress';[3] but Dr. Henry Carr suggested to me that the African compares 'Negress' with 'tigress' and 'lioness,' and objects to the likeness of the words used to describe his womenfolk and the females of animals.[4]

It is true that even the word Negro is objected to by some, who prefer to be called 'people of colour' or 'coloured men,'[5] but it is probable that no suitable name could be found which would not, in existing conditions, be objected to, sooner or later, on the ground, real or imagined, that it implied contempt.

More reasonable appears the resentment of the Negroes against the unnecessary and discourteous habit of omitting the use of 'Mr.,' 'Mrs.' or 'Miss' in writing of or speaking to Negroes.[6] A Bantu writer says that "the *average* white man of South Africa would never think of shaking hands with a black man. The ordinary terms of courtesy are purposely avoided by him, and such a prefix as 'Mr.' or 'Mrs.' in association with a black man's, or woman's,

[1] *What the Negro Thinks* (1929), by R. R. Moton, p. 187.

[2] *Ibid.*, p. 189. See also *The Menace of Colour* (1925), by J. W. Gregory, 2nd ed., preface.

[3] The word 'Negress' appears to have been first used in 1786 (*Oxford Dictionary*). Its use by a lecturer from Ceylon, at a Conference of the League of Coloured Peoples, appears to have been accepted without remonstrance, or was, perhaps, unnoticed. See report in *The Keys*, vol. 2, no. 1, p. 15.

[4] Another suggestion is that the word is disliked because it was used in advertisements of the sales of female slaves. See *Racial Pride and Prejudice* (1946), by E. J. Dingwall, p. 27.

[5] *The Menace of Colour* (1925), by J. W. Gregory, 2nd ed., preface. See also article entitled "The Negro in Barbados," by G. O. Bell, in *Negro Anthology* (1934) (edited by Nancy Cunard), p. 484: "In the society of people of Negro descent the word seems taboo, and is religiously eschewed, the term 'coloured' being used to classify the multiplicity of shades existing between the pure white and the pure black. To call the average coloured West Indian a Negro is to affront him." Another Negro writer says: "There are indeed puzzlingly subtle distinctions, to which coloured people are more or less sensitive. The adjective 'coloured' and the generic designations 'Negroes,' 'the Negro,' and 'the Negro race' are always in order; but 'a Negro man,' 'a Negro woman,' etc., are somewhat distasteful. 'Negress' is considered unpardonable." *Along this Way* (1941), by J. W. Johnson (Penguin ed.), p. 188.

[6] *What the Negro Thinks* (1929), by R. R. Moton, pp. 190, 196. See also *Christianity and the Race Problem* (1924), by J. H. Oldham, 7th ed., p. 165.

SOCIAL DISCRIMINATION AGAINST NEGROES

name never escapes his lips."[1] In 1944 a number of South African officials were dismissed or resigned their appointments because they would not comply with a Government instruction that official letters to coloured persons should be addressed in the same way as to whites, 'Sir' or 'Madam,' and that the envelopes should be addressed 'Mr.' or 'Mrs.'[2] Dr. DuBois writes bitterly of those "men who insist upon withholding from my mother and wife and daughter those signs and appellations of courtesy and respect which elsewhere he withholds only from bawds and courtesans."[3] In America this curious lack of courtesy is no doubt an unhappy survival from the old slave days, for "the Negro woman . . . still lives within the shadow of the time when to some her body was not her own but the property of her master, to be used according to his pleasure."[4] It is said that "in the United States the best class of coloured woman is subjected to insulting advances in the streets and the shops, and their husbands defend them at the risk of their lives."[5]

Another cause of offence is the use of the word 'Negro' in print without the capital 'N.'[6] This is always unfortunate, but particularly so when 'European and negro' are printed together. It will be apparent from the quotations in this book that the word 'negro,' with a small 'n' is generally used by white writers.[7]

[1] *The Bantu Past and Present* (1920), by S. M. Molema, p. 266. A French writer says that the "Negro in America" is never addressed as 'Mister,' be he a bishop or a doctor, but simply as John or Joseph. *America Comes of Age* (1927), by A. Siegfried, p. 95. This surely must be exceptional, but we know that Booker Washington was spoken of as 'Professor' or 'Doctor' by those who wished to avoid called this distinguished American 'Mr.' Washington. In this connection it is interesting to note that, in the French West Indian colonies in the eighteenth century, no coloured person could be addressed as 'sieur' or 'dame.' *The Atlantic and Slavery* (1935), by H. A. Wyndham, p. 264. [2] *The Times* of June 23, 1944.
[3] *Darkwater* (1920), by W. E. B. DuBois, p. 172.
[4] *What the Negro Thinks* (1929), by R. R. Moton, pp. 206–7. It has been suggested that "a sex relation between a slave woman and a white man was in no sense forced: it was in general a relation to which the Negro girl aspired and one which she courted." *Race Mixture* (1931), by E. B. Reuter, p. 41. This may have been due to "the slave's acceptance of the dominant world's estimate of the relative worth of black and white." See *The Story of the American Negro*, by I. C. Brown, p. 58. It is significant, however, that Negro men to-day show a marked desire to marry light-skinned women. See footnote 3 at page 124.
[5] *America Comes of Age* (1937), by A. Siegfried, p. 100.
[6] *What the Negro Thinks* (1929), by R. R. Moton, p. 188.
[7] Many 'white' newspapers in the United States are abandoning the small 'n' and capitalising 'Negro,' and this is regarded as "an important indication of a possible shift in racial etiquette." See *American Caste and the Negro College* (1938), by Buell A. Gallagher, p. 59.

Some of these 'insults,' however, are matters of comparatively trifling importance beside the effusions of the writers of a certain school, generally American,[1] who make it their business to disparage the Negro in every way possible, holding him up to ridicule and abuse for his present shortcomings and denying the possibility of his ever attaining the high standard of civilisation and culture of which they are themselves such shining examples. To quote Major Moton again, "a certain propaganda has pretty well succeeded in putting the stigma of inferiority on most things associated with the race,"[2] and Dr. DuBois says that "before that nameless prejudice . . . (the Negro) stands helpless, dismayed and wellnigh speechless: before that personal disrespect and mockery, the ridicule and systematic humiliation, the distortion of fact and wanton licence of fancy, the cynical ignoring of the better and the boisterous welcoming of the worse, the all-pervading desire to inculcate disdain for everything black."[3] The bitterness of this complaint can be understood when one reads the statement quoted in a previous chapter "that all scientific investigation of the subject proves the Negro to be an ape,"[4] or the equally remarkable suggestion that "it would doubtless be a capital thing, if it could be done, to emasculate the entire negro race and all its descendants in this country[5] and effectually stop the breed right now, and thus prevent any further danger from them, and the horrors of their crossing continually with the Anglo-Saxon stock."[6] It is only fair to add that the author from whom the last quotation is made realised that the scheme was impracticable and insisted that the alternative should be the deportation of the whole Negro population from America to Africa: if this is not done, he says, the whites will mix with "this lazy, ignorant, criminal race," and soon no one in America will be able to deny that he has in his veins "some of the blood of the Soudan cannibal."[7]

[1] See footnote 2 at page 7. [2] *Ibid.*, p. 228.
[3] *The Souls of Black Folk* (1903), by W. E. B. DuBois, p. 9.
[4] *The Negro a Beast, or in the Image of God?* (1900), by C. Carroll, p. 87. As pointed out on page 22, Herr Hitler considered the Negro to be only a half-ape.
[5] The United States of America.
[6] *The Negro, A Menace to American Civilisation* (1907), by R. W. Shufeldt, pp. 145, 154.
[7] *Ibid.*, pp. 153, 154. It should be noted that Marcus Garvey (see p. 41) advocated the return of all American Negroes to Africa. Similar proposals have been made from time to time since 1788; see *Dusk of Dawn* (1940), by W. E. B. DuBois, p. 195.

SOCIAL DISCRIMINATION AGAINST NEGROES

It has been pointed out that the Negro in the United States lives in an atmosphere of contempt and dislike, and that such advances as he may make, economically, educationally or culturally, must be in spite of it.[1] In a novel by a Negro author the return to his 'home-town' of a black youth who had been studying in Paris is described in a pathetic and significant passage: "The eyes of the white men about the station were not kind. He heard someone mutter 'Nigger.' His skin burned. For the first time in half a dozen years he felt his color. He was home."[2]

It cannot be pleasant for the segregated and almost disfranchised Negro, born a citizen of the United States, to see alien immigrants, because they are white, passing through the national and social gateways which to him are barred.[3] "As things stand to-day, even the luckiest Negro must always feel alien in the country to which he is more truly indigenous than ninety per cent of his white compatriots."[4]

As an example consider the indignation that was aroused throughout the United States when President Theodore Roosevelt invited Dr. Booker Washington to luncheon, and later when Mrs. Hoover received Mrs. DePriest at the White House.[5] Dr. Washington was at the time the President of Tuskegee Institute and one of the most distinguished Americans then living—but he was a Negro.[6]

---

[1] *Population Problems* (1923), by E. B. Reuter, p. 283.

[2] *The Ways of White Folks* (1934), by Langston Hughes, p. 36.

[3] *Nationality and Race from an Anthropologist's Point of View* (1919), by Sir Arthur Keith, p. 9.

[4] Paul Robeson, in *The Spectator* of August 8, 1931.

[5] See *Race Relations. Adjustment of Whites and Negroes in the United States* (1934), by W. D. Weatherford and C. S. Johnson, p. 516. It is suggested, however, that this indignation was deliberately worked up by Mr. Hoover's political opponents to discredit the Republic Party in the South: see *Race, Class and Party* (1932), by P. Lewinson, p. 180. In this matter of courtesy to the Negro, the action of President Roosevelt and Mrs. Hoover compares very favourably with that of Herr Hitler, who refused to receive the American Negro victors at the Olympic Games in Germany, in 1936, although he received all the others. It was announced officially that he was too tired to receive them, but "he was merely being petulant. The idea of sportsmanship is beyond him; a sporting contest is something in which a Nordic German must win." *The House that Hitler Built* (1937), by Stephen H. Roberts, p. 19.

[6] It is said that the young Negro servants at the White House gave up their posts because a Negro was eating with the whites! See *Negro Anthology* (1934), edited by Nancy Cunard, p. 28. I find it difficult to believe this; I have often had coloured guests and none of my Negro servants has ever shown the slightest objection to waiting on them.

COLOUR PREJUDICE

In South Africa the position is much the same. Lord Olivier has called attention to the offensive language and behaviour of certain South African whites in their dealings with Africans and Indians.[1] A Bantu writer says, "It is the little things that tell most in our social relationship with the whites . . . neatly dressed you arouse scowls, audible snarling interjections, or ill-mannered ridicule. . . . Posters daubed 'For Europeans only' are a standing affront to us in esplanades, botanical garden seats, parks, promenades, railway sidings, tram shelters, and public conveniences. . . . In religious circles too the colour obsession is not wanting."[2]

It is not only in the United States and South Africa that unnecessary insults are offered to the black race. As Lord Olivier says, "the symptoms of the brand of mental deficiency known as negrophobia are familiar enough"[3] in many lands. In England itself, as we have seen above, the coloured man is made to feel his position. A coloured writer says that the race prejudice of the English results "not usually in open rudeness, but in cold-shouldering and ignoring anyone different from themselves."[4] The presence of a Negro is often resented in hotels[5] and public swimming-baths, and not long ago a compartment of a train waiting at Euston was labelled 'Natives; must be separate to Europeans';[6] one of the Natives in question was the wife of a Member of the Nigerian Legislative Council, and is herself a cultured and travelled lady. Small wonder that another should write, after a visit to England:—

"We go, a disillusioned British host,
Back to the lands from which we came of late,
For ever broken by our welcome here,
And all the bitter insults that we meet."[7]

[1] *The Anatomy of African Misery* (1927), by Lord Olivier, p. 165.
[2] *Western Civilisation and the Natives of South Africa* (1934), edited by I. Schapera; article on "Bantu Grievances," by D. D. T. Jabavu, p. 298.
[3] *The Anatomy of African Misery* (1927), by Lord Olivier, p. 131.
[4] Article on "Cardiff's Coloured Population," by Nancie Sharpe, in *The Keys*, vol. 1, no. 3, p. 45.
[5] See letter to *The Times* of February 24, 1928, which referred also to the difficulty experienced by coloured girls in getting admission to hospitals in England for training as nurses. Not many years ago a well-known West Indian cricketer was unable to obtain accommodation in a London hotel because he was a coloured man.
[6] *West Africa*, of September 29, 1934. For the reported objection of a white woman to a Negro lady sharing her compartment in an English train see *The Anti-Slavery Reporter and Aborigines' Friend* of January 1940.
[7] From "Disillusionment," by Sylvia Lowe, in *The Keys*, vol. 1, no. 2, p. 28.

SOCIAL DISCRIMINATION AGAINST NEGROES

In spite of everything, our fellow-subjects of the Negro race, or at least a large proportion of them, retain a strong feeling of loyalty[1] to the British Empire and a remarkable pride in their British citizenship. Mr. Leonard Barnes says that the West Indian has "an irrational loyalty to the British connection,"[2] and, irrational or not, there can be no doubt that the West African is as loyal. It is surely a tragedy that their visits to the centre of the Empire should give cause for the weakening of that loyalty.[3]

In the British West Indian colonies there is no legal distinction between the races, although social discrimination exists, not only as between white and black but also as between the Mulattoes and the Negroes.[4] In British West Africa there is little legal discrimination that really matters. 'Natives' are subject to native law and custom and may in some cases be tried in 'Native Courts,' while non-natives may be tried only before a Magistrate or a Judge of the Supreme Court (who may be an African or a European) under English Common Law and the local statutes.

But in West Africa as in the West Indies there is social discrimination by the exclusion of Africans from 'European' clubs, and in some places from residential areas,[5] and cases occur of coloured persons being refused accommodation in hotels.[6] In both groups of colonies, however, the principal grievance lies in the failure of the Governments to appoint more Negroes to senior posts in the official hierarchy, 'European posts' as they are styled in West Africa. This failure is attributed, almost inevitably, to colour prejudice, although often enough the real cause is the difficulty of finding suitable local candidates.[7] Cases have occurred of assaults by Europeans on Africans, but these are always dealt

---

[1] I use this word with some reluctance as there should be no more need to emphasise the loyalty of British subjects in the West Indies or West Africa to their own Empire, than there is in the case of a Londoner.
[2] *The Duty of Empire* (1935), by Leonard Barnes, p. 117.
[3] Mr. Leonard Barnes has suggested that it was the inferiority of status assigned to them, no less than the friction arising from the restraints upon their trade, which in the end made the imperial tie intolerable to the American colonies. *Ibid.*, p. 74.
[4] See pages 123–4.
[5] In the Gold Coast, and probably in other colonies, African officials holding senior posts occupy the same types of quarters in the same residential areas as would be occupied by European officers of comparable rank.
[6] As in the unfortunate incident which occurred in Lagos in 1947.
[7] See page 95.

with severely when brought to official notice. Cases also probably occur of offensive remarks made to or about coloured people both in the West Indies and West Africa, but I doubt whether they are any more offensive than things written or said about the whites in the local Press or by Negro politicians.[1]

All coloured writers agree that it is among the lower class of Europeans that the greatest amount of racial prejudice exists. These 'poor whites,' or 'mean whites,' as they are often called, are the first to suffer from the economic rivalry of the blacks, and, with little but their white skins to be proud of,[2] they attach undue importance to pigmentation.[3]

One coloured writer says that "the most bitter antagonisms manifested towards the Negro are shown most frequently by those elements of the white population nearest to the Negro in status. Racial antipathies are by no means as common between Negroes and socially secure whites as between Negroes and whites who are precariously situated socially."[4] Another points out that prejudice is "rampant among the lowest ranked Europeans who employ it amongst the more timid to elevate their own position and make themselves feared. The higher a European rises the less he indulges."[5] A third says that the feeling against colour "is more marked among the lower classes and the less educated of the whites . . . the special hostility of this class is directed against the educated class of the blacks."[6] Finally we have Major Moton, who says that it is among the lower classes of whites "that the Negro finds

---

[1] People often overlook the fact that coloured people in British colonies may write or say things with impunity which in other countries would bring swift retribution.

[2] Writing in Jamaica at the beginning of the nineteenth century, Bryan Edwards refers to the "pre-eminence and distinction which are necessarily attached even to the complexion of a White Man, in a country where the complexion, generally speaking, distinguishes freedom from slavery." *The History, Civil and Commercial, of the British Colonies in the West Indies*, 4th ed., vol. 2, p. 8.

[3] Another curious but quite understandable fact is that those persons who have a small amount of coloured blood in their veins, though they may be quite white in appearance, are among the most bitter opponents of any concession to the Negroes, and are the most insistent that they should be "kept in their place."

[4] *Race Relations. Adjustment of Whites and Negroes in the United States* (1934), by W. D. Weatherford and C. S. Johnson, p. 58.

[5] *Negro Anthology* (1934), edited by Nancy Cunard; article by T. K. Utchay, "White-manning in West Africa," p. 762.

[6] *The Bantu Past and Present* (1920), by S. M. Molema, p. 270.

SOCIAL DISCRIMINATION AGAINST NEGROES

the greatest amount of prejudice and from whom he meets with the greatest amount of opposition."[1]

There is no doubt that the Negro is particularly quick in sizing up the white stranger. "He can tell almost immediately by speech, manner or appearance to which class each belongs,"[2] and he has "a keen perception for social differences among the whites."[3]

In so far as race prejudice is due to economic causes the 'poor white' is undoubtedly the real problem, and in South Africa, this problem is said to be insoluble.[4] As a result of an enquiry conducted by a Commission appointed by the Carnegie Corporation, it appears that some 300,000 whites in South Africa are living at or below the minimum essential to a European standard of living, and are either 'poor whites' or in danger of falling into this class.[5] It has been suggested that 'Native Policy' in South Africa has degenerated into a defence of the 'poor white';[6] and that the slogan 'white supremacy' really means *poor-white supremacy*.'[7] If it be true that the 'poor white' is the product of a system intended to degrade only the non-white,[8] he affords a terrible warning to those who support the system of racial repression, and, as shown above, he increases the bitterness, with all its possible consequences, of racial feeling.

While it may be admitted that the lower classes of whites are more offensive in their manner to the Negro than the better educated European, the latter is by no means free from blame. That a better educated man should be better mannered is nothing to boast about; that he has tacitly encouraged, or at least permitted, those of a lower class to insult the coloured man is at least a cause for shame.

---

[1] *What the Negro Thinks* (1929), by R. R. Moton, p. 22. Sir Ronald Storrs, in his *Orientations* (1937), p. 555, quotes André Gide: "*Moins le blanc est intelligent, plus il mèprise les noires.*" See also note 7 on page 149.

[2] *Ibid.*, p. 17.

[3] *America Comes of Age* (1927), by A. Siegfried, p. 101.

[4] *The African Today* (1934), by D. Westermann, p. 302.

[5] *Native Policy in Southern Africa* (1934), by Ifor L. Evans, p. 62.

[6] *West Africa*, of September 16, 1933.

[7] *Culture in the South* (1934), edited by W. T. Couch; article entitled "Middle Class and Bourbon," by C. E. Cason, p. 497. Mr. Cason points out that by the white man of any real prestige in the Southern States of America 'white supremacy' would be taken for granted.

[8] *The Elements of Social Justice* (1922), by L. T. Hobhouse, p. 185, note.

This chapter cannot be closed better than with a quotation from Lord Bryce. "Good feelings and good manners cannot be imposed by statute. The best hope lies in the slow growth of a better sentiment. When the educated sections of the dominant race have come to realise how essential it is to the future of their country that the backward race should be helped forward and rendered friendly, their influence will by degrees filter down through the masses of the people and efface the scorn they feel for the weaker race. . . . Manners depend upon sentiment, and sentiment changes slowly. Still it changes. It has changed as regards torture. It has changed as regards slavery."[1]

[1] *The Relations of the Advanced and the Backward Races of Mankind* (1902), by Lord Bryce, p. 43.

Chapter VI

ALLEGED INFERIORITY OF THE NEGRO

THERE are, of course, numbers of persons who justify white overlordship of the world, and the contemptuous treatment of the coloured races, by the assumption of inherent white superiority. Maintaining that western culture and civilisation, with all its imperfections, is yet the best, and that the survival of this civilisation and culture depends entirely on the white races of mankind, this school of thought argues that white supremacy must be maintained at all costs, not only for the preservation of the white race itself but in order that this race may develop and pass on to others the blessings of its culture and the benefits of its civilisation. "We now know that men are not, and never will be, equal. We know that environment and education can develop only what heredity brings . . . we now know that heredity is paramount in human evolution, all other things being secondary factors."[1] In other words we know that the white race, and especially the Nordic portion of it, is inherently superior to all others, and that no amount of education or training can raise the other races to its level. "If this great race, with its capacity for leadership and fighting, should ultimately pass, with it would pass that which we call civilisation. It would be succeeded by an unstable and bastardised population, whose worth and merit would have no inherent right to leadership and among which a new and darker age would blot out our racial inheritance. Such a catastrophe cannot threaten if the Nordic race will gather itself together in time, shake off the shackles of an inveterate altruism, discard the vain phantom of internationalism and reassert the pride of race and the right of merit to rule."[2]

The sickly sentiment of Christianity is apparently responsible

[1] *The Rising Tide of Colour against White World-Supremacy* (1920), by L. Stoddard, p. 306.
[2] Introduction by Madison Grant to *The Rising Tide of Colour* (1920), pp. xxix.-xxx.

for the present unhappy condition of the world. "Thanks to humanitarian preaching and the teaching of human equality," said a Nazi writer, "any Jew, Negro or Mulatto could be a fully qualified citizen of any European State. . . . Thanks to humanitarianism Niggers and Jews are allowed to marry into the Nordic race, yes, even to obtain important posts."[1] Herr Hitler was even more emphatic: "It does not dawn upon this depraved bourgeois world that here one has actually to do with a sin against all reason; that it is a criminal absurdity to train a born half-ape until one believes a lawyer has been made of him . . . that it is a sin against the will of the eternal Creator to let hundreds and hundreds of thousands of His most talented beings degenerate in the proletarian swamp of to-day, while Hottentots and Zulu Kafirs are trained for intellectual vocations. For it is training, exactly as that of the poodle and not a scientific 'education.'"[2] But another writer thinks that there is hope for the future. "Blood will tell. The white race must dominate. The Teutonic peoples stand for race purity. The negro is inferior and will remain so. . . . Let the lowest white man count for more than the highest negro. The foregoing statements indicate the leadings of Providence."[3] In case there should be any who doubted that Providence had come under the Nordic flag, German writers actually satisfied themselves that Christ was a Nordic and not of Jewish origin,[4] His Mother having been a blonde![5] At an earlier date Stewart Chamberlain had decided that "there is . . . not the slightest foundation for the suggestion that Christ's parents were of Jewish descent. . . . The probability that Christ was no Jew, that He had not a drop of genuine Jewish blood in His veins, is so great that it is almost equivalent to a certainty."[6]

[1] Quoted from Dr. Alfred Rosenberg's book, *The Myth of the Twentieth Century* (1930), in a pamphlet issued by "The Friends of Europe," entitled "Germany's National Religion," p. 13.
[2] *Mein Kampf*, by A. Hitler (trans. 1939), p. 640.
[3] *Race Orthodoxy in the South*, by T. P. Bailey, p. 93.
[4] Quoted from Dr. Alfred Rosenberg's book, *The Myth of the Twentieth Century* (1930), pp. 27, 76, in a pamphlet issued by "The Friends of Europe," entitled "Rosenberg's Positive Christianity."
[5] See *Genie und Rasse*, and *Der Blonde Mensch*, by Otto Hauser; quoted in *Race Relations* (1934), by W. D. Weatherford and C. S. Johnson, p. 18.
[6] *The Foundations of the Nineteenth Century* (1899), by H. Stewart Chamberlain, translated by J. Lees (1911), pp. 206, 211–12.

ALLEGED INFERIORITY OF THE NEGRO

It is extremely difficult to take seriously the modern adherents of the Nordic school, but they are merely following in the footsteps of their founder, Count Arthur de Gobineau, who asserted that "the various branches of the human family are distinguished by permanent and irradicable differences, both mentally and physically. They are unequal in intellectual capacity. . . . The dark races are the lowest on the scale. . . . Among the group of white races, the noblest, the most highly gifted in intellect and personal beauty, the most active in the cause of civilisation, is the Arian race."[1] De Gobineau's theory of racial superiority, fortified by the conclusions of Darwin, has developed into what has been called "Political Darwinism."[2] In the hands of its modern disciples it has become no more than the theory of 'the survival of the fittest,' the principle that 'might is right,' and 'the good old rule . . . the simple plan, that they should take who have the power, and they should keep who can.' At least the disciples of this creed are candid, and we know where we are with them.

Assuming for the moment that the principle of the 'survival of the fittest' can be accepted, what justification is there for the assumption by the white races that they are the fittest, and that the coloured races of mankind are inherently incapable of attaining the same standard of civilisation and culture? What in particular is there to prove that the Negroes are so far below the whites in mentality and ability to improve that they must be forever kept in a state of tutelage, if not of servitude? Writers of the Nordic school, who are emphatic in their claim of white superiority over *all* coloured peoples, admit that the yellow and brown races have attained to a certain level and are capable of going further: they deny even such qualified recognition to Negro ability.

Lothrop Stoddard, for instance, after referring to the contributions by the Asiatic races to human achievement, says that "the negro, on the contrary, has contributed virtually nothing. Left to himself he remained a savage, and in the past his only quickening has been where brown men have imposed their ideas and altered

[1] *The Moral and Intellectual Diversity of Races* (1856), from the French of Count Arthur de Gobineau, by H. Hotz, pp. 439, 443, 457. It has been said that the word 'Arian' or 'Aryan' is a linguistic expression forced by the philologists into the domain of ethnology, where it has no place or meaning. *Man, Past and Present*, by A. H. Keane, revised (1920) edition, p. 441.
[2] *Human Nature in Politics*, by Graham Wallas, 3rd ed. (1920), p. 289.

COLOUR PREJUDICE

his blood."[1] He adds that "there can be no doubt that (even the South American) Indian is superior to the negro.[2] The negro, even when quickened by foreign influences, never built up anything approaching a real civilisation."[3] "The black peoples have no historic pasts. . . . The black race has never built up a native civilisation. . . . The black man's numbers may increase prodigiously and acquire alien veneers, but the black man's nature will not change."[4]

In another book he says that "it is obvious that the black race constitutes the least advanced branch of mankind. . . . Whenever they have been left to their own devices, as in Haiti or the junglebush of the Guianas, they have quickly reverted to conditions reminiscent of their ancestral homes in West Africa or on the Congo."[5]

Discounting these opinions of an avowed adherent of the 'Nordic school,' let us see what more impartial writers, including historians, have to say. Professor Toynbee has pointed out that twenty-one different civilisations have been developed by races of various colours, but the black race alone has contributed to none. "It will be seen," he says, "that when we classify mankind by colour, the only one of the primary races, given by this classification, which has not made a creative contribution to any of our twenty-one civilisations is the Black Race."[6] Meredith Townsend asserts that "none of the black races, whether negro or Australasian, have shown within the historic time the capacity to develop civilisation. They have never passed the boundaries of their habitats as conquerors, and never exerted the smallest influence over peoples not black. They have never founded a stone city, have never built a ship, have never produced a literature, have never suggested a creed."[7]

[1] *The Rising Tide of Colour against White World-Supremacy* (1920), by L. Stoddard, p. 92.
[2] It was laid down in Brazil, in the eighteenth century, that the 'scandalous injustice' of calling the Indians 'Negroes' should be stopped, as tending to make it appear that "nature designed them to be the slaves of white men, as was believed concerning the African black." *The Atlantic and Slavery* (1935), by H. A. Wyndham, p. 143.
[3] *The Rising Tide of Colour against White World-Supremacy* (1920), by L. Stoddard, pp. 125–6.   [4] Ibid., pp. 91, 100, 102.
[5] *Clashing Tides of Colour* (1935), by Lothrop Stoddard, p. 75. See also page 83 below.
[6] *A Study of History* (1935), by Arnold J. Toynbee, vol. 1, p. 233.
[7] *Asia and Europe* (1903), by Meredith Townsend, p. 92.

ALLEGED INFERIORITY OF THE NEGRO

Field-Marshal Smuts says that among the blacks "no indigenous religion has been evolved, no literature, no art since the magnificent promise of the cave-men and the South African petroglyphist, no architecture since Zimbawe (if that is African)."[1] Professor Gregory says of the black man that "his early rock drawings in South Africa are artistically of a high order; but he has never produced an artist, a painter, or poet of first rank, or developed a great ruler or political organiser."[2]

Professor Seligman tells us that "on the artistic side the true (West African) Negro shows a skill in plastic art that is hardly found elsewhere in negro Africa, the carved ivories, wooden and ivory masks, and bronzes of Benin being especially noteworthy.... The finest of these are to be assigned to the sixteenth century and though undoubtedly negro in execution must be taken to show European, i.e. Portuguese, influence."[3] Finally we turn to an official document, which says: "It is true also that the Bantu people have never evolved an advanced civilisation of their own. They have never reduced their languages to writing. They have made no roads. One may travel through the length and breadth of tropical Africa without coming across any permanent building or monument of the past which has been constructed by them."[4]

[1] *Africa and some World Problems* (1929), by J. C. Smuts, pp. 75–6. For a discussion as to the possible builders of Zimbawe see *Man, Past and Present*, by A. H. Keane (1920 ed.), pp. 105–6.
[2] *Race as a Political Factor* (1931), by J. W. Gregory, p. 29.
[3] *Races of Africa* (1930), by C. G. Seligman, p. 56.
[4] *Report of the Commission on closer union of the Dependencies in Eastern and Central Africa* (Cmd. 3234), 1929, p. 16. For other opinions on this subject see (a) *The Caribbean Confederation* (1888), by C. S. Salmon, p. 14: "The African race have one great fact against them; there is no record of their having done anything to shape the world's history." (b) *The Control of the Tropics* (1898), by Benjamin Kidd, p. 51: "There never has been, and there never will be, within any time with which we are practically concerned, such a thing as good government, in the European sense, of the tropics by the natives of these regions." (c) *The Conflict of Colour* (1910), by B. L. Putnam Weale, p. 232: "The black man has given nothing to the world ... his hands have reared no enduring monuments, save when they have been forcibly directed by the energies of other races." (d) *Man, Past and Present*, by A. H. Keane (revised edition, 1920), p. 45: "In all the Negro lands free from foreign influences no true culture has ever been developed." (e) *Africa Emergent* (1938), by W. H. Macmillan, p. 87: "The African's own institutions have failed on the whole, not only to make much contribution to the sum of human achievement which we call civilisation, but even to furnish him with the barest necessities of existence." (f) *The Decline and Fall of the Roman Empire* (8 volumes, 1823), by E. Gibbon, vol. iii, p. 295: "Their rude ignorance has never invented any effectual weapons of

All of the above opinions are those of white men, (not all of them, be it noted, of the Nordic school) but a coloured writer has written as follows: "What then has the black man achieved in the past? What is his contribution to the worlds of science, of art, and literature? What has he done towards the advancement of civilisation and the betterment of mankind in the past? (We use the word 'past' in the sense of historical perspective.) The answer to these questions can be given in one simple word—'Nothing.'"[1]

Turning now from the achievements, or lack of achievements, of the Negro race as a whole, let us consider the personal achievements of individuals of the race. An American writer has said that "it is a well-known fact" that no Negro "has risen to a place among the great men of the world. Judged by European standards there has been no Negro of even secondary rank. No reputable student would admit that the race has produced any man whose accomplishments have not been surpassed by scores of white men working along similar lines. . . . There is an almost complete absence of Negro names in world history. Of those commonly mentioned, only a very few are of an order of merit that would bring men of other races into prominence."[2] Professor Westermann says that "cases in which the black man is the white man's equal in achievement are exceptions,"[3] and an English historian points out that "no Negro of the full blood has ever risen to first-class eminence among mankind."[4]

It is true that when the names of men and women of genius are quoted in support of the Negro claim to intellectual equality, it happens often enough that the names are those of persons with a large share of non-Negro blood. "Alexandre Dumas, beyond all question, was the most gifted man claimed by the Negroes as a member of their race. He had one-quarter or less of Negro blood. . . . The Russian poet, Alexander Pushkin, is frequently classed as a Negro, and did, in fact, have a trace of Negro blood: his maternal

defence, or of destruction; they appear incapable of forming any extensive plans of government, or conquest; and the obvious inferiority of their mental faculties has been discovered and abused by the nations of the temperate zone."

[1] *The Bantu Past and Present* (1920), by S. M. Molema, p. 329.

[2] *Race Mixture* (1931), by E. B. Reuter, pp. 107–8, 112. The Negro unwittingly acknowledges this when he over-praises the achievement of one of his race who obtains a university degree or a professional qualification.

[3] *The African Today* (1934), by D. Westermann, p. 331.

[4] *Asia and Europe* (1903), by Meredith Townsend, 2nd ed., p. 356.

great-grandfather was Hannibal, the Negro of Peter the Great."[1] Elizabeth Barrett Browning and Alexander Hamilton, who also have been claimed[2] as belonging to the race, were certainly much more white than black, and it has even been denied that Hamilton had any coloured blood at all. It has to be admitted that there have been, and are, a number of pure-blooded Negroes of outstanding ability and character, but the number is small, and it is claimed that they are no more than exceptions to the general rule.[3]

Against the statement that neither the race nor the individual African has achieved much in the past, the black man finds it difficult to give a convincing reply. He points, it is true, to Egyptian civilisation,[4] but Egypt, though geographically African, is essentially Asian both culturally and racially, and it is still to be proved that this was not always the case.[5] Professor Toynbee says that "there is some indication of a Negroid strain in certain of the occupants of the Lower Nile Valley during the twilight before the dawn of Egyptian Civilisation,"[6] and "most writers on Egyptian ethnology detect a Negro or at least Negroid element in the Caucasoid population" of ancient Egypt.[7] This is little on which to base a claim to some share in a past civilisation. Nor can the negroid characteristics of the Sphinx supply any convincing evidence of Negro control or influence in Egypt as this monument may be no more than the work of Negro slaves.[8]

Africans have even claimed the exploits of the Carthaginian generals against Rome as evidence of the past achievements of

[1] *Race Mixture* (1931), by E. B. Reuter, p. 113.
[2] *What the Negro Thinks* (1929), by R. R. Moton, pp. 204–5.
[3] An interesting list of successful coloured men and women in various walks of life is given in Chapter X of *The Story of the American Negro*, by I. C. Brown.
[4] See *The Souls of Black Folk* (1903), by W. E. B. DuBois, p. 4.
[5] "The geographers of antiquity have frequently hesitated to what portion of the globe they should ascribe Egypt. By its situation, that celebrated kingdom is included within the immense peninsula of Africa; but it is accessible only on the side of Asia, whose revolutions, in almost every period of history, Egypt has humbly obeyed." *The History of the Decline and Fall of the Roman Empire* (1823 ed.), by E. Gibbon, vol. 1, p. 30.
[6] *A Study of History* (1935), by Arnold J. Toynbee, vol. 1, p. xvii.
[7] *Man, Past and Present*, by A. H. Keane (1920 ed.), p. 482.
[8] Professor Reuter has indeed suggested that "the racial intermixture with the Negroes, brought into the Egyptian population as servile labourers, marked the beginning of the end of a great people." *Race Mixture* (1931), by E. B. Reuter, p. 11. For similar suggestions of racial deterioration caused by Negro blood see page 121.

their race, and a writer in a Lagos paper has had to point out that "the Carthaginians were no more Negroes than the Boers of South Africa, or, by the way, our good friends the Abyssinians."[1] In this connection, it is interesting to recall Sir Arthur Keith's statement that "in ancient times, as to-day, the frontiers of Europe extended to what is now desert. The Sahara is a great racial frontier; north of it we find men of the European type, south of it men of the true African or negro type."[2]

If we accept the theory that achievement is the only real test of capacity we are bound to admit that the Negro has shown little capacity in the past. But it has been pointed out that achievement in the presence of unlike conditions is not a measure of capacity for civilisation.[3] Conditions have not yet become equal for all races, though they are more equal than they were, and the past cannot be accepted as an infallible guide to the future in the matter of racial capacity. However, having examined the past, so far as is possible, it is important to consider the present condition of the Negro race.

Lord Olivier says that "the negro is progressing, and that disposes of all the arguments in the world that he is incapable of progress."[4] "The African," he maintains, "at least an important section of Africans, namely the West Indian Negroes,[5] have recently completed a hundred years of freedom and their achievements, as well as their present condition in all aspects of life, is proof that the *African can make good*."[6] In the United States, it is said "the fact remains that under extremely unfavourable conditions the race has gained considerable wealth, it has developed professional ability of a high order, it has gone North and won recognition in the arts, it has shown that it can learn when given the benefits of education."[7]

---

[1] Letter from O. Balogun, in *The Nigerian Daily Times* of September 28, 1935.

[2] *The Antiquity of Man* (1925), by Sir Arthur Keith, 2nd ed., vol. 1, p. 351.

[3] *Race Mixture* (1931), by E. B. Reuter, p. 137.

[4] *White Capital and Coloured Labour* (1905), by Lord Olivier, p. 42.

[5] I do not consider that the West Indian Negro is, on the whole, any more advanced than the African Negro *who has had the advantages of education*.

[6] "Can the African make good?" an Address delivered by Lord Olivier at the Fabian Summer School, 1935, reproduced in *The West Indian Review* of November 1935.

[7] *Culture in the South* (1934), edited by W. T. Couch; article by editor on "The Negro in the South," p. 476.

ALLEGED INFERIORITY OF THE NEGRO

As against this, Sir Harry Johnston considered that in some respects "the tendency of the Negro for several centuries past has been an actual retrograde one,"[1] while a 'Nordic' writer maintains that "whenever the incentive to imitate the dominant race is removed the Negro, or for that matter the Indian, reverts shortly to his ancestral grade of culture.[2] In other words, it is the individual and not the race that is affected by religion, education and example. Negroes have demonstrated throughout recorded time that they are a stationary species and that they do not possess the potentiality to progress or initiative from within."[3]

The present condition of independent Negro states is often quoted in support of such arguments as that preceding. In Haiti there had been almost constant revolution until American intervention established some sort of order in 1915. "Irrigation projects fell into decay; production and foreign trade dwindled. Political mismanagement increased the public debt. The courts were corrupt. Education, except that carried on by French priests, practically ceased. There was little protection of property and no industrial encouragement. Poverty and disease added to the general distress. The interior swarmed with bandits."[4] A former President of Haiti writes that "there, in the midst of a luxuriant vegetation, will be found an almost primitive population, professing a jealous love of its soil. They work, but without method, without guidance, and without capital."[5]

Abyssinia is not a Negro state but the inhabitants have a large share of Negro blood, and during the Italian invasion Negroes throughout the world sympathised with the Abyssinians as a people of the same race. Abyssinia, says a historian, writing in 1933, "is a byword for disorder and barbarity; the disorder of

[1] *British Central Africa* (1897), by Sir Harry Johnston, p. 472.
[2] See also p. 78 above. For individual examples of reversion to savagery, see the case of Hannibal (*c.* 1702) who "in spite of his fourteen years of European education ... cast away, with his French clothes, all notions of honour and of Christian faith." *The Atlantic and Slavery* (1935), by H. A. Wyndham, p. 45. Also the case of the young man, educated for some years at a mission school in the Isle of Man, who joined in a cannibal feast after the raid on Akassa (Nigeria) in 1895.
[3] *The Passing of the Great Race* (1917), by Madison Grant, p. 77.
[4] *Encyclopaedia Britannica*, 14th ed., vol. xi., pp. 82-3. See also *Voodoo Gods* (1939), by Zora Hurston, pp. 78-9.
[5] *Papers on Inter-racial Problems*, communicated to the First Universal Races Congress, London, 1911, edited by G. Spiller; article by General Legitime, p. 182.

feudal and tribal anarchy and the barbarity of the slave-trade."[1] Her culture, he says, has stagnated "at a level which is really not much higher than the level of the adjacent Tropical African barbarism."[2] Of Liberia the same author writes that she is "a republic in which a helpless aboriginal majority was being mishandled (in 1933) by a repatriated American Negro minority with an almost Abyssinian brutality."[3] That these African states are lacking in the essentials of good government has been proved, in the case of Liberia, by a League of Nations inquiry,[4] and is, indeed, admitted by the Negroes themselves. Pointing out that it is not control of the Government that the Negroes of the United States are asking for, Major Moton says that their "observations of Negro control in those countries where it does exist have not been sufficiently reassuring to make them wish to try the experiment" there.[5] Misgovernment, in fact, is held by one African writer to have positive advantages in Liberia. "Owing to a variety of reasons, such as poverty, laziness, a ridiculous superiority complex and general maladministration, the 'civilised' blacks have made very little impression on the aboriginal population. . . . There are no roads

---

[1] *A Study of History* (1935), by Arnold J. Toynbee, vol. 2, p. 365.

[2] *Ibid.* In a letter to *The Times* of July 11, 1935, Sir Hesketh Bell says that "in four-fifths of the area comprising Abyssinia the people are still living in conditions that are repugnant to all the ethics of humanity. . . . Slavery, disease, brigandage and gross superstition continue to be the main characteristics of the outlying parts of the country, and Abyssinia remains almost stagnant in all that counts for uplift and progress. The only other African country that shows similar conditions is the 'free and independent state of Liberia.' "

[3] *Ibid.* Another writer says that "the history of Liberia has consisted of ludicrous political struggles between the freed slaves and native negroes." *Environment and Race* (1937), by G. Taylor, p. 108. Yet another speaks of Liberia as being handicapped, "by the tawdry trappings of a culture to which her people never had and never could have become adapted, and now, even Liberia's best friends have to admit, made ludicrous in its incongruous setting." *The Clash of Culture and the Contact of Races* (1927), G. H. Lane-Fox Pitt-Rivers, p. 235.

[4] See *League of Nations Paper* No. C.658. M.272, 1930. VI, and also *Papers Concerning Affairs in Liberia*, Cmd. 4614 (1934), which stated that the report of the Commission appointed by the League "showed that many high officers of the Liberian State were guilty of practices analogous to slavery" (p. 3); the same Command Paper contains a report by Vice-Consul Rydings, dated April 15, 1932, which states that "operations against the disaffected tribes appear to have been conducted in a ruthless, callous and brutal manner without regard for the lives of innocent women and children" (p. 27). See also *Journey without Maps* (1936), by G. Greene, *passim.*

[5] *What the Negro Thinks* (1929), by R. R. Moton, p. 139.

ALLEGED INFERIORITY OF THE NEGRO

or railroads, the only means of communication being jungle trails and the only form of transportation being porterage. . . . Thus in Liberia we see native life in its pristine state, with its perfections and imperfections unmodified and uncorrupted by Western culture. This is one of the chief benefits of the governmental inefficiency of the civilised blacks who rule the place. . . . So far as the natives of Liberia are concerned, the failure of the incompetent ruling class of civilised blacks to develop the country along modern lines has so far proved a blessing."[1]

In the next chapter will be considered the alleged failings of the Negroes and the causes which are said to explain these failings and the general backwardness of the Negro race.

[1] *Negro Anthology* (1934), edited by Nancy Cunard; article on "Black Civilisation and White," by G. S. Schuyler, pp. 784, 787.

Chapter VII

ALLEGED SHORTCOMINGS OF THE NEGRO

WITHOUT in any way admitting that the Negro is inherently inferior to other races, and incapable of equal progress under equal conditions, it must be conceded that, for one cause or another, he lags a long way behind in the race of civilisation. There are brilliant individual exceptions to the rule, and these exceptions are becoming more numerous, but a very large majority of the Negro race is *at present* very backward. Graham Wallas speaks of "the wide intellectual gulf between the West African negro and the white man from north-west Europe."[1] A coloured writer has pointed out regarding his people that "their poverty and ignorance to-day have clear and well-known and remediable causes. All this," he says, "is true; and yet what every colored man living to-day knows is that by practical present measurement Negroes to-day are inferior to whites." The coloured people, he goes on, "are in the mass ignorant, diseased and inefficient, the governments which they have evolved, even allowing for the interested interference of the white world, have seldom reached the degree of efficiency of modern European governments."[2] Field-Marshal Smuts says of the African race that "it has largely remained a child type, with a child psychology and outlook,"[3] while anthropologists have spoken of "the negro type, with its tendency to infantile characters due to the early closing of the cranial sutures."[4] Mr. Hastings, for many years in the Administrative Service of Nigeria, has written: "For all that much has been said and written about the 'back of the black man's

[1] *Human Nature in Politics* (1920), by Graham Wallas, p. 7.
[2] *Dusk of Dawn* (1940), by W. E. B. DuBois, p. 174.
[3] *Africa and Some World Problems* (1929), by J. C. Smuts, p. 75.
[4] *Anthropology* (1911), by R. R. Marett, p. 116. See also the remarks by F. Manetta, quoted in the *Encyclopaedia Britannica*, 11th ed., vol. 19, p. 344, that in the Negro the growth of the brain is arrested by the premature closing of the cranial sutures and lateral pressure on the frontal bone. This theory is, however, not now accepted by scientists.

ALLEGED SHORTCOMINGS OF THE NEGRO

mind,' the difficulty of getting at it, and the dark, mysterious, incomprehensible corners of it, I am convinced that, in the end, it is a childish mind."[1]

In America, where it has been possible to compare Negroes with whites of approximately the same class, "great stress has been laid on the United States Army Intelligence tests in the (first) Great War, which were claimed to show that the average Negro of the United States was equal in intelligence only to the average nine-year-old white child, and that the Negro is from half to three-fourths as intellectually capable as the white."[2] Statistics have also been published with a view to demonstrating the superiority of white children over black in American schools.[3] An investigation carried out in Jamaica revealed that "in musical discrimination, in repetition of seven figures, and in certain mental arithmetic computations the Blacks surpass the Whites, but in all other mental tests the Whites are equal to or clearly ahead of the coloured groups."[4]

Professor Pintner says that "all results show the negro decidedly inferior to the white on standard intelligence tests. These results are sufficiently numerous and consistent to point to a racial difference in intelligence. The overlapping of the two races is great, and the most liberal estimate seems to be that at most 25 per cent of the coloured reach or exceed the medium intelligence of the white . . . whether educated or uneducated the negro is inferior to the white of similar status. . . . The difference between the average white man and the average negro in intelligence may not be very great, but it is quite definitely present, and this seems to be the case wherever two comparable groups of the two races have been examined, and even when we make allowance for the differences in educational opportunity."[5]

The American Army tests, on which such stress has been laid, are somewhat discounted by the fact that Professor Brigham, who

[1] *Nigerian Days* (1925), by A. C. G. Hastings, p. 178.
[2] *Race as a Political Factor* (1931), by J. W. Gregory, p. 25. It was stated in evidence by a medical man attached to United States Army hospitals in England that the average mental age of the United States Army (excluding officers and non-commissioned officers) in the last world war was twelve. *The Times*, of January 12, 1945.
[3] See *Christianity and the Race Problem* (1924), by J. H. Oldham, 7th ed., p. 73.
[4] *Race Crossing in Jamaica*, by C. B. Davenport and Morris Stegerda (Carnegie Institution of Washington Publication. No. 395, 1929), p. 369.
[5] *Intelligence Testing* (1924), by R. Pintner, pp. 345, 341, 343.

was responsible for some of the conclusions, has categorically withdrawn them.[1] But apart from this it is scarcely fair to judge of the Negro's mental capacity by tests taken directly from the environment of the white man, and we do the African an "injustice and even injury if we are content to estimate his 'intelligence' only in terms of his apparent ability to cope with the exactions of European scholastic education."[2] On the other hand, it has been suggested that the very fact that a certain test seems to be unfair may be evidence of the inferiority of the person tested.[3] It has been pointed out in the *Encyclopaedia Britannica* that "in spite of notable improvements during the last twenty years, existing instruments for measuring intelligence suffer from serious deficiencies. An intelligence examination is still a more or less undefined collection of tasks, its score is still a somewhat arbitrary summation of credits, and the correspondence of the scores to the abilities which they purport to measure is still far from perfect."[4] The question has been investigated in England by a Committee appointed by the Board of Education, which expressed the opinion that "a valid test of intelligence must be based on elements appealing to the common interests and within the common experiences of the group of persons tested."[5] The value of intelligence tests, the Committee considered, is "subject to the important condition that, in order that tests may yield valid results, the persons tested must not be drawn from environments that are widely dissimilar nor have been subjected to widely dissimilar conditions of life."[6] "Intelligence tests are to a great extent environment tests."[7]

In connection with the intelligence tests that have been made, an interesting comparison has been drawn between the abilities of boys and girls and those of whites and Negroes. Boys are held to be superior to girls in judgment and reasoning, in mathematics,

[1] In an article published in the *Psychological Review* of March 1930; see *Sociology* (1934), by Morris Ginsberg, p. 68.
[2] Article on "Amentia in the East African," by H. L. Gordon, in *The Eugenics Review* of January 1943.
[3] *Educational Psychology* (1903), by E. L. Thorndike, vol. 3, p. 221.
[4] *Encyclopaedia Britannica*, 14th ed., vol. 12, p. 461.
[5] *Report of the Consultative Committee on Psychological Tests of Educable Capacity, and their possible use in the Public System of Education*, 1924. p. 76.
[6] *Ibid.*, p. 138.
[7] *Up from the Ape* (1931), by E. A. Hooton, Professor of Anthropology, Harvard University, p. 594.

ALLEGED SHORTCOMINGS OF THE NEGRO

and in analytical processes generally, while girls are decidedly better in tests of memory; Negroes commonly excel whites in memory tests,[1] while inferior to them in those subjects in which girls are inferior to boys.[2] With the Negro emotional thinking is said to outweigh logical reasoning,[3] as with women, and it is "difficult for him to follow an argument of any length or to think out a problem for himself with all its implications."[4]

In view of the fact that the average score in intelligence tests of Negro children born and bred in American towns is higher than the average score of white children born and bred on farms in the country,[5] it is difficult to doubt that environment and opportunity affect the results of the tests as much as racial differences. Dr. Klineberg, of Columbia University, considers that if the environments were equalised the so-called inferiority of Negro intelligence, as compared with that of the whites, would disappear. He points to the fact that the Negro child born in the Southern States is inferior in intelligence to the Negro born in the north, but that, after five years' residence in New York, these southern-born Negroes are equal in intelligence to Negro children born and reared in the north.[6]

Again, it must be remembered that "no two races have been measured which do not overlap mentally whatever be the trait measured,"[7] and "individual differences within the groups are greater than the difference between the groups."[8]

In what respects, then, is the Negro held to be inferior? He is said to be lazy,[9] and "it is notorious that the employer who tries

[1] In the *Report of the Inspection Committee on Achimota College*, Gold Coast, in 1938, p. 80, reference is made to "the peculiar capacity for memorising which Africans possess."
[2] *The Philosophy of Conflict* (1919), by Havelock Ellis, pp. 172–3.
[3] *The African Today* (1934), by D. Westermann, p. 39.
[4] *Ibid.*, p. 42. See also *The Eugenics Review* of April 1917; article on "Mental Development of the South African Native," by Rev A. T. Bryant, adapted for publication by C. G. Seligman, p. 44.
[5] *Western Civilisation and the Natives of South Africa* (1934), edited by I. Schapera; article on "Race Mixture and Native Policy in South Africa," by R. F. A. Hoernlé, p. 273.
[6] See *The New York Times* of February 3, 1935. See also *The Problem of Colour in Relation to the Idea of Equality* (Supplement to vol. 1, no. 2, of the *Journal of Philosophical Studies*); paper by M. Ginsberg, p. 11.
[7] *Educational Psychology* (1903), by E. L. Thorndike, vol. 3, p. 220.
[8] *Sociology* (1934), by Morris Ginsberg, p. 71.
[9] Why then do we say of a hard-working man that "he works like a nigger"?

COLOUR PREJUDICE

to speed up the negro by offering him double wages only succeeds in making the fellow work half as long as usual."¹ Field-Marshal Smuts considers that "the easiest, most natural and obvious way to civilise the African native is to give him decent white employment. White employment is his best school; the gospel of labour is the most salutary gospel for him."² There are numbers of other white men who share the Field-Marshal's view, though few would commit themselves publicly in this matter. It is probable, however, that the Negro suffers not so much from laziness as from a lack of incentive. When he is working for himself he works hard, and the enormous production from the West African colonies, *where the African still possesses the land*, should be sufficient proof that the Negro is not inherently lazy. At work that the Negro understands and likes he will labour cheerfully and well, but he will choose his own hours for working; he has no use for the mid-day hours in the sun which are sacred to mad dogs and Englishmen. It is true that he will not work continuously, and that he gets tired and bored with routine, and it is true also that when he is underpaid he gets even with his employer by indifferent work, but it must be remembered that the wants of the Negro are comparatively few while he is living in a tropical country. He has not learnt to long for the luxuries that money can buy; his luxury is the luxury of ease. An enervating climate does not stimulate the Negro to energy any more than it stimulates the white man.³

It is, however, a fact that the Negro frequently attributes to other causes, such as unfair racial discrimination, results which are due to his own inefficiency and his easy acceptance of a slipshod standard of work as being 'good enough.' It has been said, for instance, that the efficiency of the West Indian Negroes was so low that it was decided to import white labour of southern European origin for work on the Panama Canal; although these Europeans received

¹ *A Short Introduction to the History of Human Stupidity* (1935), by W. P. Pitkin, p. 196. In the House of Commons, on July 28, 1937, a member asked the Secretary of State for the Colonies whether he was aware "of the habit of labourers in Trinidad to work only for such number of days per week as to bring them sufficient funds for their requirements, and that at the present time such labourers in the sugar plantations in Trinidad are only working an average of 4·2 days per week." The Secretary of State replied that he was "generally aware" of this practice. See *Parliamentary Debates*, 326 H.C. Deb. 5, column 3117.
² *Africa and Some World Problems* (1929), by J. C. Smuts, p. 48.
³ See *The Menace of Colour* (1925), by J. W. Gregory, 2nd ed., preface.

twice as much for exactly the same work as that done by the Negroes their efficiency was estimated to be three times as great.[1] 'Portuguese,' Chinese and Hindus in the West Indies, and Syrians in West Africa, have by their greater industry and efficiency ousted the Negroes from lucrative occupations. Too often the Negro considers himself fully qualified to do work for which he has not been trained, and feels a sense of grievance if he is unable to obtain, or retain, a post for which he is quite unfitted.[2]

That the Negro lacks continuity of purpose and stability cannot, unfortunately, be denied. A coloured writer says that though his people are "quicker in intellect and spirit than the English, they pay for it by being less continent, less stable, less dependable."[3] Lord Bryce has said that the difference between the Negroes and the white races "lies not so much in intelligence as in force of will and tenacity of purpose."[4] To some extent, but not altogether, this may be a result of slavery.[5] Dr. DuBois says that "slavery fosters certain virtues like humility and obedience, but these flourish at the terrible cost of lack of self-respect, shiftlessness, tale-bearing, theft, slovenliness and sexual looseness."[6]

Dr. Miller, for many years a medical missionary in northern Nigeria, considers that there is "another and deeper reason which covers the field of mental dishonesty, habitual deceit, and apparently ineradicable lying in the Hausa.[7] It is hard for us to realise what the petrifying and demoralising influence of centuries of insecurity of

[1] *White Settlers in the Tropics* (1939), by A. Grenfell Price, pp. 154–5.
[2] "I learned my first lesson about Jamaican labour. It considers itself as capable, if not superior, to white labour, even though it may not have learned the rudiments of the job." *Caribbean Nights* (1939), by W. J. Makin (former Editor of the *Jamaican Standard*), p. 42.
[3] *The Case for West Indian Self-Government* (1933), by C. L. R. James, p. 7. For examples of Negro unreliability, see *On the Edge of the Primeval Forest*, by A. Schweitzer, trans. by C. T. Campion (1931), p. 133.
[4] *The Relations of the Advanced and the Backward Races of Mankind* (1902), by Lord Bryce, p. 44.
[5] "The heritage of slavery is irresponsibility and lack of forethought." *An African Survey* (1938), by Lord Hailey, p. 636.
[6] *Morals and Manners among Negro Americans*, by W. E. B. DuBois, p. 16. (Quoted in *Race Relations* (1934), by W. D. Weatherford and C. S. Johnson, p. 279.) See also *The Fall of the Planter Class in the British Caribbean* (1929), by L. J. Ragatz, p. 27: "The West Indian negro had all the characteristics of his race. He stole, he lied, he was simple, suspicious, inefficient, irresponsible, lazy, superstitious, and loose in his sex relations."
[7] The Hausa is Negroid, but not pure Negro.

life from tyrants can mean; nor what it can induce of meanness in the character of a people."[1] However this may be, the fact remains that the black man too often fails to tell the truth, and, indeed, he frequently lies for no apparent reason.[2]

Booker Washington considered that the greatest injury done to the Negroes by slavery was to deprive them of a sense of self-independence, habit of economy, and executive power.[3] The West Indian Negro particularly is apt to waste his money, when he has any, on 'sweetmeats and trinkets,'[4] and a West African has observed that the West Indian Negroes "will spend money which they haven't got, and are always out for a good time without seeming to worry much about the upkeep of a family or looking after living expenses . . . they will spend one whole day's wages on grog (rum), although they might have to go hungry on the next."[5]

The further charge has been levied against the Negro that, even when sufficiently educated, he is unfitted for posts of responsibility owing to a lack of character. Admitting that his personal experience was limited to Lagos, Lord Lugard has said that he was "reluctantly compelled to admit that so far as my own experience goes, it is extremely difficult at present to find educated African youths who are by character and temperament suited to posts in which they may rise to positions of high administrative responsibility."[6] A very large number of experienced officials in the African colonies would endorse this statement, and the Report of Vice-Consul Rydings, in 1932, in its reference to Liberian officials, is of importance in this connection. After referring to certain excesses committed by Liberian troops against the Kru tribe, which inhabits the southern part of the country, he states that "the responsibility for the events which have occurred can be laid only to the door of the Liberian Government, who have given evidence of their utter inability to administer native territory.

[1] *Yesterday and Tomorrow in Northern Nigeria* (1938), by W. Miller, p. 95.
[2] "I am assured that, unless a negro has an interest in telling the truth, he always lies—in order to keep his tongue in practice." See *Journal of a Residence among the Negroes in the West Indies* (1845), by M. C. ("Monk") Lewis, p. 68.
[3] *Selected Speeches of Booker T. Washington* (1932), by E. D. Washington, p. 27.
[4] See *Colonial Policy* (1931), by A. D. A. DeKat Angelino, vol. 1, p. 70.
[5] See *West Africa* of September 2, 1939.
[6] *The Dual Mandate in British Tropical Africa* (1922), by Lord Lugard, 2nd ed., p. 88.

ALLEGED SHORTCOMINGS OF THE NEGRO

The Liberian officials who are entrusted with this onerous task possess neither the requisite moral qualities, intelligence, experience or training, and it is, I submit, impossible to see whence the material for a well-organised, intelligent and incorruptible administrative body can be obtained among the Americo-Liberians."[1]

It is an undoubted fact that the senior Negro clerk or foreman frequently lacks the moral courage to reprove his subordinates, or to report them in cases of serious irregularities.[2] I have had personal experience of the failure of a trusted Negro head-servant to reveal to me that one of the other servants was grossly dishonest; my head-servant was himself absolutely honest, and would, I believe, have been incapable of stealing from me, but he lacked the courage to report his fellow-African. It is remarkable, also, how much sympathy is extended by Negroes to those of their own colour who, for one reason or another, have fallen foul of white authority. Until the culprit is discovered there is a conspiracy of secrecy to protect him, although his wrong-doing may not be approved of. When his conduct is under investigation or trial[3] this sympathy is out-spoken, even though the offence may be one against persons of his own race and the white man is concerned in the matter merely as the instrument of justice and authority. It has been said that "the arrested Negro often acquires the prestige of a victim, a martyr, or a hero, even when he is simply a criminal."[4] And the

---

[1] *Papers concerning Affairs in Liberia*, Cmd. 4614 (1934), pp. 30–1.

[2] In the *Report of the Commission on the Civil Services of British West Africa, 1945–46* (para. 18), Sir Walter Harragin stated that too many clerks were being employed who were inefficient. "It is not," he said, "understood by Chief Clerks the harm that they are doing themselves and the country by failing to report passengers in their department.... Quality is being sacrificed to quantity because of the intense fear that one clerk has of incurring the enmity of his fellows (and his fellows' families) by pointing out incompetency."

[3] An outstanding case was that of an African elected member of the Gold Coast Legislative Council, who was convicted on a charge of having offered to refrain from making a speech in Council (attacking the Association of West African Merchants) in March 1944, if he were given a bribe of £25,000. One African of standing, although convinced of his guilt, thought that it was a shame to 'persecute' the accused as he was an old man! A fund was raised in Accra to finance his defence, and the people were exhorted to stand together in his support. The local Press reported everything connected with the trial at such length that other events had to go unrecorded; a reader of the local papers at this time might have been excused for thinking that there was no war raging in Europe—or in Burma, where Gold Coast troops were fighting.

[4] *An American Dilemma* (1944), by G. Myrdal, vol. 1, p. 525.

punishment is always considered excessive, although the guilt may be manifest. It was particularly striking, some years ago, to observe the almost universal sympathy expressed in Lagos for certain Negro lawyers who were accused of conduct to their Negro clients which was, to say the least, highly irregular; and still more striking were the universal rejoicings which followed when a surprisingly light penalty was imposed on one of the erring lawyers.[1] Even a term of imprisonment for such anti-social crimes as "bribery, embezzlement and even petty theft" seldom affects the social standing of the culprit.[2]

An American writer suggests that this attitude may be due to the fact that the Negro is suspicious of white justice. "The fact that a Negro may be 'framed' or that he may not get a fair trial undoubtedly tends to make all Negroes think of those arrested as martyrs rather than as criminals. . . . He is in some places a policeman, and sometimes a juror, but he is never the judge."[3] I do not believe that in British colonies there is any serious distrust of British justice, although it is very often imperfectly understood. Other, and less easily described, reasons exist for the apparent sympathy for wrong-doing among the Negro population. In the first place, there is the school-boy horror of 'sneaking,' and it must be remembered that the Negro is sometimes in much the same relation to the white man as the school-boy is to his master. Then there is the feeling, particularly among the educated classes, that the failings of their brethren should be concealed, so that the white man should not have fresh occasion to point the finger of scorn. Again, there is the fear that the one who gives away the Negro culprit to the white authorities or openly blames him will be

[1] The African needs to be saved from those friends who consider that his shortcomings should be condoned, and that allowances must be made for him when he goes wrong. If he constantly receives concessions, which would be withheld from his white brother in similar conditions, he will never advance. It is said that at the Universities, the Bar and the Medical Schools, a lower standard is demanded of African students; I consider this, if it be true, as a serious wrong done to the African. It has been pointed out that "some whites are inclined to have a double standard in judging Negro achievements; they applaud mediocrity and thereby foster it." See *An American Dilemma* (1944), by G. Myrdal, vol. 2, p. 991.

[2] This point was made by the *Nigerian Eastern Mail*, in an article reproduced in *West Africa* of August 13, 1938.

[3] *Race Relations, Adjustment of Whites and Negroes in the United States* (1934), by W. D. Weatherford and C. S. Johnson, p. 340. In the British West Indies and British West Africa there are a number of Negro judges and magistrates.

dubbed a 'white man's nigger' and a traitor to his race. And lastly there is the dread of vengeance, through physical or supernatural force, from the culprit or his friends. It is easy enough to sneer at such a dread, but we do not, perhaps, fully understand the conditions under which these people may be living.[1]

This problem, the problem of finding a sufficient number of Negroes of character and courage (there are plenty with the education and ability required) is one of the most important of those facing colonial Governments to-day. Provided that adequate care is taken in making the necessary selection, I am hopeful that such men will be found in increasing numbers. It must be admitted that a few disastrous failures would have a most unfortunate effect on future progress, but I feel that the risk must be run, and a few mistakes must be accepted as inevitable, if we are to honour our repeated pledges to advance Africans to 'European' posts in West Africa when the right men can be found.[2]

It is unfortunate that the Negro, and especially the half-educated Negro, should so often alienate the sympathy of well-wishers by a bombastic manner, or by equally bombastic speech. Professor Westermann speaks of the "feeling of inferiority in the black man from which the educated classes in particular suffer, and which they try to counteract. The way of doing this is often naïve. The wearing of European clothes, whether rags or the most up-to-date style; using European furniture and European forms of social intercourse; adorning the Native language with European expressions; using bombastic phrases in speaking or writing a European language; all these contribute to a feeling of equality with the European and his achievements."[3] An African writer says of his own people that, "attempting to emulate Europeans, they practised

---

[1] Sir Bernard Bourdillon points out that "it is no exaggeration to say that in West Africa the great majority of the people have either an open or a secret belief in witchcraft." *The Future of the Colonial Empire* (1945), p. 67. A great many in the West Indies are afraid of "Obeah."

[2] It is not, however, an easy problem. "Another difficulty facing those anxious to Africanise the services is tribal jealousy. This exists not merely in the rural parts of West Africa, but in the oldest of its towns in the littoral. Even among the well educated, there is the feeling that whoever is in authority, it should be either a member of the tribe to which those affected belong, or it must be a European. Under no circumstances would an African foreigner (in the tribal sense) be welcomed to hold any independent command." *West Africa* of October 2, 1937.

[3] *The African Today* (1934), by D. Westermann, p. 331.

only the external things and wasted their money on woollen suits in a hot climate, carrying their idiosyncrasies in dress far enough to give them the aspects of comic opera characters."[1] Another writer points out that aggressiveness, boasting and loud talk are forms of the ordinary reaction of the suppressed individual who tries to overcome his inferiority complex,[2] but it is a pity that the flamboyance and vulgarity of certain Negroes should be allowed to over-shadow the dignity and other virtues of the less prominent members of the race.

The Negro attaches undue importance to long words, and values a speech by its length rather than by its quality. He prefers "fluency in the use of words to originality in ideas."[3] Like the white man, he is over-fond of the sound of his own voice, but he differs from the white man in the patience with which he will listen to long-winded speeches from others, whether or not these others have anything to say. It was an African who wrote: "The Negro race abounds with orators: would that it had more logicians."[4] White sympathisers with the race must share his view.

[1] *Negro Anthology* (1934), edited by Nancy Cunard; article on "Britain and the Africans," by Ladipo Odunsi, p. 773.
[2] *Alien Americans* (1936), by B. Schrieke, p. 92. It is amazing how loudly the African can talk. Two men walking side by side and carrying on an ordinary, friendly conversation, can often be heard by others fifty or a hundred yards away.
[3] *A Hundred Years of the British Empire* (1940), by A. P. Newton, p. 228.
[4] *The Negro Question, or Hints for the Physical Improvement of the Negro Race, with special reference to West Africa* (1892), by J. Renner Maxwell, p. 177. See also "This Race of Talkers," in *The Nigerian Daily Times* of July 3, 1936.

Chapter VIII

PHYSICAL AND MENTAL DIFFERENCES BETWEEN THE RACES

IN view of the suggestion that the Negro race is inherently inferior to the white race and incapable ever of reaching the level of the other, it is important to examine in what way the races differ in physical and mental characteristics, and to study the views of impartial and competent scientists on the subject.

The most obvious way in which the various races of mankind differ one from another is in the colour of the skin, and, indeed, where other physical dissimilarities between races are found there is invariably a marked difference in colour. As we have seen in a previous chapter, the principal races of the world, according to the colour classification, are the whites or Caucasians, the yellows or Mongolians, the blacks or Negroes, the browns, and the reds. The two races with which we are mainly dealing are those conveniently labelled as 'black' and 'white,' though the latter is often as much red as white, and the Negro is seldom really black, being generally of a dark brown complexion.[1]

Although colour is the most convenient method of classification, "the most definite physical distinction between the races is based on the hair;[2] that of the Mongolian is round in cross-section, so that it hangs loose and lank. . . . The Negro hair is flattened in cross-section so that it coils up like a piece of ribbon and produces

[1] "While it is true that all Negroes are not black and that all black people are not Negroes, it is also true that the darkest skin colour found among mankind occurs in this race. Even among the Negroes of Africa there is a wide variation of colour, which ranges from an intense black to a light yellow": *The Biology of the Negro* (1942), by J. H. Lewis, p. 27. See also *The Races of Man and their Distribution*, by A. C. Haddon (1929 ed.), p. 7.

[2] It may be possible later to distinguish races by their blood. For a brief but interesting reference to the world distribution of the blood-groups see *Evolution and Genetics* (1925), by T. H. Morgan, pp. 197–8. The proportion of those belonging to the four blood-groups in a population recently mixed may give a clue to their racial past.

the woolly hair of the Negro . . . the Caucasian hair has an intermediate shape; it is oval in cross-section; it is wavy."[1] Professor Haddon says that "the most convenient character to employ for preliminary grouping of mankind is the nature of the hair."[2]

Racial antagonism based on a difference of colour is the more remarkable if we accept Darwin's theory that all the races of man are descended from a single primitive stock,[3] and the opinion of Professor Gregory that the complexion of this primitive stock was probably dark, but that after the Caucasian stem had branched off from the Negro and Mongolian the change in food and climate caused the pale skin of the European.[4] If this opinion is correct we shall be forced to believe that the Ethiopian *can* change his skin in the course of time, if he first changes his place of residence and the food he eats.[5] Even if the first man was white, as is suggested by Professor Marett,[6] and those living near the equator subsequently became black, colour-antagonism is no less remarkable. It has been established that, in all human beings, the pigment secreted in the skin is the same in quality and the shades of colour are due only to the quantity of pigment secreted.[7] Sir Arthur Keith, referring to the supposed negroid traits of the remains of those early burials found in Europe at Cromagnon and elsewhere, has expressed the opinion that they are not more negroid than many pure-bred representatives of the Mediterranean type now alive. The European, he says, "has been evolved north of the Sahara, and the Negro types to the south of it; the farther we trace them into the past,

[1] *Race as a Political Factor* (1931), by J. W. Gregory, p. 20. It should be noted that the Australian aborigines have the same wavy hair as the white races!

[2] *The Races of Man and their Distribution*, by A. C. Haddon (1929 ed.), p. 5. See also *Man, Past and Present*, by A. H. Keane (1920 ed.), p. 38.

[3] *The Descent of Man* (1874), by C. Darwin, 2nd ed., p. 273.

[4] *Race as a Political Factor* (1931), by J. W. Gregory, pp. 18-19.

[5] It is said that recent investigations have proved that, where black and white have crossed, the fourth generation from the original mixture is born white, and its descendants remain white thereafter. See *Western Civilisation and the Natives of South Africa* (1934), edited by I. Schapera: article on "Race Mixture and Native Policy in South Africa," by R. F. A. Hoernlé, p. 271. The Negro baby is sometimes nearly white at birth.

[6] See *Race, Sex and Environment, A Study of Mineral Deficiency in Human Evolution* (1936), by J. R. de la H. Marett, p. 218: "If Man is a foetalised ape produced by severe iodine-deficiency, it is probable that the first man was white. . . . I consider it probable that the white skin was retained as a palaeanthropic character, and that pigmentation was re-evolved by the first emigrants who made their habitat in the South." [7] *A Study of History* (1935), by Arnold J. Toynbee, vol. 1, p. 227.

the more the white and black ancestral forms should come to resemble each other."[1]

It is generally assumed that skin colour in mankind is dependent on climate, and this belief seems to have been held from very ancient times if we are to judge from the myth of Phaeton driving the chariot of the sun over Africa. Losing control of his horses, he came too near the earth, burning the land, drying up the rivers, and turning Libya into a desert; "it was then, men say, that the Ethiopians got their black colour, owing to the heat driving their blood to the very skin."[2] It is true that so far as the Old World is concerned the darker races are to be found near the equator and the fairer races farther away from it, but on the American continent this general rule does not apply, the aborigines of Canada and Argentina, as well as of the tropical regions that lie between, being all of the same general colour. Professor Haddon thinks that a plausible explanation of this lies in the time-factor, on the assumption that the American Indians have not been in their present habitat long enough for climatic conditions to have taken effect.[3] He also points out that two views might be taken of the possible reasons for colour variations. "One view would be that adaptive pigmentation . . . has resulted from the action of the environment extending over many generations and presumably at a time when the tissues were more susceptible or elastic than at present; the variation so acquired having at length become transmissible. . . . The other view . . . is that pigmentation . . . arose as a spontaneous variation, that is as a sport or mutant, independently of the action of the environment, at a period perhaps when variability and mutation were more prone to occur, and the individuals so pigmented, being more fitted to sustain the solar heat, at length outlived the rest."[4]

[1] *The Antiquity of Man* (1925), by Sir Arthur Keith, 2nd ed., vol. 2, p. 719.
[2] Ovid: *Metamorphoses*, Book II.
[3] *The Races of Man and their Distribution*, by A. C. Haddon, revised edition, 1929, p. 8. It is possible, however, that the uniform colour of the American aborigines may be due to the fact that the main mountain chains of America run north and south, and thus do not form barriers to large scale migration from one latitude to another; nor are there any large deserts or seas to handicap movement northward or southward from equatorial regions. In the Old World, on the other hand, the main mountain ranges run east and west, while the Sahara desert and the Mediterranean Sea are formidable barriers to movements from the equator northwards.
[4] *Ibid.*, pp. 144–5.

Another writer says that "speaking generally, it may be conceded that many coloured races have shown their capacity to become gradually acclimatised to cold latitudes, while fair races have not proved so adaptable when they move to the tropics. This may perhaps be explained on the general grounds that blondness is a later acquired specialisation, and therefore less adaptable to modifications of environment than more generalised characters."[1]

There seems to be no doubt that blonds suffer the most from the effects of tropical light, having less protection against the short rays of the sun than dark-skinned people. A dark skin screens out the ultra-violet rays and radiates heat in a way that the white cannot do.[2]

However distasteful it may be to followers of the Nordic school and other supporters of the theory of white superiority, the consensus of scientific opinion seems to point to the fact that we are all descended from the same stock, and that the earliest members of this stock were of a dark complexion. The Yoruba word for a European means 'a peeled man,'[3] and even the formation of the nose of the white man may be an acquired characteristic, as Professor Haddon points out that "wide nostrils and a broad nose are frequently associated with hot, moist conditions, whereas in regions of cold, dry climate the nasal apertures are narrowed so as to warm the inhaled air."[4]

We have seen in a previous chapter that Darwin, after careful consideration, rejected the theory that the different races were actually of distinct species and expressed the opinion that all were descended from a single primitive ancestor. "There is, however, no doubt," he says, "that the various races, when carefully compared and measured, differ much from each other—as in the texture of the hair, the relative proportions of all parts of the body, the capacity of the lungs, the form and capacity of the skull, and even in the convolutions of the brain."[5] In some of these characteristics, such as the length of arm, prognathism, the heavy, massive cranium

[1] *The Clash of Culture and the Contact of Races* (1927), by G. H. Lane-Fox Pitt-Rivers, p. 109. [2] *Ibid.*, pp. 107–8.

[3] Article by Pastor M. Agbebi, of Lagos, Nigeria, in Papers on Inter-racial Problems communicated to the *First Universal Races Congress held at the University of London*, July 1911, p. 344.

[4] *The Races of Man and thei. Distribution*, by A. C. Haddon, revised ed., 1929, p. 12.

[5] *The Descent of Man* (1874), by C. Darwin, 2nd ed., p. 259.

with large zygomatic arches, and the flat nose,[1] the black man appears to be on a lower evolutionary level than the white, and to be nearer in his relationship to the higher apes; in the important matter of hair, however, which, as we have seen above, is the most definite physical distinction between the races, the white man is closer to the ape.[2] The hairy skin of the whites, of the Australian 'blackfellows,' and of a few tribes, such as the Ainus, is close in its nature to the hairy coats of the apes: the Negro skin is far less hairy, and the Mongolian has less body hair than either. The thin lips of the whites are similar to the thin lips of the ape: "the most contrastingly 'human' development is the full lips of the Negro."[3] It is clear from this that "no race has a monopoly of evolutionary end products, and no arguments for superiority can be based on single traits selected just because they favour the White race."[4]

It has, of course, been suggested that the lack of achievement of the Negro race is due, not to environment or climate or to any other external influence, but to an inherent deficiency in brain power. The difference in size and shape of the black man's brain as compared with that of the white, has been held to prove that his intellectual endowment is inferior. For instance, in a letter to *The Times*,[5] it was pointed out that the average cubic capacity of the brains of 3,444 adult male natives of Kenya was 1,316 cubic centimetres, as compared with an average European capacity of 1,481 cubic centimetres,[6] and it was suggested that, while the mental

[1] "In apes, as in all primitive races of mankind, the nasal spine is but a stout, low, ridge-like elevation with, on each side of it, a broad gutter leading from the floor of the nose to the front of the jaw above the incisor teeth." *The Antiquity of Man* (1925), by Sir Arthur Keith, 2nd ed., vol. 1, p. 85.
[2] See *Encyclopædia Britannica*, 14th ed., vol. 16, p. 193.
[3] *Race and Racism* (1942), by Ruth Benedict, p. 65.   [4] *Ibid.*
[5] From Dr. H. L. Gordon, Visiting Physician to Mathari Mental Hospital, Nairobi, in *The Times* of December 8, 1933. Dr. Gordon has also tentatively suggested that it is the 'New Brain,' with its 'myriad cells of late evolutionary origin' in which the Negro is lacking. He says that "a highly technical skilled examination of a series of 100 brains of normal Natives has found naked eye and microscopic facts indicative of inherent new brain inferiority. . . . Quantitively the inferiority amounts to 14·8 per cent: qualitatively the cells of the new brain compared with those of the average normal European show defect and deficiency." See article on "The Intentional Improvement of Backward Tribes," by H. L. Gordon, in *The East African Medical Journal*, vol. 11, no. 5, August 1943, pp. 148–50.
[6] As the result of an investigation in Jamaica it was found that, on the average, the cranial capacities of the Jamaican blacks were exceptionally high, and that, in this island, the usually inferior skull capacity of the blacks surpassed that of the whites.

affliction known as *dementia praecox* is never encountered among natives living in primitive circumstances, the effect of European education on the under-sized brain of the Kenya native was conducive to this disease.

Other letters to *The Times* challenged the deductions of the writer of the original letter. Professor Leakey questioned whether brain capacity, measured in terms of cubic centimetres, bore any relation to actual or potential mental ability. "I am not aware," he said, "that this has ever been scientifically demonstrated, and, in fact, I am inclined to believe that there is no correlation between these two things. . . . So far as we know, males of the brutish Neanderthal race have a very high 'brain capacity' figure, and . . . such direct evidence as is available shows that some at least of the very clever men England has produced had small 'brain capacities,' but great mental ability, and that English women who have a small average 'brain capacity' can hardly be denied to have great mental ability in many cases."[1]

Referring to an address by Dr. Gordon to the Eugenics Society, the *British Medical Journal*[2] says that the findings "seem to show a definite cerebral deficiency in the native as compared with the European," but Sir Arthur Keith says that size of brain, "is a very imperfect index of mental capacity." "We know," he continues, "that certain elements enter into the formation of the brain which take no direct part in our mental activity. A person who has been blessed with a great, robust body, and strong, massive limbs requires a greater outfit of nerve tracts and nerve cells for the purpose of mere animal administration than the smaller person with trunk and limbs of a moderate size."[3]

See *Race Crossing in Jamaica*, by C. B. Davenport and Morris Steggerda (Carnegie Institution of Washington Publication no. 395, 1929), pp. 164–5.

[1] In *The Times* of December 13, 1933. See also a letter from Professor Julian Huxley in *The Times* of December 18, 1933. Sir Arthur Keith has also pointed out that Cromagnon man, who appears to have had negroid characteristics, had a larger brain than the modern Englishman. *The Antiquity of Man* (1925), 2nd ed., vol. 1, p. 74. In an amusing letter to *The Times* published on December 19, 1933, Professor J. B. S. Haldane pointed out that the average cranial capacity of the Eskimos was greater than that of Europeans; "Charity," he says, "begins at home, so let us hope that, if the natives of Kenya are to be protected from European education, steps will be taken at the same time to safeguard Europe from the disintegrating effects of Eskimo culture, which may well prove too complex for beings of smaller cranial capacity." [2] Of November 18, 1933.

[3] *The Antiquity of Man* (1925), by Sir Arthur Keith, 2nd ed., vol. 2, pp. 605–6.

PHYSICAL AND MENTAL DIFFERENCES BETWEEN RACES

Professor Ginsberg draws attention to interesting tables that have been compiled giving the measurements of the cranial capacity of different races,[1] and, admitting that the higher values occur with greater frequency among the civilised peoples, maintains that "there is no real ground for assuming any correlation between cranial capacity and cultural level."[2] "In essentials," he says, "there appears to be no difference between the mental structure of primitive and civilised man. . . . The differences in their achievements are due to differences in the range of experience, in the degrees of systemisation, in the power of logical self-criticism, and, above all, in the degree in which the flow of thought is dominated by subjective factors."[3] It is perhaps safest to accept the opinion of another writer who points out that although "there may be racial differences in mentality they have not yet been satisfactorily established by any scientific test."[4]

One fact, frequently remarked on by European observers in Africa, is worthy of attention. There appears to be little doubt that Negro children, in their early years, are fully equal to white children in intelligence and capacity for acquiring knowledge in school and elsewhere; it appears almost equally certain that, at about the age of puberty, the mental development of Negro children, in a great many cases, is definitely arrested, and that they fall behind white children in energy and capacity. This phenomenon is generally accepted as being due to the fact that sexual matters take an unduly prominent place in the life and thoughts of the Negro at a very early age. One who has been resident in Africa for many years in official positions has said: "I have over and over again been the

[1] By Martin, in *Lehrbuch der Anthropologie*, Jena, 1914, pp. 642-3. For further information regarding the comparative weights and sizes of brains in Africans and others, see "The Brain of the Kenya Native," by F. W. Vint, in *The Journal of Anatomy*, vol. 68, part 2, January 1943, pp. 216-23; *Sociology* (1934), by Morris Ginsberg, pp. 66-7; *The Antiquity of Man* (1925), by Sir Arthur Keith, 2nd ed., vol. 2, pp. 604, 659.
[2] *Sociology* (1934), by Morris Ginsberg, pp. 65-6.
[3] *Ibid.*, p. 224.
[4] *Race Relations, Adjustment of Whites and Negroes in the United States* (1934), by W. D. Weatherford and C. C. Johnson, p. 8. Lord Olivier says that his "conviction after some fifty years' experience with Negro peoples is that if you look after the nutrition, health and economic conditions of Negroes, whether in Africa or elsewhere, their brain will take care of itself." Address to the Fabian Summer School in 1935, published under the title "Can the African make good?" in *The West Indian Review* of November 1935.

COLOUR PREJUDICE

witness of the sudden and astonishing change which takes place among the young male house-servants as youth approaches manhood. Brightness and initiative disappear; they go about their duties in the most casual manner; they are unable to remember the clearest and simplest instructions."[1] Another official of long African experience has said: "When the youth arrives at puberty there is undoubtedly the tendency towards an arrested development of the mind. At this critical period many bright and shining examples fall off into disappointing nullity. As might be imagined, the concentration of their thoughts on sexual intercourse is answerable for this falling away."[2] My own experience in Africa forces me to agree with this evidence.[3]

While sexual excess is undoubtedly a contributing cause to this arrest of mental development, it has been suggested that while with white children the volume of the brain grows with the expansion of the brain-pan, in the case of Negro children "the growth of the brain is, on the contrary, arrested by the premature closing of the cranial sutures and lateral pressure of the frontal bone."[4] This belief is, however, now discredited.[5]

Even assuming that this arrest, or even deterioration, in mental development is due entirely to precocious sexual obsession, it by no means follows that this obsession is inevitable in the race, and could not be eradicated by different living conditions and the right educational effort. In a poor or isolated community, or where the lack of education debars the people from intellectual interests, and the climate or custom forbids youth from finding an outlet for its energies in physical exercise, it is not surprising that sexual adventures should be pursued to relieve the monotony of life.[6]

[1] *Portuguese East Africa* (1906), by R. C. F. Maugham, pp. 268–9.
[2] *British Central Africa* (1897), by Sir Harry Johnston, p. 408.
[3] Several other statements regarding the loss of mental energy by African boys after puberty are quoted in *Sex and Culture*, by J. D. Unwin, p. 606. See also *The Yellow and Dark-Skinned People of Africa south of the Zambesi* (1910), by C. McCall Theal, p. 264.
[4] *Encyclopædia Britannica*, 11th ed., vol. 19, p. 344.
[5] See page 86.
[6] It is said that "many pass all the way from the last stage of infancy, through childhood and youth, right into maturity, without ever having experienced voluntary sexual abstinence." See *The African as Suckling and as Adult*, by J. F. Ritchie, Principal of Barotse National School, Northern Rhodesia (1943), p. 40.

This opinion is endorsed by Professor Leakey, in a comment on the statement that "after puberty the development of the native brain almost ceases." He writes: "From certain observations that I have made on a mission station, I am inclined to believe that, whereas this may be true of natives living under normal tribal conditions, it is far less true among children born of educated native parents who start their education at about the same age as an ordinary English child. Leaving aside the undoubted effect of early education upon mental development, I suggest the additional possibility that the reason for the stunting of mental and brain growth at puberty in natives living under tribal conditions is that for them sex life starts almost directly after puberty, and that this sex activity in some way inhibits development. Native children born and educated on mission stations are less subject to this inhibiting factor, and have, I believe, a far more normal development."[1] The Reverend A. T. Bryant, admitting that "a mental change for the worse does really take place about the age of puberty," considers that the loss of mental vigour and power is not nearly so marked in the case of boys who are sent to school at an early age.[2] Another writer suggests that the arrest of mental development at the age of puberty "may not be so much an inevitable result of the kind of mental faculties which are inherited as the result of the coming into play of a peculiar tradition. This conclusion is supported by the fact that, when African education begins earlier, when, that is to say, there is more of a break with native tradition, the arrest is less well marked. Further, in America, it is still less marked though it can be detected. The conclusion would thus seem to be that, though there may be some tendency for intellectual development to stop at a rather lower stage than among European races, it is nothing like so well marked as the observations of residents in South Africa would seem at first sight to show."[3]

It is clear that it has not yet been proved that the relative size.

[1] In *The Times* of December 13, 1933.
[2] *The Eugenics Review*, April 1917. Article on "Mental Development of the South African Native," by Reverend A. T. Bryant; adapted for publication by C. G. Seligman. See also *Christianity and the Race Problem* (1924), by J. H. Oldham, 7th ed., p. 74.
[3] *The Population Problem, A Study in Human Evolution* (1922), by A. M. Carr-Saunders, p. 398.

of brain is an index to mental capacity,[1] nor has science given us evidence, in any other direction, of the alleged inherent inferiority of the black man's intellectual endowment. As Professor Malinowski points out, science has done little or nothing in spite of the clash of colour and the confusion of cultures, which he refers to as "the most important process, if not the greatest catastrophe of modern times," to elucidate the effective value of race. "The task, indeed," he says, "was too formidable, the practical preoccupations too acute, the changes too rapid, to make the problem attractive to the detached academic man; and anthropology has almost deliberately entrenched itself behind a wall of antiquarian detachment. Half of the work on race has been devoted to the study of a few skulls of Piltdown man and Neanderthal man. Hundreds of thousands of skulls were measured, classified and labelled. But what happens within these skulls while they are alive, the passions the prejudices, the desires—all this has yet been largely left out of the field of research. Racial research has not gone beyond a mere classification of man's bodily characteristics. . . . And yet it is obvious that, until we can definitely connect certain bodily characteristics—colour of the skin, character of the hair, size and form of the skull—until we can connect these indices with cultural efficiency and intellectual capacity all the study of physical characteristics is well nigh valueless. The failure of anthropology has left the field to practical bias, vested interest, and to those prejudices which so easily crop up in racial matters."[2]

One biologist has said that all the existing genuine scientific knowledge on the subject could be written out on the back of a postage stamp,[3] and it has been recognised in an official document that "there are no strictly scientific grounds on which a judgment regarding the degree of progress of which African peoples are capable can be based. All that we have to guide us are the broad facts of history and of personal experience, and it is not surprising

[1] "So far as concerns conclusions drawn from brain measurements it must be realised that nothing is definitely known regarding any correlation between the physical characteristics of the brain and intellectual or moral qualities." *An African Survey* (1938), by Lord Hailey, p. 37.
[2] Article on Race and Labour, by B. Malinowski, in Supplement No. 8 to *The Listener* of July 16, 1930.
[3] Preface by Lancelot Hogben to *Half-Caste* (1937), by C. Dover, p. 9.

PHYSICAL AND MENTAL DIFFERENCES BETWEEN RACES

that opinions should widely differ."[1] "Least of all," writes Professor Morgan, "should we feel any assurance in deciding genetic superiority or inferiority as applied to whole races, by which is meant not races in a biological sense but social or political groups bound together by physical conditions, by religious sentiments, or by political organisations. The latter have their roots in the past and are acquired by each new generation as a result of imitation and training. If it is unjust 'to condemn a whole *people*,' meaning thereby a political group, how much more hazardous is it, as some sensational writers have not hesitated to do, to pass judgment as to the relative genetic inferiority or superiority of different *races*. If within each human social group the geneticist finds it impossible to discover, with any reasonable certainty, the genetic basis of behaviour, the problems must seem extraordinarily difficult when groups are contrasted with each other where the differences are obviously connected not only with material advantages and disadvantages resulting from location, climate, soil and mineral wealth, but with traditions, customs, religions, taboos, conventions and prejudices. A little goodwill might seem more fitting in treating these complicated questions than the attitude adopted by some of the modern race-propagandists."[2]

[1] *Report of the Commission on Closer Union of the Dependencies in Eastern and Central Africa* (Cmd. 3234), 1929, pp. 15–16.
[2] *Evolution and Genetics* (1925), by T. H. Morgan, pp. 206–7.

Chapter IX

PHYSICAL REPULSION BETWEEN RACES

SINCE we are unable to accept as scientifically proved the theory that the black man is inherently inferior to the white, or that he comes from a different stock, how are we going to explain the prejudice that undoubtedly exists, and what Graham Wallas describes as "the irrational race-hatred which breaks out from time to time on the fringes of empire?"[1] And how are we to justify the attitude of those whites who deny that black men have any rights which can override the privileges of the more powerful race? A German writer held that the "rights of natives, which can be recognised only at the cost of holding back the evolution of the white race at any point, simply do not exist . . . such an idea is absurd."[2] A South African politician expressed the same view in a letter to *The Times*: "The white man, English as well as Dutch, is determined to do all he can to remain, and what is more, to rule . . . this matter is, to us in South Africa, such a vital and fundamental matter that no ethical considerations such as the rights of man and equal opportunities for all non-Europeans, will be allowed to stand in the way."[3]

The situation is highly complex. "White and black alike are being driven blindly by forces which they do not sufficiently understand, and are unable therefore intelligently to control."[4]

[1] *Human Nature in Politics* (1920) by Graham Wallas, 3rd. ed., p. 295.

[2] *Deutsche Kolonialwirtschaft*, by P. Rohrbach, p. 44. Quoted by J. H. Oldham in *Christianity and the Race Problem* (1924), p. 95.

[3] Sir Thomas Watt, in *The Times* of March 30, 1926. See also article by J. T. Graves in *The Virginia Quarterly Review* (Autumn 1942), pp. 504–5, quoted in *An American Dilemma* (1944), by Gunnar Myrdal, p. 663: "There is no power in the world . . . which could now force the Southern white people to the abandonment of the principle of social segregation. It is a cruel disillusionment . . . for any of their (the Negroes') leaders to tell them that they can expect it, or that they can exact it as the price of their participation in the war."

[4] Speech by Mr. J. H. Oldham at the International Conference, in September 1926, at Le Zoute. Quoted in *The Christian Mission in Africa* (1926), by E. W. Smith, pp. 168–9.

The tragedy is that so few will take the trouble to try to understand. "I have always felt," says Major Moton, "that much of the friction between races, as well as between nations and individuals, is due to misunderstanding, that if people would take the time to understand one another's point of view they would frequently find that things are not so bad as they imagine."[1] Lord Bryce thought that where the races meet "antagonism is sure to arise. It arises from Inequality, because as one of the races is stronger in intelligence and will, its average members treat members of the weaker race scornfully and roughly, when they can do so with impunity. It arises from Dissimilarity of character, because the sense of not comprehending one another makes each suspect the other of faithlessness or guile."[2]

Racial prejudice may be due to economic causes or to political conditions, to the superiority complex of one race or an inferiority complex in another, or to biological differences and hereditary instinct. Whether it is due to any one of these causes or to a combination of several, there can be little doubt that the prejudice is aggravated to a large degree by a lack of knowledge, and a tendency to accept, as facts, theories which are incapable of proof.

Realising then that colour prejudice does exist, to the general disadvantage of all and more particularly to the disadvantage of the coloured races, it is important to discover whether such prejudice is natural and inevitable or whether it is due to causes which can be removed. Are individuals of different races naturally repulsive to one another, and is this a wise provision of nature designed to preserve purity of race?[3] Or is racial antipathy due to the clash of interests and inequality of culture? If the former alternative must be accepted the position would indeed be hopeless, and nothing could prevent the adoption of the policy of the "survival of the fittest"; sooner or later the weakest peoples, whichever they might be,

[1] *Finding a Way Out* (1920), by R. R. Moton, p. 143.
[2] *The Relations of the Advanced and the Backward Races of Mankind* (Romanes Lecture, 1902), by Lord Bryce, p. 29.
[3] Sir Arthur Keith thinks that the answer to this question is in the affirmative. "Nature," he says, "endowed her tribal teams with this spirit of antagonism for her own purposes. It has come down to us and creeps out from our modern life in many shapes, as national rivalries and jealousies and as racial hatreds. The modern name for this spirit of antagonism is race prejudice. . . . Race prejudice, I believe, works for the ultimate good of mankind." *The Place of Prejudice in Modern Civilisation*, (1931), pp. 35, 48.

would go to the wall—to absorption or annihilation. But if, as I believe, there are no inevitable causes for racial prejudice, it will be possible, though admittedly difficult, to eradicate the causes which now exist, given the necessary understanding of those causes and the goodwill of all concerned.

If colour prejudice were instinctive, it is probable that it would be shown by children at an early age. It is well known, however, that white infants go readily to Indian, Chinese or Negro nurses, and that young children seldom evince any signs of racial or colour prejudice. It is true that a child, seeing a person of a coloured race for the first time, might show signs of surprise or fear, but "a child's fear of a strangely shaped or coloured face is more easily obliterated by familiarity than it would be if it were the result of a specific instinct of race-hatred."[1] It has, however, been suggested that the absence of colour prejudice in a child is due to the fact that the sexual instincts, which produce this prejudice, have not yet been developed.

It would, however, be a mistake to assume that the apparent absence of an instinctive race prejudice among children is proof of its non-existence among adults. There does exist, for one cause or another, a real physical repulsion between individuals of different races. Lord Bryce remarks that there "is always a slight repulsion between peoples speaking different tongues and with characters markedly unlike,"[2] and he points to the feeling between the Welshman and the Englishman, or the Lowland Scot and the Highlander, as examples. That the feeling should be more intense between persons of different colour is not remarkable. White dislike for the colour, smell and customs of other races is most heartily reciprocated.

An American writer says that several of the most devoted friends of the Negro race have admitted to him that the first impression made on them by contact with a black was one of painful revulsion,[3] and Lord Lugard has quoted a Bishop as saying that, although he had striven and prayed all his life, he had been unable to overcome his instinctive aversion from coloured people.[4] On the other hand,

[1] *Human Nature in Politics* (1920), by Graham Wallas, 3rd ed., p. 56.
[2] *Race Sentiment as a Factor in History* (1915), by Lord Bryce, p. 20.
[3] *The Neighbor. The Natural History of Human Contacts* (1904), by N. S. Shaler, pp. 164-5.
[4] *The Problem of Colour in relation to the Idea of Equality* (Supplement to vol. 1, no. 2, of the *Journal of Philosophical Studies*), p. 7.

PHYSICAL REPULSION BETWEEN RACES

"the unsophisticated African entertains aversion to white people, and when, on accidentally or unexpectedly meeting a white man he turns or takes to his heels, it is because he feels that he has come upon some unusual or unearthly creature ... an aquiline nose, scant lips and cat-like eyes afflict him."[1] The uncivilised Bantu has a horror of any skin that is not the same colour as his.[2] Even the cannibal will turn in horror from the white man, who is held to be indigestible because he is not 'ripe,'[3] and "it has been noted by certain ethnologists that whiteness of skin, to certain African peoples who had never seen a white person before, suggested the unsightly discolouration of a person who had been dead long in the water."[4] The Japanese find our large eyes and our high noses 'horrid.'[5] Professor Malinowski says that "a great many members of other non-European races feel race prejudice as strongly as we do, and would welcome an effective colour bar protecting them from Europeans. Those natives whom I have known well and for a long space of time admit to a genuine dislike of our European smell, colour, features and manners, a dislike as pronounced as that manifested by some Europeans towards other races."[6]

It has been pointed out that most of us still judge one another as do cats and dogs—chiefly by the nose.[7] By this test, apparently, the white man is no better than the coloured. Professor Toynbee quotes an example of the disgust felt by the vegetarian Japanese at the "rank and foetid odour of the carnivorous peoples of the West."[8] "To many an African the white man exudes some rancid odour not agreeable to his olfactory nerves."[9] A white writer who has

[1] *Papers on Inter-racial Problems*, communicated to the First Universal Races Congress held at the University of London, July 1911, edited by G. Spiller; article by Pastor M. Agbebi, p. 344.
[2] *The Bantu Past and Present* (1920), by S. W. Molema, p. 310.
[3] *Selections from the Travels of Ibn Batuta, 1325-1354* (Broadway Travellers), p. 332. The complaint has also been made that the flesh of the white man is too salty.
[4] *Race Relations. Adjustment of Whites and Negroes in the United States* (1934), by W. D. Weatherford and C. S. Johnson, pp. 543-4.
[5] *Papers on Inter-racial Problems*, communicated to the First Universal Races Congress held at the University of London, July 1911, edited by G. Spiller; article by Dr. Felix von Luschan, p. 14.
[6] Article on "The Colour Bar," by B. Malinowski, in *The Spectator* of June 27, 1931.
[7] *A Short Introduction to the History of Human Stupidity* (1935), by W. P. Pitkin, p. 352.
[8] *A Study of History* (1935), by Arnold J. Toynbee, vol. I, p. 231.
[9] *Papers on Inter-racial Problems*, communicated to the First Universal Races Congress held at the University of London, July 1911, edited by G. Spiller; article by Pastor M. Agbebi, p. 344.

travelled in West Africa says that when the Negroes sweat "they undoubtedly do emit a rather pungent cat-like smell, but I cannot see that it is essentially more disagreeable than the acrid sour-milk sweat of Europeans. To my nose a cup final crowd smells both nastier and stronger than any crowd of negroes with whom I have been in contact."[1]

If the white man in Africa finds the Negro untidy, dirty and noisy, and there is admittedly much in his habits repulsive to Europeans,[2] "there is much in our institutions and morals that horrifies him as profoundly as much in his horrifies us."[3]

Even in the matter of physical beauty the white man has claimed superiority over those of other races, and has assumed that this superiority is admitted. It is true that in a curious book, published in 1892, a West African Negro, educated at Oxford and later the holder of a responsible official position, ascribed most of the troubles of his race to its ugliness. "Why," he says, "is the Negro so despised? Let truth be told. It is because he is ugly, because his woolly pate is not so becoming as the flaxen hair of the Anglo-Saxon, because the flat nose of the Negro is more like the nasal organ of the ape than is the aquiline nose of the Aryan races, because blubber lips are not as pretty as thin ones, because a black complexion is displeasing compared with a fair or olive one. . . . Will the Negro himself deny that he is uglier than the other races of mankind or that this ugliness is the origin of all his troubles, the source of the torrent of ridicule, of abuse, of calumny, of injustice, which he experiences? . . . I am a Negro of pure descent . . . but I must confess with regret that, except the Chinese, I have never seen another race approaching even within a measurable distance, the Negro in ugliness."[4] The author proceeds to recommend miscegenation, on the grounds that "the fine physique of the Negro

[1] *Africa Dances* (1935), by G. Gorer, p. 11. A European long resident in Nigeria has pointed out that the accusation that Negroes smell is made by Europeans who commonly come in contact with them when they are working under a hot sun, and therefore sweating profusely. See *Dark Subjects* (1939), by H. L. Ward Price, p. 155. See also *The Biology of the Negro* (1942), by J. H. Lewis, p. 94.

[2] *The Anatomy of African Misery* (1927), by Lord Olivier, p. 73.

[3] *Ibid.*, p. 151. It is said that among primitive peoples the native sculptor often shows the European holding a bottle, which he regards as an appropriate label. See *The Savage Hits Back* (1937), by J. E. Lips, p. 115.

[4] *The Negro Question, or Hints for the Physical Improvement of the Negro Race, with special reference to West Africa* (1892), by J. Renner Maxwell, pp. 10, 40, 41.

PHYSICAL REPULSION BETWEEN RACES

race blended with the beauty of the Caucasian race should produce a progeny both robust and beautiful."[1]

There seems every reason to believe, in spite of the above quotation, that the Negro *would* deny that his race is uglier than others. Darwin points out that "the sense of beauty obviously depends on the nature of the mind, irrespective of any real quality in the admired object; and that the idea of what is beautiful is not innate or unalterable. We see this, for instance, in the men of different races admiring an entirely different standard of beauty in their women."[2] Put more shortly, beauty lies in the eye of the beholder. It is well known that the Negro is not, as a rule, an admirer of white beauty, and he probably shares the views held by the Melanesians and reported by Professor Malinowski in the following words: "Europeans, the natives frankly say, are not good-looking. The straight hair . . . the nose, 'sharp like an axe blade,' the thin lips, the big eyes 'like water puddles,' the white skin with spots on it like those of an albino—all these the natives say (and no doubt feel) are ugly."[3] We have seen above what the Japanese think on the subject.

At the same time it must be admitted that the Negro has given some grounds for the unthinking to believe that he admires white beauty. By bleaching their skin and by straightening their hair coloured women try hard to lessen their unlikeness from white women, and it has been remarked that the most race-conscious of all the Negro owned newspapers in the United States carried the largest proportion of space devoted to advertisements for obliterating the marks of difference.[4] A Negro physician has had to point out to his own people that "when a white man believes the white people are the best looking people in the world, he is wise and in harmony with nature. When a Negro believes that, he is a fool and out of harmony with nature."[5] But it is difficult to believe that the Negro is really a fool in this matter, or that any number of Negroes admit the superiority of white beauty. It is

---

[1] *The Negro Question, or Hints for the Physical Improvement of the Negro Race, with special reference to West Africa* (1892), by J. Renner Maxwell, p. 105.

[2] *The Origin of Species* (1888), by C. Darwin, 6th ed., p. 251.

[3] *The Sexual Life of Savages in North-Western Melanesia* (1932), by B. Malinowski, 3rd ed., p. 258.

[4] *Race Relations. Adjustment of Whites and Negroes in the United States* (1934), by W. D. Weatherford and C. S. Johnson, p. 544.   [5] *Ibid.*, p. 284.

probable that the desire to resemble the whites, and the phenomenon of 'passing over,' to which reference will be made later,[1] are due to nothing more than the desire to be inconspicuous and normal[2] in a 'white' country, to escape the inconvenience of colour where colour is a handicap, and to obtain a share of the prestige which is to-day the prerogative of the whites.[3] A coloured man is reported to have said: "it's no disgrace to be black, but it's often very inconvenient."[4] It must, however be admitted that the argument is weakened by the fact that, although there is no colour line in Brazil,[5] the desire to be white is no less marked in that country than elsewhere in Latin America.[6]

There is undoubtedly an association of ideas which makes his colour a handicap to the Negro in his dealings with the white race. To nearly every race and in nearly every language whiteness is the emblem of purity and goodness,[7] while blackness is associated with death and dirt and wickedness.[8] The God who made man in His

[1] See page 122.
[2] *A Study of History* (1935), by Arnold J. Toynbee, vol. 1, p. 228.   [3] *Ibid.*
[4] *The Autobiography of an Ex-Coloured Man*, by J. W. Johnson, 1927 ed., p. 155.
[5] Or, at any rate, the discrimination there is "much milder." See *An American Dilemma* (1944), by G. Myrdal, vol. 1, p. 134. An authority on the colour question in Brazil speaks of "that obvious inferiority complex that even in Brazil, a land so favourable to the mulatto, is to be observed under a number of forms." *The Masters and the Slaves*, by Gilberto Freyre, trans. by S. Putnam (1946), p. 453 (published in Portuguese in 1933).
[6] *Clashing Tides of Colour* (1935), by L. Stoddard, p. 97; quoted from an article by L. L. and J. S. Bernard in the "Annals of the American Association of Political and Social Science." November 1928.
[7] An American clergyman has assured us that God agrees with this! "As to the intrinsic superiority of a white complexion over that of black, there is no question; for by the common consent of all ages among men, and even of God himself in heaven, there has been bestowed on white the most honourable distinction. White has become the emblem of moral purity and truth." *A Bible Defence of Slavery* (1852), by the Reverend Josiah Priest, p. 164. Mr. Peter Nielsen says that he has been told by a minister of the Dutch Reformed Church in South Africa that "according to the scriptures, the separation of the white and the black races will be continued in Heaven as upon earth—he said nothing about hell—and that those Natives who are permitted to enter the heavenly abodes will be separately accommodated in some of the many mansions of which mention is made in the New Testament." *The Colour Bar* (1937), pp. 43–4.
[8] Compare "We are the chosen people; look at the hue of our skins.
     Others are black or yellow: that is because of their sins."
See also *An American Dilemma* (1944), by Gunnar Myrdal, p. 697: "Blackness of skin remained undesirable and even took on an association of badness" (in the United States, after emancipation).

own image[1] is assumed to be white, the devil to be black, and the Negro himself will speak of a good man as one whose heart is white.[2]

"The great thing about the African, and the real objection to him in the eyes of European races, is the fact that he is black, and, in most cases, his features are of the Negro type, and he has wool instead of hair. . . . This question of colour, of features, and of wool requires explanation, because it obviously has nothing to do with the mental capacity of the man; they are, perhaps, consequences due more to climate than to anything else. But with Europeans the association of ideas leads all of them to deem this colour, these features, and this wool, to be signs of permanent inferiority."[3]

One does not need to be a student of psychology to realise that these associations of ideas, unfair though they may be in their results, do in fact occur. It has been pointed out that each one of us likes, or dislikes, a certain type of man, and although such types are found in every race of mankind, we "find in actual experience a much larger number of the type we like in our own race, and of the type we dislike in a different race."[4] Furthermore, it is almost inevitable that unthinking persons should associate with another race the traits which he dislikes in an individual of that race. Two Englishmen, disliking one another intensely, would confine that dislike to the individual who had caused it; an Englishman and a Frenchman disliking one another would probably, in expressing their dislike, dwell on the nationality of the other in no complimentary terms; a white man thinking or speaking of a black man whom he disliked would import into a matter of personal and individual feeling an entirely irrelevant feeling of racial antipathy, attributing to racial rather than to personal shortcomings the causes of his dislike. Such an unreasonable attitude must be due to prejudice and not to any inherent racial repugnance.

[1] The 'Nordics,' of course, created God in *their* own image.
[2] Major Moton speaks of the better "class of the white race who have made the term 'white' the hall-mark of excellence so commonly used by Negroes." *What the Negro Thinks* (1929), p. 19.
[3] *The Caribbean Confederation* (1888), by C. S. Salmon, Preface. Mr. Salmon served in responsible official posts both in West Africa and the West Indies.
[4] *Christianity and the Race Problem* (1924), by J. H. Oldham, 7th ed., p. 39.

Chapter X

MISCEGENATION[1]

IT is, of course, in the matter of sexual relationship that the question of physical attraction or repulsion becomes of the greatest importance, and it is with regard to sexual relationships between white and black that prejudices are the most bitter. The desire of the whites to "keep the race pure" is given as the reason for much discrimination against the Negro, and as the excuse for much brutality and bloodshed. It has been stated that the crossing of the races results in inferior progeny, both mentally and physically, and in some countries the law has been invoked in the vain attempt to put a stop to inter-racial sexual union.

Lord Bryce says that "nothing really arrests intermarriage except physical repulsion, and physical repulsion exists only where there is a marked difference in physical aspect, and especially in colour. While all the races of the same, or a similar, colour intermarry freely, those of one colour intermarry very little with those of another. This is most marked as between the white and the black races."[2]

It must not be thought that the objection to miscegenation is on the part of the whites alone. Professor Gregory says that "the aversion to marriage with people of a different colour is not limited to the whites. Mixed intercourse is regarded with even more intense repulsion by some of the higher classes of Indians, who regard every half-caste as an insult to their national pride."[3] He adds that the feeling against miscegenation "is firmly expressed by some of the most influential leaders such as Gandhi and Rabindranath Tagore."[4] Lord Olivier pointed out that in South Africa "dominant social feeling condemns miscegenation and neither

[1] For an interesting discussion on this subject, see *Population Problems of the Pacific* (1927), by S. H. Roberts, pp. 352–86.
[2] *The Relations of the Advanced and the Backward Races of Mankind* (1902), by Lord Bryce, p. 18.
[3] *The Menace of Colour* (1925), by J. W. Gregory, 2nd ed., p. 228.
[4] *Race as a Political Factor* (1931), by J. W. Gregory, p. 38.

MISCEGENATION

race desires it,"[1] while we have the statement of Major Moton, one of the leaders of Negro thought in America, that "it is generally accepted, on both sides of the color line, that it is best for the two races to remain ethnologically distinct. Theoretically," he says, "Negroes would all subscribe to the right of freedom of choice in marriage even between the two races,[2] but practically they have never ceased to resent the action of those very few individuals of the race, particularly the men, who have chosen to cross the color line for wives. To the race as a whole it constitutes active disloyalty to the Negro race itself, as well as a reflection on its womanhood."[3] In South Africa, "the feeling within the white group against race-mixture is met by the Bantu with an equally strong condemnation of race-mixture from their side."[4]

The attitude of the white man towards sexual relations with Negroes is very peculiar. A marriage between white and black, and especially between a white woman and a black man, is regarded with horror, but illicit intercourse, and even permanent concubinage, in the case of a white man and a black woman is looked upon with tolerance.[5] Mr. Oldham has pointed out that "it too often happens that those who would resort to the most violent measures to prevent or punish intermarriage between white and black are not averse to keeping black women as concubines."[6] During the days of slavery there was a considerable amount of illicit intercourse between white men and women slaves, and the large half-caste populations of the United States, the West Indies and South Africa are living witnesses to this fact. Lord Olivier has suggested that there has been a decrease in the amount of illicit intimacy between white men and black or coloured women, in proportion to their respective numbers, since the abolition of slavery,[7] but such intimacy does

[1] *The Anatomy of African Misery* (1927), by Lord Olivier, p. 221.
[2] This refers to the legal prohibition in certain States of inter-racial marriage.
[3] *What the Negro Thinks* (1929), by R. R. Moton, p. 241.
[4] *Western Civilisation and the Natives of South Africa* (1934), edited by I. Schapera; article on "Race-Mixture and Native Policy in South Africa," by R. F. A. Hoernlé, p. 278.
[5] It is said that this is not the case among the Dutch in South Africa. "Since the great trek, the pioneer Dutch have regarded any social and sexual intercourse between the black and white races as the last descent in degradation and very few have transgressed. Entire social ostracism would inevitably follow any breach." *Black and White in South Africa* (1911), by Sir M. S. Evans, p. 218.
[6] *Christianity and the Race Problem* (1924), by J. H. Oldham, 7th ed., p. 150.
[7] *The Anatomy of African Misery* (1927), by Lord Olivier, p. 219.

continue, and is particularly frequent in those tropical lands where there are few white women, or where the general standard of sexual morality is low.[1]

In view of the strong feeling, on both sides, against inter-racial marriage, it is not surprising that so many of these marriages prove to be unsuccessful. There are, of course, notable exceptions, but it is, as a rule, difficult for personal affection and esteem long to survive the hostility of relatives and the complete change of environment. Even between persons of the same race but of different social status these difficulties arise. Examples of unhappy marriages between white women and Indians are given by Mrs. Sarangadbar Das, herself Swiss and married to a high-caste Hindu, in her interesting book.[2] An Egyptian, writing of the marriages between Egyptian men and European women, says that "the majority of these unions are not happy. The reason is simple: it is owing to the difference in ways, customs, characters, cast of mind."[3] Anyone who has lived in the colonies can testify to the unhappiness of most of the white women who have married Negroes. On the other hand an Australian writer says that Australian women married to lower class Chinese *in Australia* are as happy as their neighbours.[4] He sees no harm in the crossing of the European and Chinese stocks, but, he says, "as regards the *negro peoples*, theirs is a very different and very difficult problem. On every count they stand on a lower plane than white or Mongolian. Racial mixture with them may be a deterioration for the other races."[5]

In the very early days of American settlement there appears to have been no strong feeling against racial mixture, as not infre-

[1] It is said that in the southern United States "one of the most complex aspects of life ... is the indescribable attraction of the black woman" for the white man. *America Comes of Age* (1927), by A. Siegfried, p. 99. A writer of the 'Nordic' school deplores man's "perverse predisposition to mismate." *The Passing of the Great Race* (1917), by Madison Grant, p. 22.

[2] *A Marriage to India* (1931), by F. Hauswirth (Mrs. Das). See especially Chapter XI.

[3] *Papers on Inter-racial Problems*, communicated to the First Universal Races Congress held at the University of London, July 1911; article by Moh. Sourour Bey, p. 170. Lord Cromer has said that marriages between Egyptians and Europeans led generally to such unhappy consequences that he endeavoured to prevent them. *Ancient and Modern Imperialism* (1910), p. 138. See also *Colour Conflict: Race Relations in Africa* (1943), by G. W. Broomfield, General Secretary, Universities Mission to Central Africa, p. 126.

[4] *Environment and Race* (1937), by G. Taylor, p. 339.

[5] *Ibid.*, p. 340.

MISCEGENATION

quently white indentured women became the mothers of children by Negro slaves,[1] in spite of the fact that there must have been more white men than white women in the settlements. At a later date legislation was necessary and "Forasmuch as divers free-born English women, forgetful of their free condition, and to the disgrace of our nation, do intermarry with negro slaves," an Act was passed by the General Assembly of Maryland, in 1661, to put a stop to the scandal.[2] To-day, it is said that in the Southern States "miscegenation is rightly held to be an offence far worse than manslaughter, and when the guilty couple have gone through the formality of marriage it is punished by life-imprisonment."[3] In more than half of the States of the Union there are laws which forbid the intermarriage of black and white, and the constitution of Florida contains a provision that "all marriages between a white person and a Negro, or between a white person and a person of Negro descent to the fourth generation, inclusive, are forever prohibited."[4] It is interesting to compare these laws, and the similar laws in the Union of South Africa, with the law in force in Ireland in the fourteenth century, when marriage between an English and an Irish person was declared to be an act of treason.[5]

Is there any instinctive biological reason for the almost universal condemnation of mixed marriages? Two eminent anthropologists think that there is not, and that the disapproval of miscegenation is primarily social, not biological.[6] It is probable, then, that the reason is to be found in the children of these marriages. Lord Bryce says that "where two races are physiologically near to one another, the result of intermixture is good. Where they are remote, it is less satisfactory, by which I mean not only that it is below the level of the higher stock, but that it is not generally and evidently better than the lower stock . . . the mixture of whites and negroes, or of whites and Hindus, or of the American aborigines and negroes,

---

[1] *Race Relations. Adjustment of Whites and Negroes in the United States* (1934), by W. D. Weatherford and C. S. Johnson, p. 403.
[2] *Race Mixture* (1931), by E. B. Reuter, p. 78.
[3] *The Conflict of Colour* (1910), by B. L. Putnam Weale, p. 231.
[4] *Race Mixture* (1931), by E. B. Reuter, p. 86.
[5] *History of the English People*, by J. R. Green, vol. 1, p. 519. The object of this law was to stop the increasing sympathy of the English settlers for the Irish people and for Irish customs.
[6] *We Europeans* (1935), by Julian S. Huxley and A. C. Haddon, p. 280.

COLOUR PREJUDICE

seldom shows good results."[1] Mr. Oldham observes that "crossings between the more distantly related stocks do not give good results,"[2] while Professor Gregory says that "the main practical conclusion from the study of inter-racial relations is that both from analogy with cross-breeding in animals and plants, and from observation of human cross-breeds, the intermarriage of members of the three primary races of mankind produces in general inferior and unreliable progeny."[3]

Another writer concludes that "crossings between widely different races can lower the physical and mental level. . . . Until we have more definite knowledge of the effect of race-crossings we shall certainly do best to avoid crossings between widely different races."[4] Professor Ginsberg considers that the evidence for the opinion that the crossing of widely different races is biologically undesirable is far from conclusive, "since it is generally impossible to make allowance for the social handicaps of such mixed marriages and to disentangle the purely biological effects. . . . Intermarriage generally seems undesirable, from the sociological point of view, when one of the parties is likely to suffer from a conscious or unconscious attitude of inferiority. Until therefore the coloured peoples attain to greater social and economic equality a policy of

[1] *The Relations of the Advanced and the Backward Races of Mankind* (1902), by Lord Bryce, pp. 24–5. An interesting comparison has been drawn between the various Central American republics where the population is of mixed Spanish and Indian origin, with a small percentage of Negro blood. "It is a striking fact that the progress, civilisation and culture of the five Central American republics, Costa Rica, El Salvador, Guatemala, Honduras and Nicaragua, appear to vary in proportion to the percentage of white blood. Costa Rica and El Salvador possess the smallest areas and the poorest natural resources. Yet they contain the highest percentage of white population and they are far in advance of the three larger republics inhabited by a blend in which the Indian element predominates. *White Settlers in the Tropics* (1939), by A. Grenfell Price, p. 122.

[2] *Christianity and the Race Problem* (1924), by J. H. Oldham, 7th ed., p. 145.

[3] *Race as a Political Factor* (1931), by J. W. Gregory, p. 70. This result has, however, been attributed to social rather than to biological factors. "Sweeping assertions are often made to the effect that half-castes are always unreliable, that they share the defects of both parent stocks, and so on and so forth. Such statements usually have no biological foundation. In so far as they are based on facts at all, the facts are social. . . . 'Racial crossing' may be inadvisable, but chiefly because the ethnic groups involved happen to be in different national worlds or on different cultural levels." *We Europeans* (1935), by Julian S. Huxley and A. C. Haddon, pp. 280, 282–3.

[4] *Eugenics in Race and State*: The Second International Congress of Eugenics (1921); article on "Harmonic and Disharmonic Race-crossings," by Jon Alfred Mjoen, vol. 2, p. 60.

MISCEGENATION

intermarriage on a large scale is neither desirable nor practicable."[1]

It is, of course, true that "half-caste children are mostly of low-caste parentage,"[2] and, very often, of illegitimate birth,[3] factors which must militate against them in later years. "Interbreeding," as Lord Olivier says, "has always been most rife where the two races have been in the position of master and slave respectively,"[4] and the superiority of the Mulatto to the pure-blooded Negro in America has been attributed to a long course of sexual selection, the most intelligent and physically attractive of the Negro women having been selected as household servants with a view to concubinage.[5]

It has been asserted that the decline of the Portuguese nation from the days when it was pre-eminent in science and intellect, and led the way in exploration and adventure, is due in large measure to the dilution of Portuguese by Negro blood which followed the voyages of discovery along the West African coast and the bringing to Portugal of African slaves.[6] That the Portuguese have a considerable strain of Negro blood is well known[7] and to this fact may perhaps be attributed their greater fertility, as compared with other European races, when mated with Negroes. Again, as we have seen above, Professor Reuter considers that "the racial admixture with the Negroes, brought into the Egyptian population as servile laborers, marked the beginning of the end of a great people."[8]

Professor McDougall points out that the Arabs who were the founders of the Moslem culture and civilisation "freely mixed their blood with that of many other races, and especially with

[1] *The Problem of Colour in Relation to the Idea of Equality* (Supplement to vol. 1, no. 2, of the *Journal of Philosophical Studies*); paper read by Morris Ginsberg, pp. 20–1.
[2] *Race as a Political Factor* (1931), by J. W. Gregory, p. 44.
[3] "The hybrid is generally born of a vicious father, who deserts the mother and leaves the offspring to be spurned by other races." *White Settlers in the Tropics* (1939), by A. Grenfell Price, p. 143.
[4] *The Anatomy of African Misery* (1927), by Lord Olivier, p. 220.
[5] See article by Professor E. B. Reuter on "The Superiority of the Mulatto," in *The American Journal of Sociology*, XXIII (1917), referred to by Professor J. W. Gregory in *Race as a Political Factor* (1931), p. 45.
[6] See *The Menace of Colour* (1925), by J. W. Gregory, 2nd ed., p. 19. See also page 81 above.
[7] *Man, Past and Present*, by A. H. Keane (1920 ed.), p. 528.
[8] *Race Mixture* (1931), by E. B. Reuter, p. 11. See also Sir G. Elliot-Smith in *The Eugenics Review*, vol. 7, p. 181.

that of the Negro race—a race which never yet has shown itself capable of raising or maintaining itself unaided above a barbaric level of culture. It seems to be probable in the highest degree that this miscegenation, and especially perhaps the large infusion of Negro blood into the peoples bearing the Moslem culture, was a principal factor in bringing about the rapid decline of that civilisation."[1]

The process of admixture between the white and black races has been going on steadily for centuries, and it still continues. In the United States the 'passing' of light-coloured persons into the white race is a well-known phenomenon.[2] It is said to be quite easy for those with an eighth or less of Negro blood to pass as white,[3] especially as their families and friends usually aid rather than hinder the passage, being "glad to have their light-skinned relations escape the insults and economic disadvantages whose deadening and tragic effects they know only too well."[4]

Professor Toynbee reminds us, however, of "the agony with which a modern American citizen who knows that there is a tincture of Negro blood in his veins, keeps watch and ward over his secret when he has surreptitiously violated the 'colour-bar' by 'passing' from the black to the white side of the caste-line."[5] In South Africa also, coloured persons 'pass over' to the white race;[6] in the West Indies, where the communities are smaller, it is not so easy, and, owing to a less severe colour-bar, not so advantageous as in the United States and South Africa.

Apart from the economic advantages of being 'white' in a country where Negroes are discriminated against, there is no

---

[1] *Ethics and Some Modern World Problems* (1924), by W. McDougall, p. 17.

[2] It has been calculated that from 10,000 to 20,000 'pass' each year from the coloured group into the white. See *Brown America* (1932), by Edwin R. Embree, p. 46. It is difficult to believe that the number can be so great.

[3] *Race Mixture* (1931), by E. B. Reuter, p. 56. It is said, however, that a relatively small proportion of Negroid blood becomes increasingly recognisable as age advances, and that this is particularly true in the case of women; *Race, Sex and Environment* (1936), by J. R. de la H. Marett, p. 197.

[4] *Negro Anthology* (1934), edited by Nancy Cunard; article on "America's Changing Color Line," by H. Jannath, p. 84.

[5] *A Study of History* (1935), by Arnold J. Toynbee, vol. 2, p. 219.

[6] See *Western Civilisation and the Natives of South Africa* (1934), edited by I. Schapera; article on "The Economic Position of the Bantu in South Africa," by W. H. Hutt, p. 267; and *The Keys*, the Official Organ of the League of Coloured Peoples, vol. 2, no. 4, p. 78.

MISCEGENATION

doubt that the Mulattoes and other persons with a mixture of white and black blood[1] feel themselves superior to the Negro.[2] We have seen in Chapter II that there is much discrimination among the coloured peoples themselves. A West Indian writer says that the population of the West Indies "is composed of a large percentage of actually black people, and about fifteen or twenty per cent of people who are a varying combination of white and black. From the days of slavery, these have always claimed superiority to the ordinary black, and a substantial majority of them still do so (though resenting as bitterly as the black assumptions of white superiority). . . . There are the browns, intermediates who cannot by any stretch of imagination pass as white, but who will not go one inch towards mixing with people darker than themselves. . . . Fair-skinned girls who marry dark men are often ostracised by their families and given up as lost."[3] In Harlem

[1] In referring generally to Mulattoes I include Quadroons, Octoroons, and all other shades between black and white. See footnote 5 on page 22 above.

[2] "The same or a greater degree of superiority which the Whites assume over *them*, the free Mulattoes lay claim to over the Blacks." *The History, Civil and Commercial, of the British Colonies in the West Indies*, by Bryan Edwards, 4th ed., vol. 2, p. 24. This was written in 1807. See also *The Story of the American Negro*, by I. C. Brown, p. 127, and *Voodoo Gods* (1939), by Zora Hurston, p. 3: "The colour line in Jamaica between the white Englishman and the blacks is not as sharply drawn as between the mulattoes and the blacks."

[3] *The Case for West Indian Self-Government* (1933), by C. L. R. James, pp. 8–9. It has been charitably suggested by Miss Cunard and those associated with her that this attitude of the Mulatto to the black man is the result of the British policy of 'Divide and Rule,' the Mulatto being deliberately put against the Negro. See *Negro Anthology* (1934), edited by Nancy Cunard, note by Editor on page 517, and article on "How Britain Governs the Blacks," by G. Padmore, p. 812.

(Mr. Padmore has also written a book, *How Britain Rules Africa* (1936), criticising British administration in Nigeria and other Colonies. He states on page 27 that the Royal Niger Company governed the Oil Rivers Protectorate, with their headquarters at Calabar; and he refers at page 203 to the Alafin of Abeokuta. These may be trifling inaccuracies, but they leave the reader who has some knowledge of Nigeria with grave doubts as to the accuracy of other statements made. An American writer describes this book as "not particularly reliable" and "superficial and inaccurate"; see *British Enterprise in Nigeria* (1943), by A. N. Cook, pp. 286, 293.)

Lord Olivier, reviewing *Negro Anthology*, speaks of Miss Cunard's references to conditions in Jamaica as "wildly untrue" and "gross nonsense"; he adds that "when Miss Cunard writes the manifest nonsense and displays the one-sidedness which cannot but appal any instructed sympathisers she prejudices the whole case of her clients." See *The New Statesman and Nation* of March 10, 1934.

Miss Cunard says that the "Communist world-order is the solution of the race problem for the Negro" (p. iii.); I have too great a respect for the intelligence of the Negro to think that he will believe this, and in Miss Cunard's book itself reference "there are near-white cliques, mulatto groups, dark-skinned sets who will not invite each other to their houses. . . . The light-skins and browns look down on the black."[1] "In the smart Negro churches the best pews are reserved for the palest of the faithful,"[2] and in Negro colleges "groupings among students often follow the colour line."[3]

It appears to be generally accepted by white writers that the Mulattoes are superior to the Negroes in intellect and ability. It is said that wherever the Negro has interbred with the white, the Mulatto shows the same superiority over the Negro, in the West Indies, in Brazil and in Africa.[4] In Brazil, where there is no colour prejudice, black labour "is deemed inefficient and unreliable. Alike in town and country, the mass of full-blooded Negroes lie at the bottom of the social scale, remaining poor and backward."[5] In the United States, "with only a very few exceptions Negro leadership has come from those with mixed blood."[6] "Inquiry into the actual facts show the assertion that 'the coloured people of America have produced as many remarkable black men as mulattoes' to be completely erroneous. The mulattoes, comprising at present less than 20 per cent of the population, have produced more than 80 per cent of the superior men of the race."[7] Such superiority as may

is made to "blacks who joined the Communist Party only so they could dance with white women." *Ibid.*, p. 329. A Negro writer shares my view. "Will the Negro turn to Communism? I do not think so. A restless fringe in the larger cities may go over, but the race shows practically no inclination to do so, either among the intellectuals or the masses." *Along this Way* (1941), by J. W. Johnson (Penguin Ed.) p. 206.

[1] *Negro Anthology* (1934), edited by Nancy Cunard, p. 73.

[2] *American Comes of Age* (1927), by A. Siegfried, p. 101. In South Africa also we have "the unlovely exclusiveness of the Coloured to the Bantu Christian, modelled on the equally unlovely exclusiveness of the European to the Coloured Christian." *The Colour Problems of South Africa* (1934), by E. H. Brookes, p. 170.

[3] *Alien Americans* (1936), by B. Schrieke, p. 153. Gunnar Myrdal says that after emancipation "darker Negroes who rose from the masses to distinction in the Negro community by getting an education or by conducting successful business enterprises showed an almost universal desire to marry light-skinned women and so to become adopted members of the light-colored aristocracy and to give their children a heritage of lighter color. Blackness of skin remained undesirable." *An American Dilemma* (1944), p. 697.

[4] *A Short Introduction to the History of Human Stupidity* (1935), by W. P. Pitkin, p. 194.

[5] *Clashing Tides of Colour* (1935), by Lothrop Stoddard, p. 97.

[6] *Culture in the South* (1934), edited by W. T. Couch; article by the editor on "The Negro in the South," p. 469. [7] *Race Mixture* (1931), by E. B. Reuter, p. 126.

exist, however, may well be due to the greater opportunities available to the Mulattoes. There is an obvious inconsistency in attributing the superiority of the Mulatto over the Negro to the white mixture in his blood, and at the same time arguing that the crossing of the two races lowers the quality of both and produces inferior offspring; yet these conflicting arguments are advanced from time to time by those who are anxious to maintain the racial purity of the whites.[1]

It is the fierce desire for white racial purity that is so often traded upon by those who are anxious, for one reason or another, to "keep the black man in his place." In America, "in spite of the complexity of its causes, the race hatred in the last analysis is always concentrated on the physical protection of the race.[2] Any discussion of the problem reveals the widespread existence of a sexual apprehension that cannot be quieted, and which penetrates every thought and act."[3] Most of the lynching in the United States is due to the belief that the white woman must be protected from the abnormally strong sexual desires of the Negro. Lord Olivier says that "the danger, such as it is, of sexual assaults, is enormously increased, if indeed it is not entirely created, by the extreme race-barrier theory."[4] In British tropical colonies, where the danger is not thought of, it does not in fact exist[5] and it is significant that during the Civil War in America, when most of the Southern white men were with the Confederate armies, their wives and daughters were often left on the plantations, alone save for Negro slaves who, in no case, betrayed their trust. It has been said that the Negro is over-sexed,[6] but Sir Harry Johnston has pointed out of those in

[1] This point is brought out by Professor Ginsberg in his paper included in *The Problem of Colour in Relation to the Idea of Equality* (Supplement to vol. 1, no. 2, of the *Journal of Philosophical Studies*), p. 20.

[2] "The men of the superior race have everywhere been quick to apprehend the danger of losing their women to the men of the race below." In South Africa "from old Natives one still hears of what befell some of the men of the tribes indigenous to the country that is now Rhodesia when they dared to aspire to the favour of women of the invading Matabele." *The Colour Bar* (1937), by Peter Nielsen, p. 1.

[3] *America Comes of Age* (1927), by A. Siegfried, p. 98.

[4] *White Capital and Coloured Labour* (1905), by Lord Olivier, p. 75.

[5] This is confirmed by an American writer—see *Race Questions, Provincialism and other American Problems* (1908), by Josiah Royce, pp. 19, 29.

[6] This was stated, for example, with some vehemence in *A Bible Defence of Slavery*, by the Reverend Josiah Priest, an American clergyman, in 1852; see p. 174 et seq.

COLOUR PREJUDICE

Africa that being "almost without arts and sciences, and the refined pleasures of the senses, the only acute enjoyment offered them by nature is sexual intercourse."[1] Yet, he says, "the negro is very rarely knowingly indecent or addicted to lubricity."[2] Another writer says that far from being over-sexed they are by European and Asiatic standards frigid; sex plays a proper part "without indecency and without fuss."[3] Some Negro dances may be indecent, but so is some of the stage and ball-room dancing of the whites. There is probably not as much indecency and sexual immorality in a tropical Negro town as there is in many European and American cities, and the conversation of the Negro is no more pornographic than that of the white man, though the language may be more crude.

[1] *British Central Africa* (1897), by Sir Harry Johnston, p. 408.
[2] *Ibid.*
[3] *Africa Dances* (1935), by G. Gorer, p. 245.

Chapter XI

THE EFFECT OF ENVIRONMENT AND HISTORY ON THE NEGRO RACE

THOSE who maintain that the Negro is not inherently inferior to the man of any other race, and is capable of equal progress in civilisation and culture, attribute his present backwardness to past environment and lack of opportunity. Assuming that the Negro race originated in tropical Africa, or at any rate that it moved to this habitat at an early stage of evolution, it must be admitted that there is considerable excuse for a later lack of achievement[1] and that, in the circumstances, potentiality cannot be judged from this lack. It is, of course, conceivable that the Negroes were 'pushed' into the tropical jungles by races already their superiors in strength and intelligence,[2] and that environment is, in their case, a result rather than a cause of inferiority; but such a theory is incapable of proof and need not be pursued.

The tropical regions of the African continent are particularly inaccessible and inhospitable. They are cut off from the north, and thus from land communication with Asia and Europe, by the barren wastes of the Sahara desert, the swamps of the Upper Nile, and the mountains of Abyssinia. The coast line is little indented, there are few good harbours, and the rivers are obstructed by sand-bars and rapids to such an extent that navigation, in early days, was extremely difficult. Much of the coast was swampy, and further inland dense forests barred the way to travellers. The proximity to the equator made the climate extremely hot, and a multitude of insect pests, the mosquito, the tsetse fly and the hookworm among them, ensured the prevalence of disease.

[1] "Mere survival in tropical Africa is a great human achievement"; see *Up from the Ape* (1931), by E. A. Hooton, p. 592.
[2] Or, alternatively, if the tropics were the original home of mankind, that the more enterprising tribes left, at an early date, for more temperate lands.

In these circumstances it was impossible for the inhabitants of tropical Africa to receive the external stimulus which is so necessary for every race. They were unable to borrow ideas from others as the white race has done. The English alphabet is of Semitic origin, our language is a mixture of Latin, French and Anglo-Saxon, our numerals come from the Arabs, our religion from the Hebrews.[1] For our civilisation and culture we are largely indebted to the Greeks and Romans, and some of our modern art and music seems to have come to us from the Negroes themselves. Without all these, which we were able to acquire because our geographical environment was suitable, can there be any certainty that we should to-day be better than the Negroes? In our own time we have seen in Japan an example of the rapid material development of a country once the barriers (artificial in this case) to contact with other cultures were removed.

In the matter of climatic environment also the European races have been more fortunate than the Negroes. In the tropics less energy is required for the business of living, food (of a sort) is abundant, clothing and heating are almost unnecessary, and little ingenuity need be exercised in order to maintain a bare existence. The intense damp heat encourages mental and physical laziness (in white as in black), and there is every incentive to do nothing beyond what cannot be avoided. The colder climate of the north, with its invigorating winters, is more productive of human energy than the hot, moist climate of the tropics which is more favourable to vegetable activity.[2] It is true that the Maya civilisation of Central America arose in an environment which is to-day not unlike that of tropical Africa, and that on the American continent the higher civilisations arose in the tropical zone and not in the temperate zone as in the Old World.[3] But this fact may be explained, as the similarity of colour throughout the continent may be explained, by the late arrival of man in America and the advance of the more energetic peoples from the northern land-bridge southwards, along the western coast, in search of a suitable country in which to settle.

[1] The debt of European civilisation to ancient Greek and Hebrew thought is emphasised by Professor A. N. Whitehead, in *Adventures of Ideas* (1933).

[2] See *Colonial Policy* (1931), by A. D. A. DeKat Angelino, vol. 1, p. 197.

[3] The best known of the ancient American civilisations were the Peruvian, Maya and Aztec. The two former flourished entirely, and the last almost entirely within the tropics.

Another explanation may be found in Dr. Huntington's theory that civilisations rose and fell on account of a periodic shifting of climatic zones.[1]

That centuries of residence in the tropics should have limited the energy of the Negroes is not remarkable. It has been pointed out that the climate reduces the physical vigour of the coloured as well as the white man.[2] Whites who have been settled for some generations in the tropics compare unfavourably in energy and physique with newcomers from temperate lands. Dr. Huntington says of the white inhabitants of the Bahama Islands (which are only partly within the tropics) that the result of residence for several generations "has been disastrous.... My own observations lead to the conclusion that the average white farmer is scarcely ahead of the average negro."[3] "Part of the white people," in the Bahamas, he says, "are like their race in other regions, but a large portion have unmistakably degenerated."[4]

It has been suggested that dampness, especially in warm lands, causes as much stupidity as any other single influence, and makes more comprehensible "those amazing changes of personality which take place in the white man who goes to the damp tropics."[5] Tropical neurasthenia, although more common among Europeans, is not entirely confined to them, being found among the educated native officials in West Africa and other tropical colonies.[6]

It is, however, in the matter of insect-borne diseases that the Negro inhabitant of tropical Africa has been most heavily handicapped. These diseases are especially inimical to mental and physical efficiency, and being endemic throughout the country must have a debilitating effect on the race as well as upon the individual. Ignoring the more spectacular diseases such as yellow fever, conveyed by the *stegomyia* mosquito, and trypanosomiasis, conveyed by the tsetse fly, which have killed millions,[7] and are endemic in

---

[1] *Civilisation and Climate* (1924), by E. Huntington, 3rd ed., *passim*.
[2] *The Menace of Colour* (1925), by J. W. Gregory, 2nd ed., preface.
[3] *Civilisation and Climate* (1924), by E. Huntington, 3rd ed., p. 46.
[4] *Ibid.*, p. 33.
[5] *A Short Introduction to the History of Human Stupidity* (1935), by W. P. Pitkin, p. 72.
[6] *Manson's Tropical Diseases* (11th ed., 1940), edited by P. H. Manson-Bahr, p. 605.
[7] Trypanosomiasis, commonly known as 'sleeping sickness,' has completely depopulated many islands in the Victoria Nyanza. The population of certain districts in Uganda was reduced in six years from 300,000 to 100,000 by this disease. *Ibid.*, p. 118. See also *The Tsetse Flies of East Africa* (1936), by C. F. M. Swynnerton.

tropical Africa, it will be sufficient to consider two only (malaria and hookworm) of the diseases which afflict the tropical dweller and lower his vitality without actually, in the majority of cases, directly causing immediate death. It has, indeed, been said that malaria has the disastrous effect of permitting human existence while precluding the possibility of human health or happiness.[1] Acute diseases sometimes tend to strengthen the race by killing off the weak; malaria and hookworm debilitate the race by attacking both the weak and the strong.[2]

Malaria fever, which is conveyed by the *anopheles* and other mosquitoes, is found in many parts of the world outside of the tropics, but especially in tropical regions where probably every single inhabitant has suffered from it at some time or another in his life.[3] Malaria has long been recognised as a disease of worldwide incidence and the cause of a higher sickness and death rate than any other disease.[4] "The amoeba of malaria . . . has become Enemy No. 1 of mankind."[5]

It is not improbable that the decline of Greek civilisation and the fall of the Roman Empire may have been due very largely to the debilitation of the people by malaria,[6] and it may well be that the Fascist revival of Italian energy was due as much to the discovery of the cause of malaria as to the driving force of Mussolini. It

[1] *Malaria in Europe* (Heath Clark Lectures, 1934; London School of Hygiene and Tropical Medicine), p. 175. The death-roll from malaria, is, however, considerable. It is said that 300,000 abortions due to malaria occur annually in Bengal alone, and that directly and indirectly malaria is believed to be responsible for at least two million deaths annually in India. In Ceylon, in 1936, an epidemic of malaria caused 80,000 deaths in seven months. *A History of Tropical Medicine* (1942), by H. H. Scott, pp. 216–17.

[2] See *White Settlers in the Tropics* (1939), by A. Grenfell Price, p. 205.

[3] "The natives of malarious districts acquire their immunity from repeated and persistent infection in childhood. In such places the blood of practically every child up to three or four years of age contains malaria parasites." *Manson's Tropical Diseases* (11th ed., 1940), edited by P. H. Manson-Bahr, p. 9.

[4] *Encyclopædia Britannica*, 14th ed., vol. 14, p. 706. Malaria appears to have been recognised by Hippocrates in the fifth century B.C.

[5] *Malaria in Europe* (Heath Clark Lectures, 1934, London School of Hygiene and Tropical Medicine), p. 201.

[6] On this subject see *Malaria, a Neglected Factor in the History of Greece and Rome* (1907), and *Malaria and Greek History* (1904), by W. H. S. Jones, and the remarks of Sir Ronald Ross in the *Report on the Work of the Greek Anti-Malaria League During the Year 1907* (reprinted from the *Annals of Tropical Medicine and Parasitology*, vol. 2, no. 2, June 1908). Also *Roman Fever* (1896), by W. North, and note at the beginning of *Health Problems of the Empire* (1924), by A. Balfour and H. H. Scott.

must not be forgotten that less than two generations ago the part that the mosquito plays in transmitting malaria was unknown to science, and the disease was attributed, as the name shows, to the bad air, or miasma, from swampy land.

Some years ago the State Board of Health of California estimated that the annual cost to the State from malaria, directly or indirectly, was $2,820,000.[1] If this is the case in the twentieth century in a rich country like the United States, which has at its command immense resources with which to fight the disease, it is easy to understand what little chance the people of Africa had to overcome the scourge. Even the prophylactic of quinine, which has been known to the white races since the seventeenth century,[2] was not available to the Negroes until comparatively recent times, and indeed, owing to its high cost, it is even now available to only a small proportion of the population of tropical lands.[3]

The second of the two diseases to be considered is that caused by the hookworm.[4] It is said that "hookworms affect the health and destroy the vitality of millions of people living in tropical and warm climates. In badly infested countries hookworm disease stunts the growth of children, cripples agriculture, handicaps the progress of the race, and is a great economic disadvantage ... when the symptoms are well developed, hookworm disease is characterised by anaemia, mental and physical weakness."[5] It has been estimated that in the tropics at least ninety-five per cent of those engaged in agriculture are, in greater or less degree, infected by the hookworm parasite.[6] It is known as the 'lazy man's disease' on account of the apathy and langour of its victims,[7] who are already predisposed to lethargy by the hot, damp climate. The larvae of

[1] *Transactions of the Commonwealth Club of California*, vol. 11, no. 1, March 1916.
[2] Cinchona bark, from which quinine is made, first became known to the Spaniards in Peru. The first recorded instance of its use was in 1638.
[3] In the Gold Coast and other colonies quinine is imported by the Government for sale to the public at cost price. The new drug, paludrine, which is said to be more effective and much cheaper than quinine, may make a revolutionary change in the general health and consequent prosperity of tropical peoples.
[4] Ankylostomiasis. This disease was, at one time, prevalent in Europe, especially among miners working in damp mines, where the sanitary arrangements were inefficient.
[5] *Preventive Medicine and Hygiene* (1935), by M. J. Rosenau, 5th ed., pp. 142, 144.
[6] *A Short Introduction to the History of Human Stupidity* (1935), by W. P. Pitkin, p. 89.
[7] *Ibid.*, p. 88.

the hookworm enter the human body through the skin; in countries where a large proportion of the population goes barefoot, larvae from the infested soil would commonly enter through the soles of the feet.¹

Besides the existence of specific tropical diseases to which reference has been made, it must be remembered that the dweller in tropical lands is often under-nourished, or at least wrongly nourished.² It is only in recent years that the rôle played by mineral deficiencies in producing disease has been recognised, but it is now appreciated that the people in tropical lands are, in general, under-nourished, and that their diets are often insufficient in quantity and unsatisfactory as regards quality in that they contain inadequate amounts of animal protein, mineral salts and vitamins.³ "Apart from the recognised food deficiency diseases, there can be little doubt that a vast amount of ill-health in the tropics and the East is due to the consumption of diet deficient in vitamins and other food factors."⁴ The African usually consumes an entirely unbalanced diet, consisting chiefly of starchy foods, such as yams and cassava.

While it is true that "few of the constituents considered necessary in Europe for a nutritionally adequate diet are generally available in sufficient quantities in the Colonial Empire,"⁵ or, indeed, any-

[1] Mr. Leonard Barnes has suggested that "two square meals a day and two pairs of shoes a year are the African's prime need. The one would give him strength to fight disease, and the other would give him full protection from the life-draining plague of hook-worm." *Empire or Democracy* (1939), p. 147. It was with this in mind that I was able in 1945 to secure the exemption from customs duties of boots and shoes imported into the Gold Coast.

[2] See the *First Report on Nutrition in the Colonial Empire* (Cmd. 6050-1).

[3] *The Quarterly Bulletin of the Health Organisation of the League of Nations*, vol. 4, no. 2, June 1935. Off-print No. 2: "Nutrition and Public Health," by Et. Burnett and W. R. Aykroyd, pp. 27, 126-7. See also *An African Survey* (1938), by Lord Hailey, p. 1: "Over immense areas the African soil lacks the constituents which make possible a continuous occupation for agricultural or even pastoral purpose: 'shifting cultivation' is less a device of barbarism than a concession to the character of a soil which needs long periods of recovery for regeneration."

[4] *The Quarterly Bulletin of the Health Organisation of the League of Nations*, vol. 4, no. 2, June 1935. Off-print No. 2: "Nutrition and Public Health," by Et. Burnett and W. R. Aykroyd, p. 129. It has been stated that "neither alfalfa nor the vitamin-rich cereals and grasses grow in tropical heat," and the suggestion is made that the tendency of people in the tropics to eat highly spiced food is due to the fact that "most spices are ground from small seeds rich in B vitamins, so here may be an unwitting effort to remedy a dietary defect." See *Climate Makes the Man*, by C. A. Miles (second impression, 1946), pp. 21, 32.

[5] *First Report on Nutrition in the Colonial Empire* (Cmd. 6050), p. 154.

where in the tropics, it is the natural poverty of these countries which forms the chief obstacle to improvement.[1] Sir Donald Cameron has said that some Africans "live, and have always lived, in very primitive surroundings, inadequately nourished and in a position to do little more than to keep starvation from the door."[2] The native of the tropics will not be able, without outside assistance[3] to improve his diet and his health, until his economic condition has been materially improved.

It has been suggested that the heavy rainfall has denuded tropical countries of certain minerals, especially lime and phosphorous, which, through plant foods, are consumed by men in other regions;[4] and that mineral economy has been secured through an increase of sexuality, mechanical efficiency being sacrificed to meet this requirement.[5]

Another writer also has suggested that the development of a race, and its rise in cultural condition, is dependent upon the extent to which the potential social energy of the race is used sexually. He points out that it is those races which have adopted absolute monogamy which have displayed the greatest amount of social energy, and that, as soon as the sexual opportunity of the race was extended, the energy decreased.[6] "In the records of history," he says, "there is no example of a society displaying great energy for any appreciable time unless it has been absolutely monogamous. . . . There is only one example of a polygamous society displaying productive social energy, that of the Moors; but in their case the women whom the men took to wife had been reared in an absolutely monogamous tradition. The energy of the Moors faded away when the mothers spent their early childhood in a less rigorous tradition."[7] The African races have always practised polygamy.[8]

[1] See *Statement of Policy on Colonial Development and Welfare* (Cmd. 6175), paragraph 4.

[2] *My Tanganyika Service and Some Nigeria* (1939), p. 245. See also *The Future of the Colonial Empire* (1945), by Sir B. Bourdillon, Chapter 2, *passim*.

[3] Which is now being given through grants to British colonies from the Imperial Treasury, under the authority of the Colonial Development and Welfare Act.

[4] *Race, Sex and Environment. A Study of Mineral Deficiency in Human Evolution* (1936), by J. R. de la H. Marett, p. 74.

[5] *Ibid.*, p. 20.

[6] *Sex and Culture* (1934), by J. D. Unwin, p. 382.

[7] *Ibid.*, p. 343.

[8] "In most parts of Africa polygamy has been the custom, and insistence on monogamy is one of the great bars preventing the entrance of men into the Christian

Yet another writer, with a long experience of Africa, has suggested that "because of a long period of unbroken indulgence as a nursling, ended by an unbearably sudden and severe weaning, the African has two diametrically opposite convictions about himself, reflected in an equivalent unbalanced attitude to the world."[1] He points out that whereas the European child is fed at regular hours, and loses and regains the breast periodically over a long period, while it is often separated from its mother for hours at a time, the African child is carried on its mother's back at all times, even when she is working, and is fed whenever it is hungry. To the African child, therefore, weaning comes as a great shock, and "this is one of the main bases of the African's deep feeling of inferiority (which contrasts sharply with his occasional illusions of personal power and perfection), of his notorious poverty of creative imagination, and of his general disinclination to make efforts to help himself."[2] Africans, he says, "are typically lacking in initiative, in ability to think independently and objectively,"[3] and "it can hardly be denied that the African is generally greedy and abnormally acquisitive, but this is easily understandable if he suffers permanently from a sense of having been deprived of something."[4] This something is not only the mother's milk, but the mother herself, as the father resumes relations with his wife as soon as the child is weaned, and, in the conditions existing in the average African house, the child soon becomes aware of this.

Deprived by geographical position and physical obstacles from contact with other races, and thus prevented from learning and borrowing from other cultures (as the white peoples have learnt and borrowed), living in a region where the damp heat discouraged mental or physical energy, and where an apparently bountiful nature made effort largely unnecessary, afflicted with terrible diseases the causes of which have only been known to science for a couple of generations, and unable to obtain a sufficiency of suitable food, it is small wonder that the Negro race had made little progress towards civilisation when it first came into considerable contact

Church. . . . In some areas men brought up in a Christian atmosphere are reverting to polygamy." *The World Mission of the Church* (findings and recommendations of the International Missionary Council, 1938), p. 157.

[1] *The African as Suckling and as Adult*, by J. F. Ritchie, Principal of Barotse National School, Northern Rhodesia (1943), p. 61.

[2] *Ibid.*, p. 28.   [3] *Ibid.*, p. 61.   [4] *Ibid.*, p. 60.

with Europeans in the fifteenth century. Treated by them as beings of an inferior race, encouraged to war among themselves to secure prisoners for sale as slaves, and brutalised by the trade spirits for which the slaves were sold, the natives of Africa for over three hundred years were almost deliberately held back from progress by the highly civilised and 'superior' race which grew rich on the slave trade. Those Negroes who were carried across the sea to America or the West Indies were torn from their families and environment, and taken to a strange country to work for strange masters who, when they were not actually cruel, were at the best unsympathetic. In the nineteenth century the slave trade was slowly stamped out, but slavery lingered on in the United States till 1865[1] and in Brazil till 1888. In practically every part of the world the Negro is to-day politically powerless; he is economically helpless everywhere. In this twentieth century educated Negroes are still subjected to unnecessary and humiliating insults, and as late as the year of Grace 1947 Negroes were still being lynched in the United States of America.

Under similar conditions it is doubtful whether any other race would have advanced farther than the Negro has advanced, or have survived the natural difficulties with which the Negro race was confronted. Through it all the Negro race has shown amazing patience and self-control in face of insult and remarkable fortitude in its struggle against adversity. The Negro has retained his sunny good-natured disposition, a natural courtesy, an impulsive and open-handed generosity, an intense love of music.[2] An old writer has said that Negroes are seldom unjust, and have a greater abhorrence of injustice than any other people.[3] Explorers like Mungo Park have experienced the disinterested kindness of Africans.[4] From African clerks, soldiers and servants I have myself received faithful and loyal service through many years. In my

---

[1] *The Times* of November 27, 1936, records the conviction of a planter in Arkansas who was also a Town Marshal, for a breach of the anti-slavery laws. This man caused a party of Negroes to be arrested for vagrancy and induced the local magistrate to sentence them to work on his plantation, thus securing a supply of free labour. The Judge who tried the case, in summing up, observed that such breaches of the anti-slavery laws occurred frequently.
[2] *Population Problems* (1923), by E. B. Reuter, p. 270.
[3] *Selections from the Travels of Ibn Batuta, 1325-1354* (Broadway Travellers), p. 329.
[4] *Travels of Mungo Park*, vol. I, pp. 197-8.

opinion the lack of achievement by Negroes in the past is attributable to conditions over which they had no control, and their present low position in the scale of civilisation is due to the short period during which they have had contact with the outer world and the advantages of education. There is no reason why, in the future, if they are given a fair chance economically and socially, they should not advance in civilisation and culture, and contribute their undoubted qualities to a world which has not yet reached perfection under white domination.

Chapter XII

LACK OF UNITY AND INFERIORITY COMPLEX AMONG NEGROES

GRANTED that he has been held back in the past by natural and artificial barriers, and that these barriers have not yet been entirely removed, it is doing no service to the race for the Negro and his friends to assume that the black man is in no way responsible for his present position. The Negro, like the men of other races, has many imperfections. If it be wrong to regard Negroes as inferior and undesirable beings, capable of nothing good, it is equally wrong to consider them, as some are apt to do, as entirely "blameless Ethiopians." It would be far better if the friends of the Negroes, as well as their enemies, could disregard their colour and their race and think of them only as 'men in a world of men,' with the vices and the virtues of men.[1]

Perhaps the most serious failing of the educated Negro, so far as the advancement of his own race is concerned, is his lack of the will for co-operation, the inability to follow for long a leader of his own colour, and the jealous vanity which prompts him to criticise and pull down his brother Negro who has ascended a few rungs higher than himself on the ladder of culture and progress. Frederick Douglass,[2] long recognised as a leader of the Negro race in America, and prominent in the fight against slavery, is now held to have failed his people.[3] Booker Washington,[4] who probably

[1] Sir Bernard Bourdillon speaks of "the sentimentalists, who, in their desire to protect their 'black brother,' do him the disservice of crowning him with a halo which he would be the last to claim for himself." See *The Future of the Colonial Empire* (1945), p. 11.

[2] Born 1817, died 1895. His father was a white man and his mother a Negro slave. He held several official posts, including that of United States Minister to Haiti.

[3] See *Negro Anthology* (1934), edited by Nancy Cunard; article entitled "Blacks turn Red," by E. Gordon, p. 237.

[4] Born 1859, died 1915. Dr. Washington is chiefly famous for his work in connection with the Tuskegee Institute.

did more real service to the Negroes of the United States than any other man, is blamed for his moderation, and accused of treachery to his race.[1] Dr. DuBois blames him for accepting for the black man a position of inferiority and "the old attitude of adjustment and submission,"[2] and, in view of this, it is interesting to observe that Dr. DuBois, in his turn, has been accused of the same thing.[3] Dr. Harold Moody, the President of the League of Coloured Peoples, was accused of being 'sycophantic,' and the 'militant coloured students' in London were invited to break away from his leadership.[4] I was once speaking to an African friend, a reasonable and well-educated man, of the great loss his race had suffered by the death of Dr. J. E. K. Aggrey; he agreed, but with an obvious reservation, and I was surprised to learn from him, on enquiry, that Africans generally regarded Aggrey as being too much on the side of the white man, and not sufficiently loyal to his own people.[5]

This failing is recognised by the Negroes themselves. Dr. Moody speaks of "the painful divisions which at present exist in our group where every man's hand is against his brother's and no one will come in and push our chariot up the hill, merely because he thinks he will not get sufficient praise and he may be giving undue honour to his brother."[6] Again we hear that "most of the educated great African men, who are highly praised by the whites, are not generally loved by their own brethren and race."[7] In South Africa, "it has

[1] See *Negro Anthology* (1934), edited by Nancy Cunard; article entitled "Blacks turn Red," by E. Gordon, p. 237. See also *The Negro in the Future* (1934), by Harold A. Moody, p. 7.

[2] *The Souls of Black Folk* (1903), by W. E. B. DuBois, p. 50. Dr. DuBois says that "among his own people Mr. Washington has encountered the strongest and most lasting opposition amounting at times to bitterness." *Ibid.*, p. 145. See also *Dusk of Dawn* (1940), pp. 70–2, by the same author.

[3] *Negro Anthology* (1934), edited by Nancy Cunard, pp. 146–7, 238. See also *The Crisis*, the official organ of the National Association of Coloured People, for August 1943.

[4] *Negro Anthology* (1934), edited by Nancy Cunard, p. 555 (quoted from an article on "Race Prejudice in England," in *The Negro Worker* of March 1932).

[5] Dr. Aggrey was born on the Gold Coast in 1875 and died in 1927. He served on the Phelps-Stokes Commission on education in Africa and was later appointed to the staff of Achimota College, Gold Coast. For his biography see *Aggrey of Africa* (1929), by E. W. Smith.

[6] *The Negro in the Future* (1934), by Harold A. Moody, p. 3.

[7] *Negro Anthology* (1934), edited by Nancy Cunard; article entitled "White-manning in West Africa," by T. K. Utchay, p. 766.

LACK OF UNITY AND INFERIORITY COMPLEX

nearly always happened that when one Bantu attains a position where he could use power for the benefit of his race he is either pulled down by the jealousy and faction of his fellow-countrymen or abuses the power he has obtained, for the sake of fraud or tyranny or excess."[1] An African writer says that "with the exception of the Fantees, . . . I do not know of any tribe of Negroes in West Africa amongst those who have come in contact with Europeans at least, who do not betray petty jealousies and heart-burnings at the successes of their compatriots."[2] I have myself seen many examples of this failing, and, so far as this is concerned, I agree with the African writer who says that "Africans still constitute their own public enemy No. 1, to be conquered first before they can make one iota of sound national progress."[3] The failing is undoubtedly the cause of an unimportant but significant phenomenon which I have personally observed. I refer to the numerous clubs and societies which come into being from time to time, each with a galaxy of office-holders (and a new blazer), each celebrating, with some circumstance, its "First Annual" social evening, and passing out of active existence within the year, to be replaced by another under a different leader and with a new set of office-holders.[4]

The Negro untouched by European culture accepts readily enough the superior position and leadership of his chiefs, and shows little of the jealousy of his educated brother. It has been suggested that the objection of American Negroes to having other Negroes in a position of authority over them is due to basic convictions instilled during slavery, which makes the admission that a Negro may be as capable as a white man an admission of double personal inferiority.[5] Whatever the cause, there can be no doubt that the Negroes distrust their most capable leaders, who, although they may be bitter in their attitude to the whites, are yet possessed of a sufficient sense of responsibility, and of realities,

[1] *Negro Anthology* (1934), edited by Nancy Cunard; article entitled "From an African Notebook," by W. Plomer, p. 650.
[2] *The Negro Question* (1892), by J. Renner Maxwell, p. 172.
[3] L. Solanke, in a letter to *West Africa* of May 30, 1936.
[4] Reference is made to this phenomenon in *Yesterday and Tomorrow in Northern Nigeria* (1938), by Dr. Walter Miller, p. 78. See also *An American Dilemma* (1944), by G. Myrdal, p. 954: "There is an intense rivalry between clubs for status and an equally intense rivalry between members within any given club for office."
[5] *Race Relations. Adjustment of Whites and Negroes in the United States* (1934), by W. D. Weatherford and C. S. Johnson, p. 283.

to abstain from useless vituperation and to work patiently for the end which all men of good will must desire. The inevitable effect of this is that the unthinking mob of Negroes will follow the noisy and irresponsible persons who freely express their hatred of the white man and promise the people fantastic and impossible things.¹

The educated Negro is, unfortunately but perhaps naturally, obsessed by the white attitude to his race, and by his own inferiority complex. It is generally true that the better educated a black man may be the greater is the prejudice he encounters, while his education and culture make him more sensitive to insults.² That the Negro suffers from an inferiority complex is generally admitted,³ and Professor Macmillan* says that "the attitude of the more self-conscious classes has been paraphrased 'I'm as good as you are, only I'm not and won't admit it'."⁴ This complex makes the Negro

¹ In the Gold Coast *Spectator* of April 25, 1941, a certain politician was referred to as "a fearless, independent, outspoken, conscientious and self-sacrificing patriot and leader, hero of the people, and a terror at the Legislature. Above all," went on the article, he "aims at one great thing in life for the politician, press and people: purity and the highest probity in thought and action." Three years later, as already mentioned at p. 93, this politician was convicted of demanding from an official of a certain Association the sum of £25,000 as the price of his refraining from making a speech in the Legislative Council attacking the Association. See also page 43, note 4.
"To the Negro people dishonest leadership is a most important cause of weakness in concerted action.... If a generation of young Negroes could be brought up to understand how scrupulous honesty could tremendously strengthen the Negro cause ... this would mean a great deal for Negro progress." *An American Dilemma* (1944), by G. Myrdal, vol. 2, p. 857. The real trouble, as Professor Myrdal points out, is that "the Negro leader, the Negro social economist, the Negro man of arts and letters, is disposed to view all social, economic, political, indeed even aesthetic and philosophical issues from the Negro angle. What is more, he is expected to do so. ... The Negro genius is imprisoned in the Negro problem.... The difference in this respect between the Negro and other 'racial' minorities—the Jews, for example—is notable.... A Jewish economist is not expected to be a specialist on Jewish labour." *Ibid.*, vol. 1, p. 28.

² *The Bantu, Past and Present* (1920), by S. M. Molema, p. 264. See also *The Autobiography of an ex-Coloured Man* (1927), by J. W. Johnson, p. 145: "I can imagine no more dissatisfied human being than an educated, cultured and refined coloured man in the United States."

³ Dr. Harold Moody speaks of "the inferiority complex with which our race is afflicted, not only our masses but our intelligentsia as well." *The Negro in the Future* (1934), p. 2. Miss Margery Perham has pointed out in *The Spectator* of August 23, 1935, that wherever the Negroes are in close touch with white civilisation the dominating factor in their lives is the sense of inferiority.

⁴ *Warning from the West Indies* (1936), by W. M. Macmillan, p. 45.

LACK OF UNITY AND INFERIORITY COMPLEX

suspicious, ever on the look-out for slights, and perhaps, by the aggressive manner assumed as an armour against these slights, actually provoking them. No white man realises how often he unintentionally wounds the susceptibilities of Negroes; it is equally certain that the Negro does not appreciate how often his own manner has alienated the sympathy of whites who would like to be friendly. That a large proportion of educated Negroes hate the white people, with a bitter hatred, cannot be denied, but there is no reason for such hatred to be inevitable, and every reason why it should be removed.

It is in their poetry, their novels and particularly in their newspapers, that the obsession of the Negroes regarding the colour question is so obvious, and it is not impossible that this obsession affects the literary value of their writing. Some Negro poets have succeeded in expressing the sorrows of their race without any loss of poetic quality,[1] but it is too true that most of the novels of Negro authors[2] are "intensely propagandist: they are often bitter, frequently sarcastic, they are lacking in power of sustained plot."[3] In 1926 a Negro journalist published an analysis of the American Negro Press. "From a pile of 220 Aframerican weeklies," he wrote, "one may drop 197 as little more than waste paper. Of the remaining twenty-three ten are mediocrities . . . Aframerican journalism is violently race-conscious."[4] Even Miss Cunard says that "the Negro race in America has no worse enemy than its own Press,"[5] and another writer speaks of the "vulgarity and blatancy" of certain newspapers which are constantly "spitting and growling" at white domination and at Negro leaders, "to the great glee of a race which rejoices at such impudences. It is an expression of the inferiority complex."[6]

In some British colonies, also, the Negro-owned newspaper is apt to overlook essentials in the interests of anti-white propaganda,

---

[1] See, for example, *From the Dark Tower*, by Countee Cullen.
[2] There have been numerous successful books by Negro authors; see, for example, *Porgy*, by D. Heywood.
[3] *Race Relations, Adjustment of Whites and Negroes in the United States* (1934), by W. D. Weatherford and C. S. Johnson, p. 483.
[4] See article entitled "The Negro Press," by E. Gordon, in *The American Mercury* of June 1926, quoted in *Culture in the South* (1934), edited by W. T. Couch (article entitled "Journalism in the South," by J. D. Allen), pp. 156–7.
[5] *Negro Anthology* (1934), edited by Nancy Cunard, p. 73.
[6] *Alien Americans* (1936), by B. Schrieke, p. 150. See also page 43, above.

and to display a reckless disregard for journalistic responsibility.[1] It seems certain that such propaganda must, in the end, defeat its own object. It would surely be better to encourage their own race to greater progress and consistency than to harp continually on the iniquities of other races. A little self-criticism might not be amiss, although, for the reasons given above,[2] it is doubtful whether any Negro-owned newspapers which referred to Negro failings would long survive. I do honestly believe, however, that the attitude of the Negro Press in the colonies is one of the main causes of the continued existence of, and possibly of the increase in, colour prejudice. Anti-white feeling is deliberately whipped up by many writers in these papers, every action of a white man is adversely and bitterly criticised, every attempt by the whites to help the Negroes is treated with suspicion, and the most unfair personal attacks are made on white officials who are not in a position to defend themselves. The better type of Negro may dislike this policy, but, I regret to say, has not the moral courage to take a public stand against it. That this persistent vilification of the white race increases coloured hatred of the whites cannot be doubted, but there is also another result which the newspaper editor cannot or will not appreciate. White men in tropical colonies are inclined at first to treat as a joke the effusions of this type of newspaper, which are often badly written and full of ludicrous errors. But gradually they come to resent these unrestrained, unfair, and

[1] The Commission which reported on the Trinidad Disturbances of 1937 wrote as follows as regards the local Press: "It is in no spirit of criticism that we would urge upon editors in the Colony the necessity for proper moderation of expression with a view to the formation of a healthy public opinion." Cmd. 5641, p. 57. The Recommendations of the West India Royal Commission of 1938-39 contained the following: "In view of the very important and growing influence which many organs of the Press in the West Indies now exercise in the relations between the public and the Civil Service, and on the important questions of colour prejudice and colour discrimination, we consider it most important that the value of restraint and moderation should be fully appreciated by those responsible for the conduct and tone of the Press." Cmd. 6174, p. 28. An article entitled "The Nigerian Student," by R. A. Henson, which appeared in *The Spectator* of February 23, 1945, p. 166, says: "A further important point is the African's love of words and argument. He is inclined to speak and write rashly and without due thought, not giving himself time to weigh judiciously the merits of any particular question. This quality is well exemplified by the ill-advised and sometimes scurrilous nature of the matter published in the local press." A Dutch writer has also referred to the need for self-control in the Press of tropical colonies; see *Colonial Policy* (1931), by A. D. A. DeKat Angelino, vol. I, pp. 98, 490. [2] See page 43.

cowardly attacks, and their attitude to coloured persons is unconsciously affected by the exasperation caused by them, and the contempt they feel for the writers, whom they come to regard (in the absence of any declaration to the contrary) as typical of their race. If a 'white' newspaper were to publish anything half as offensive about coloured people as the Negro Press frequently publishes about whites, there would be an outburst of indignation throughout the coloured world, but, *and here is the difference*, white people also would join in the protests.

In spite of the bitter feelings among Negroes, and especially among educated Negroes, against the white race, there is a keen desire to acquire 'white' culture and education, which is regarded "as the white man's talisman in the acquisition of power and wealth and position."[1] It is said that the African has no greater desire than to resemble the white man as far as possible,[2] and it must be difficult for him to understand why this desire should be resented.[3]

The fact remains, however, that in some quarters the desire of the Negro for white culture and education *is* resented, and the attitude of certain whites has in many cases turned the naturally cheerful, good-tempered Negro into a suspicious and embittered hater of everything white. The innate qualities of the Negro still remain, and it is not too late, by a change of attitude, to bring out these qualities and secure the co-operation of the dark races in the building up of a better civilisation. That the Negro has something to contribute to such a civilisation cannot be doubted, in spite of his admitted lack of achievement in the past. He can, for instance, contribute his delightful sense of humour[4] to a white world which is sadly lacking in this gift; more than one European in Africa has

---

[1] *What the Negro Thinks* (1929), by R. R. Moton, p. 40.
[2] *The African Today* (1934), by D. Westermann, p. 281.
[3] Perhaps the reason may be found in the words of Dr. Moody: "When the imitative African who has just emerged from the bush, dresses up in some ridiculous manner and appears bombastic, this is just his interpretation of how the white man appears to him, and he is merely trying to produce as faithful a copy of his white boss as possible." *The Negro in the Future* (1934), by H. A. Moody, p. 1. An English writer says that "if you watch a man's negroes you will know the chief points of his character. They mirror their masters faithfully and terribly." *Africa Dances* (1935), by G. Gorer, p. 143.
[4] I cannot agree with the remark in *Race Relations* (1934), by W. D. Weatherford and C. S. Johnson, p. 284, that "since the native African is not a very humorous person it seems most likely that this quality of humour was developed in slavery."

been cheered, when he badly needed cheering, by the spontaneous humour of African soldiers and servants. "The African has more than other races the divine gift of liberating laughter, an inborn gaiety and carefreeness, a keen sense of humour, and a capacity for seeing the best in everything and everyone."[1] To the loyalty and faithful service of Africans, I have already paid tribute.[2] The Negro is artistic and musical by nature, he is deeply religious, and his social sense is highly developed.[3] Sir Michael Sadler has pointed out that it is "only within the last thirty years that works by indigenous sculptors and carvers in West Africa have been acclaimed by many European artists and critics of eminent and indisputable authority for the masterpieces which they are."[4] Until he is spoilt by contact with the whites the Negro has good manners.[5] We would do well to abandon our self-complacency and learn from Africa what it has to teach.

[1] *Africa and Christianity* (1937), by D. Westermann, p. 14.

[2] I should like to take this opportunity of paying tribute to Joseph Agbake, one of my African servants, who was with me throughout most of my service in Nigeria. When I was transferred from Nigeria to the Bahamas in 1924 he wrote to ask me to send him money to pay for his passage to the Bahamas, as he wished to join me there. I wrote back pointing out that I did not think he would be happy so far from his family and friends, and that I could not afford to pay for his passage from Nigeria to the Bahamas and back. Without any further reference to me, he, who had never left Nigeria before, joined a cargo steamer as steward and worked his way across the Atlantic, in mid-winter, from Lagos to New York, and from there came to the Bahamas. He rejoined me later in Nigeria.

[3] Speech by Mr. J. H. Oldham at the International Conference, in September 1926, at LeZoute. Quoted in *The Christian Mission in Africa* (1926), by E. W. Smith, p. 15.

[4] *Arts of West Africa* (1935), edited by Sir Michael Sadler, p. 8.

[5] "The white man may travel the length and breadth of Africa and be received as a gentleman by gentlemen, but the black man travelling in England, America, Australia and other white lands is treated as a churl by churls." *Negro Anthology* (1934), edited by Nancy Cunard; article on "Black Civilisation and White," by G. S. Schuyler, p. 787. I wish that I were able to deny this statement.

Chapter XIII

CONCLUSION

IT may be, as Lord Olivier maintains, that colour prejudice is an instinctive and active affliction independent of economic relations,[1] but it has been suggested that nine-tenths of what is known to-day as colour prejudice is no more than a veil to cover the white man's economic fears. It has been well said that "Negrophobia is, like anti-Semitism, a substitute for economic thought,"[2] and the black man has some grounds for thinking that white hostility to educated Negroes is based, in some countries at least, on the fear of competition. As we have seen, this is also the explanation of the greater hostility to colour shown by the "Poor Whites" who see in the Negro a dangerous competitor who may rob them of employment. This is the reason why, in the northern United States, as the numbers of Negroes increase, the traditional Northern tolerance fades away.[3] This explains why white prejudice against the Oriental is stronger in California and British Columbia than in the rest of the United States and Canada.

The Oriental and the Negro, who are willing to work for smaller wages than the white man, depress the standard of living, and even Socialist writers admit that it is natural for the white man to wish to preserve his own standards.[4] "Much of the race hatred so prevalent in America is due to economic causes and the fear of a lowering of the standard of life through cheap negro labour,"[5]

[1] *The New Statesman and Nation* of March 10, 1943.
[2] *The Colour Problems of South Africa* (1934), by E. H. Brookes, p. 20.
[3] It has been suggested that the North was "never thoroughly convinced of the equality of the Negro," and that the Northern attitude which culminated in the Civil War was prompted by a desire for the maintenance of the Union and "the frustration of the power of the Southern oligarchy." See *Alien Americans* (1936), by B. Schrieke, p. 127.
[4] *Labour's Way with the Commonwealth* (1935), by George Lansbury, p. 84. See also *Christianity and the Race Problem* (1924), by J. H. Oldham (7th ed.), p. 37.
[5] *The Problem of Colour in Relation to the Idea of Equality* (Supplement to vol. 1, no. 2, of the *Journal of Philosophical Studies*); paper by M. Ginsberg, p. 20. See also *The Keys* (official organ of the League of Coloured Peoples) of January–March 1936, p. 30: "As a matter of fact, colour prejudice is not really spontaneous. It is the result of a deliberate policy, executed for sound economic reasons."

and there was certainly no hostility to Chinese immigrants into California until they began seriously to compete with the white inhabitants.[1] One writer asserts that in Africa and in the Pacific there is no real race problem, but merely an economic one.[2]

Perhaps the best proof of this lies in the change of attitude of Socialists when the force of circumstances makes them abandon theory for practice. A Labour writer says that "it is generally agreed that no class is so free from race or colour prejudice as the working class,"[3] but while this is perhaps true of those living in Great Britain, who experience no competition from coloured workers, he admits that in South Africa the Labour Party does not live up to these principles.[4] Another writer points out that in South Africa white Labour insists on the colour-bar,[5] and another that the policy of the South African Labour Party exemplifies the rankest apostasy from every principle of honest socialism.[6] In the United States there is persistent opposition on the part of white Labour Unions to Negro competition,[7] and it is said that white Labour has not hesitated to murder Negroes in order to terrorise and eliminate them from competition.[8] A Communist writer admits that white Labour in America has been unfair to the coloured worker in the past, but attributes this to the results of capitalist exploitation![9] We have already seen that greater hostility is shown towards Negroes by 'Poor Whites' than by whites of better position, and these white workers prefer to join with white capitalists against their coloured fellow-workers.[10] Even in Great Britain the Labour Unions abandoned their theories when faced by the compeition of coloured seamen at the time of the shipping depression, and Cardiff

---

[1] *Alien Americans* (1936), by B. Schrieke, pp. 10–14.

[2] *The Clash of Colour* (1924), by B. Matthews, pp. 54, 107, 121, 122.

[3] *Labour's Way with the Commonwealth* (1935), by George Lansbury; Chapter on the colonies, by C. R. Buxton, p. 96.

[4] *Ibid.*, pp. 104–5.

[5] *The Clash of Colour* (1924), by B. Mathews, p. 70.

[6] *The Duty of Empire* (1935), by Leonard Barnes, p. 286.

[7] The Labour Unions in California were also prominent in the agitation against Chinese and Japanese immigration. See *Alien Americans* (1936), by B. Schrieke, pp. 26, 28.

[8] *Culture in the South* (1934), edited by W. T. Couch, p. 457.

[9] *The Negro Question in the United States* (1936), by J. S. Allen, p. 16.

[10] *The Colour Problems of South Africa* (1934), by E. H. Brookes, p. 29.

CONCLUSION

has been the scene of discrimination based on colour which was as bad as anything that South Africa could show.[1]

It seems probable that race and colour prejudice must always have existed to some degree, being no more than the original family and tribal instinct which binds together those with similar interests in a defensive or offensive alliance against strangers. As one tribe, or collection of tribes, grew stronger and overcame others the tendency would be to look down upon the vanquished, and, as the stronger tribe became more civilised, to regard weaker and less cultured peoples as barbarians. England itself has seen repeated examples of this, and the experiences of their ancestors should make Englishmen more sympathetic to the present position of the Negroes. The Roman soldiers and administrators despised the ancient Britons, and probably thought them incapable of any advance in civilisation.[2] The Romanised and comparatively civilised Britons of later days were despised by the Danes and Saxons who so easily overcame them. The Saxons were in their turn despised by their Norman conquerors, who for many years excluded them from high office either in church or state. However this may be, we know that through a combination of circumstances and geographical environment, the 'white' tribes of north-western Europe became stronger than all others,[3] and probably because colour provided an easy and obvious mark of distinction, the whites adopted it as the criterion.[4] At a slightly later date, in order to justify the aggression of the stronger 'white' nations, the theory of racial inferiority was advanced, and was greatly fortified by the fact that the whites were Christians while the coloured races were infidels as well as barbarians. The cause of this aggression was economic. To increase their own wealth the European nations

[1] See *The Keys* (official organ of the League of Coloured Peoples), of October–December 1935, p. 20.

[2] The cruelties of Druidical worship were suppressed, in the same way as human sacrifice has been almost stopped in British African colonies, although in the former case it may have been the political strength of Druidism, rather than its savagery, which caused Roman action. See, on this point, *The History of the Decline and Fall of the Roman Empire* (1823 ed.), by E. Gibbon, vol. I, p. 38.

[3] Aristotle remarked that "those who live in cold countries, as the north of Europe, are full of courage, but wanting in understanding and the arts"! *Politics*, Book VII, Chapter VII.

[4] Sir Arthur Keith, comparing human tribes to football teams, has suggested that the differing skin colours are like the jerseys of the players. See *The Place of Prejudice in Modern Civilisation* (1931), p. 35.

seized the rich lands occupied by the coloured races, and enslaved Negroes to provide labour for these newly-acquired lands. When the ethics of slavery were questioned the theory was launched of the specific distinctness of the Negro race, and of its general inferiority to the whites. We have seen that the theory of distinctness was seriously maintained up to comparatively modern times.

It was almost inevitable that the stronger races should look with disdain on those whom they had conquered and enslaved, and, as the centuries passed, a dark skin came to be considered as a mark of inferiority, and as depriving its owner of human rights. At the beginning of the nineteenth century, however, there was a revulsion of feeling which led to the outlawry of the slave trade and the abolition of slavery in the British colonies and elsewhere though in the United States, Cuba and Brazil slavery still continued. It was, unfortunately, just at this time, when the future of the black races looked more hopeful than ever before, that the writings of DeGobineau, Darwin and Mendel emphasised the importance of natural selection and heredity, and revived the slowly dying theories of racial superiority and inferiority. It is perhaps not a coincidence that within a generation Africa was partitioned between the European Powers, in order that the blessings of civilisation might be imparted to the 'inferior' inhabitants of that continent.

The conquest of America, the slave trade, and the partition of Africa, were all undertaken for economic reasons, to increase the trade and wealth of the 'white' nations. As the Negroes progressed, however, under white tutelage, and the fact that they did so progress cannot be denied, there began an insistent clamour from them for some share in the growing wealth. Negroes and the men of other coloured races became dangerous competitors in the labour market, and claimed the social and material advantages which had previously been the monopoly of the whites. The white conscience had gradually been growing more tender, and it was therefore necessary to conceal the stark economic materialism, which refused to yield to the coloured peoples any share of the privileged position held by the whites, under a cloak of prejudice. This seems to be the true explanation of the revival of 'Nordic' race-consciousness, of the desire for the purity of the race, and of the sexual apprehension which prompts the citizen of the United States to kill black men on the mere suspicion of transgression.

CONCLUSION

It is said that for the colour problem there is no solution,[1] and if the problem is really one of colour this may be true. I do not believe, however, that colour prejudice is entirely natural and inherent, but that it is to some extent a cultivated growth based on economic fallacies. The consensus of scientific opinion appears to be that the Negro is not lacking, or markedly inferior, in mind or capacity for improvement;[2] that his retarded development was originally the outcome of his environment,[3] and, later, the outcome of the treatment he received from the more advanced races; and that he is capable of full development when conditions render such development possible.[4] However much the white races may despise those of a different colour and affect to regard them as inferior, they cannot argue away the fact that they are closely related,[5] and that rich men are not necessarily better men than their poor relations. It is not the equality of endowment but the equality of right which has to be considered,[6] and a civilisation which denies such equality of right to men of a certain colour, *because of that colour*, is not logical and cannot be enduring.

It is impossible, as has been admitted in an early chapter, to remove at once all the disabilities under which Negroes, in various parts of the world, are suffering to-day. It should be possible, however, without expense and without much trouble, to remove one of the most potent causes of racial discord, by an immediate change in our attitude to those of coloured blood. It is not suggested that Englishmen should abandon their traditional reserve (even if they were capable of doing so) and make violent demonstrations of brotherly love; such demonstrations would certainly be misunderstood and quite unwelcome to the Negroes. But it is suggested that we should avoid, in manner, speech and writing, an attitude of disdain for everyone who does not possess a white skin, and that we should show to such people a simple courtesy.[7]

---

[1] *America Comes of Age* (1927), by A. Siegfried, p. 108.
[2] See *Population Problems* (1923), by E. B. Reuter, p. 275.
[3] *Man, Past and Present*, by A. H. Keane (1920 ed.), p. 17.
[4] *Sex and Culture* (1934), by J. D. Unwin, p. 101.
[5] *Social Morality* (1869), by F. D. Maurice, p. 88.
[6] *The Elements of Social Justice* (1922), by L. T. Hobhouse, pp. 94-5.
[7] "Discourtesy to Africans does an immense amount of harm. In the first place, it creates resentment and therefore hinders, and may make impossible, that co-operation of black and white upon which so much may depend. Secondly, it diminishes the prestige of the white race. To Africans good manners are of primary importance.

Such courtesy would be in accordance with our professed Christian belief, and would be a better hall-mark of civilisation and culture than any material progress that we may have made. I have every confidence that it would be appreciated and reciprocated, and I cannot see any possible evil result that could ensue.

White men and women of different nations, religions and classes, are, as a rule, mutually courteous one to another without necessarily mixing socially. Jew and Gentile live as neighbours in England and other civilised lands without intermarrying. Catholics and Protestants can, in most countries, remain on the best of terms though differing from one another in religion. I see no reason why black men and white men should not live as fellow-citizens on terms of mutual respect and consideration, without either race sacrificing its identity. It is, after all, natural for those with common interests to seek one another's companionship rather than the companionship of those whose interests are different,[1] but there is nothing wrong in this,[2] and I do not believe that Negroes in tropical countries are desirous of forcing their way into the social life of the white residents.[3] What they resent, and with some reason, is their exclusion on account of their colour, especially when they see white men of inferior education and culture admitted without question. They would understand readily enough a distinction based on culture rather than on colour.

The present unhappy condition of affairs is, however, not entirely the fault of the white races. It can be made better, as I have tried to show, by an improvement in the manners of white people. But if any material and lasting improvement is to be accomplished it must be with the co-operation of the Negroes,[4] who must endeavour

... The absence of good manners is a sign of ill-breeding. It would be a shock to some of us to learn how greatly discourtesy lowers the European in the African's estimation." *Colour Conflict: Race Relations in Africa* (1943), by G. W. Broomfield, General Secretary of the Universities' Mission to Central Africa, p. 131.

[1] See *Christianity and the Race Problem* (1924), by J. H. Oldham (7th ed.), pp. 161-2.

[2] Mr. Oldham points out that such "social separateness does not differ from that which may be found between different social groups in England." *Ibid.*, p. 162.

[3] "All that the African desires is sympathetic co-operation with the European, which includes no ambition to mix in his social life." *Dark Subjects* (1939), by H. L. Ward Price, p. 272.

[4] Attention has been drawn to the fact that at the Congress of representatives of Coloured Peoples held at Manchester in 1946, "emotion, rather than reason, was the order of the day and one listened in vain for a constructive suggestion as to how problems of the colonies should be met. I should have thought myself that the main

CONCLUSION

to forget the past and credit their white neighbours with good intentions, when they give evidence of such intentions. The old brooding on past injuries, the suspicious attitude to white advances, and the bitter and sometimes outspoken hatred of everything white, must be controlled, if a true spirit of friendship and respect is to be established between the races. Above all, the Negroes must cultivate an intellectual honesty which will make them realise that all the handicaps under which their race labours are not due to the machinations of others[1] but in a very large measure to their own shortcomings. They must also develop that other form of honesty which will ensure that they can be trusted to do good work or hold responsible positions without the constant need of supervision, and they must build up a public opinion, and a moral courage, which will enable them to oppose the evil-doers—even those of their own race—without fear or favour.

purpose of the conference was to enlist the support of the world to the cause of the African, but it seemed to me that many of the speeches would antagonise even sympathetic listeners." *The West African Review* of March 1946, p. 265.

[1] "Let us cease to believe in the bogey that others are keeping us down and that we have to look to others for our liberation. Our liberation will depend largely upon ourselves." Dr. H. Moody, in *The News Letter* of the League of Coloured Peoples for May 1946. As a matter of fact, "the indigenous exploiter has often fewer scruples than his prototype in western countries," see essay by Sir Drummond Shields, in *Fabian Colonial Essays* (1945), p. 109. Dr. W. R. Miller has pointed out that the Africans "have been supine, callous and indifferent to the things which are a blot on their own country, and they should not think that by vociferous condemnation of European officials they can absolve their consciences from ignorance or neglect of such pressing needs." He asks also "Where are the scholarships for promising but needy African boys contributed or bequeathed by wealthy Africans?" *Have we failed in Nigeria?* (1947), pp. 129, 22.

INDEX TO AUTHORS, PERSONS AND PUBLICATIONS

(For General Index see page 156)

African Morning Post, 48
Agbake, J., 144
Agbebi, M., 62, 100, 111
Aggrey, J. E. K., 138
Alakija, O. A., 35
Allen, J. D., 141
Allen, J. S., 146
American Journal of Sociology, 121
American Mercury, The, 141
Angelino, A. D. A. DeKat, 39, 50, 92, 128, 142
Anti-Slavery Reporter, 70
Aristotle, 147
Association of West African Merchants, 93, 140
Aykroyd, W. R., 132.

Baden-Powell, Lord, 62
Bailey, T. P., 76
Baldwin, Lord, 65
Balfour, A., 130
Balfour, Lord, 52
Balogun, O., 82
Barnes, L., 10, 16, 17, 26, 30, 33, 51, 71, 132, 146
Batten, T. R., 48
Beaconsfield, Lord, 33
Bell, G. O., 66
Bell, Sir H., 84
Benedict, R., 101
Bernard, L. L. and J. S., 114
Blunt, Sir W. S., 34
Bosman, W., 21
Bourdillon, Sir B., 17, 48, 95, 133, 137
Brearley, H. C., 53, 54
Brigham, Professor, 87
British Medical Journal, 102
Brogan, D. W., 36, 55
Brookes, E. H., 34, 36, 57, 58, 59, 61, 124, 145, 146
Broomfield, G. W., 49, 118, 150
Brown, I. C., 61, 67, 81, 123
Browning, E. B., 81
Bryant, A. T., 89, 105
Bryce, Lord, 18, 20, 29, 38, 74, 91, 109, 110, 116, 120
Buell, R. L., 30
Burgess, J. W., 24
Burnett, Et., 132
Buxton, C. R., 25, 50, 146

Caines, J. E., 52
Cameron, Sir D. C., 11, 133
Campbell, T. M., 48
Carmer, C., 55
Carr, H., 12, 36, 66
Carroll, C., 22, 68
Carr-Saunders, A. M., 32, 105
Caseley-Hayford, A., 17
Cason, C. E., 73
Census of India, 20
Chamberlain, H. S., 24, 76
Churchill, W. S., 10
Cicero, 5
Clare, L. A., 26
Clark, W. E. Le G., 24
Clemenceau, G., 10
Collins, A., 24
Commission on Closer Union in East Africa, 79, 107
Commission on Trinidad, 142
Commission on West Indies, 142
Confucius, 5
Cook, A. N., 123
Cortez, 21
Couch, W. T., 53, 54, 73, 82, 124, 141, 146
Coupland, R., 15, 41
Craige, J. H., 43
Crisis, The, 41, 138
Crocker, W. R., 11
Cromer, Earl of, 9, 11, 18, 21, 118
Cullen, C., 28, 141
Cunard, N., 17, 35, 43, 66, 69, 72, 85, 96, 122, 123, 124, 137, 138, 139, 140, 141, 144
Curtis, L., 57

Daily Express, The, 65
Darwin, C., 23, 98, 100, 113, 148
Das, Mrs. S., 33, 118
Davenport, C. B., 87, 102
Davis, J., 48
DeGobineau, Count, 24, 77, 148
Delano, I. O., 64
DePriest, Mrs., 69
Dibelius, W., 39, 55
Dingwall, E. J., 66
Disraeli, B., 33
Douglass, F., 137
Dover, C., 40, 106

INDEX TO AUTHORS, PERSONS AND PUBLICATIONS

Driberg, J. H., 19, 33
DuBois, W. E. B., 15, 41, 67, 68, 81, 86, 91, 138
Du Bos, Abbé, 24
Dumas, A., 80
Durham, Earl of, 43

East African Medical Journal, 101
East, E. M., 42
Economist, The, 54, 58
Edwards, B., 49, 72, 123
Elizabeth, Queen, 46
Elliot-Smith, Sir G., 121
Ellis, Sir A. B., 36
Ellis, Havelock, 89
Embree, E. R., 34, 122
Encyclopædia Britannica, 19, 24, 53, 64, 83, 86, 88, 101, 104, 130
Eugenics, Review, The, 88, 89, 105, 121
Evans, I. L., 55, 73
Evans, Sir M. S., 117
Eybers, G. W., 55

Fabian Society, 151
Farson, N., 9
Fouillee, A., 32
Freeman, E. A., 52
Freyre, G., 114
Friends of Europe Publications, 76

Gallagher, B. G., 62, 67
Gandhi, M., 116
Garvey, M., 41, 68
Genesis, 19
Gibbon, E., 79, 81, 147
Gide, A., 73
Gilbert, Sir H., 46
Ginsberg, M., 88, 89, 103, 121, 125, 145
Gordon, E., 137, 138, 141
Gordon, H. L., 88, 101
Gorer, G., 30, 34, 49, 112, 126, 143
Grant, M., 24, 75, 83, 118
Graves, J. T., 108
Green, J. R., 119
Greene, G., 84
Gregorovius, F., 50
Gregory, J. W., 17, 20, 52, 53, 61, 66, 79, 87, 90, 98, 116, 120, 121, 129

Haddon, A. C., 22, 97, 98, 99, 100, 119, 120
Hailey, Lord, 10, 34, 51, 91, 106, 132
Haldane, J. B. S., 102
Hamilton, A., 81
Hamilton, Mrs. G. W., 50
Hamilton, M. A., 39, 55

Hannibal, 81, 83
Harlech, Lord, 29
Harragin, Sir W., 93
Harris, Sir J. H., 16, 29
Hastings, A. C. G., 87
Hauser, O., 76
Hauswirth, F., 33, 118
Headlam, C., 56
Henson, R. A., 142
Heywood, D., 141
Hippocrates, 130
Hitler, A., 22, 39, 68, 69, 76
Hobhouse, L. T., 73, 149
Hoernlé, R. F. A., 62, 89, 98, 117
Hogben, L., 106
Hooton, E. A., 88, 127
Hoover, Mrs., 69
Hotz, H., 24, 77
Hughes, L., 69
Huntington, E., 129
Hurston, Z., 36, 83, 123
Hutt, W. H., 57, 122
Huxley, J., 22, 102, 119, 120

Ibn Batuta, 37, 111, 135

Jabavu, D. D. T., 70
James, C. L. R., 91, 123
Jannath, H., 122
Johnson, C. S., 54, 69, 72, 76, 91, 94, 103, 111, 113, 119, 139, 141, 143
Johnson, Jack, 39
Johnson, J. W., 36, 66, 114, 124, 140, 141
Johnston, Sir H. H., 83, 104, 151
Jones, W. H. S., 130
Journal of Anatomy, 103
Journal of Philosophic Studies, 16, 56, 89, 110, 121, 125, 145

Keane, A. H., 77, 79, 81, 98, 121, 149
Keith, Sir A., 56, 69, 82, 99, 100, 101, 102, 109, 147
Keys, The, 65, 66, 70, 122, 145, 147
Kidd, B., 79
Klineberg, Dr., 89

Lansbury, G., 25, 56, 145, 146
Lawrence, T. E., 29, 34, 35
League of Nations Bulletin, 84, 132
Leakey, L. S. B., 105
Legitime, General, 83
Levy-Bruhl, L., 26
Lewinson, P., 53, 69
Lewis, J. H., 97, 112
Lewis, M. G., 49, 92

153

Lindley, M. F., 46, 47
Lips, J. E., 112
Listener, The, 106
Louis, Joe, 39
Lowe, S., 70
Lugard, Lord, 11, 28, 47, 92, 110

MacCrone, I. D., 18, 55
McDougall, W., 35, 53, 122
Macmillan, W. M., 12, 31, 79, 140
MacMunn, Sir G., 19
Mahabharata, 19
Makin, W. J., 91
Malinowski, B., 106, 111, 113
Manchester Guardian, The, 50, 65
Manetta, F., 86
Manson-Bahr, P. H., 32, 129, 130
Marett, J. R. de la H., 98, 122, 133
Marett, R. R., 86
Markham, V. R., 56
Marson, U. M., 65
Martin, Professor, 103
Marvin, F. S., 20
Mathews, B., 16, 39, 41, 44, 146
Maugham, R. C. F., 104
Maurice, F. D., 149
Maxwell, J. R., 96, 112, 113, 139
Mendel, G. C., 23, 148
Miles, C. A., 132
Miller, D. H., 40, 52
Miller, W. R., 92, 139, 151
Milner, Lord, 56
Mjoen, J. A., 120
Molema, S. M., 43, 67, 72, 80, 111, 140
Moody, H., 26, 36, 65, 138, 140, 143, 151
Moore, F., 19, 52
Morgan, T. H., 97, 107
Moses, 18
Moton, R. R., 5, 35, 36, 38, 49, 60, 62, 63, 65, 66, 67, 73, 81, 84, 109, 115, 117, 143
Mumford, W. B., 10
Muret, M., 41
Murphy, E. G., 61
Mussolini, B., 40, 130
Myrdal, G., 53, 93, 94, 108, 114, 124, 139, 140

Negro Worker, The, 138
New Statesman and Nation, The, 123, 145
New York Times, The, 89
News Letter, 151
Newton, A. P., 96
Nielson, P., 20, 114, 125
Nigerian Daily Times, The, 35, 36, 82, 96
Nigerian Eastern Mail, The, 94
Noel-Baker, P. J., 16

North, W., 130
Northern Nigeria Lands Committee, 50

Oakley, R. R., 11
Odunsi, L., 96
Oldham, J. H., 5, 15, 28, 29, 30, 31, 32, 33, 60, 66, 87, 105, 108, 115, 117, 120, 144, 145, 150
Olivier, Lord, 20, 25, 30, 61, 70, 82, 103, 112, 117, 121, 123, 125
Orde-Browne, G. St. J., 10
Ormsby-Gore, W. G. A., 29
Ovid, 99
Oxford Dictionary, 64, 66

Padmore, G., 123
Park, M., 135
Parliamentary Debates, 89
Perham, M., 11, 57, 140
Pintner, R., 87
Pitkin, W. P., 32, 90, 111, 124, 129, 131
Pitt-Rivers, G. H. L., 16, 44, 84, 90
Pizarro, A., 17, 21
Plomer, W., 139
Poteat, E. M., 54
Prescott, W. H., 17, 19
Price, A. G., 51, 91, 120, 121, 130
Priest, Rev. J., 19, 22, 114, 125
Psychological Review, The, 88
Pushkin, A., 80
Putnam, S., 114
Putnam-Weale, B. L., 43, 79, 119

Quaranta, F., 30, 51

Radhakrishnan, Sir S., 32
Ragatz, L. J., 22, 91
Rand Daily Mail, 58
Reuter, E. B., 67, 69, 80, 81, 82, 119, 121, 122, 124, 136, 149
Rhodes, C., 56
Rice, S., 19, 33
Ritchie, J. F., 104, 134
Roberts, S. H., 69, 116
Robeson, P., 69
Rohrbach, P., 108
Roos, T., 51
Roosevelt, President, 69
Rosenau, M. J., 131
Rosenberg, A., 76
Ross, Sir R., 130
Royal Institute of International Affairs, 15, 30
Royce, J., 125
Rydings, Vice-Consul, 84, 92

Sadler, Sir M., 144
St. Johnston, Sir R., 63

INDEX TO AUTHORS, PERSONS AND PUBLICATIONS

Salmon, C. S., 79, 115
Schapera, I., 57, 62, 70, 89, 98, 117, 122
Schmeling, M., 39
Schrieke, B., 35, 43, 61, 96, 124, 141, 145, 146
Schuyler, G. S., 85, 144
Schweitzer, A., 27, 48, 91
Scot, Dred, 52
Scott, H. H., 130
Seligman, C. G., 79, 89, 105
Shahani, R. G., 32, 33, 34, 60
Shaler, N. S., 110
Sharkey, J., 39
Sharpe, N., 70
Shields, Sir D., 151
Shufeldt, R. W., 68
Siegfried, A., 17, 67, 73, 118, 124, 125, 149
Simon, Lord, 48
Sinclair, W. A., 63
Smith, A., 30
Smith, E. W., 108, 138, 144
Smuts, J. C., 16, 58, 79, 86, 90
Solanke, L., 139
Sourour, M., 118
Spectator, The, 19, 33, 69, 111, 142
Spectator, The (Gold Coast), 140
Spiller, G., 32, 62, 83, 111
Stark, F., 29
Stegerda, M., 87, 102
Stevens, A. H., 19, 52
Stoddard, L., 19, 24, 42, 75, 78, 114, 124
Storrs, Sir R., 28, 34, 73
Swinny, S. H., 20
Swynnerton, C. F. M., 129

Tagore, R., 116
Taylor, G., 51, 84, 118
Temple, C. L., 50
Theal, C. McC., 104

Thompson, T., 21
Thorndike, E. L., 88, 89
Times, The, 28, 30, 58, 62, 64, 67, 70, 84, 87, 101, 102, 105, 108, 135
Townsend, M., 78, 80
Toynbee, A. J., 18, 19, 29, 32, 33, 34, 35, 47, 51, 78, 81, 84, 98, 111, 114, 122
United Empire, 10, 34
Unwin, J. D., 104, 133, 149
Utchay, T. K., 35, 72, 138

Victoria, Queen, 55
Vint, F. W., 103
Virginia Quarterly Review, 108
Von Luschan, F., 111

Wagner, 24
Wall, O. A., 23
Wallas, G., 23, 53, 77, 86, 108, 110
Ward-Price, H. L., 112, 150
Washington, B., 63, 67, 92, 137, 138
Washington, E. D., 92
Watt, Sir T., 108
Weale, B. L. P., 43, 79, 119
Weatherford, W. D., 54, 69, 72, 76, 91, 94, 103, 111, 113, 119, 139, 141, 143
West Africa, 70, 73, 92, 94, 95, 139
West African Review, 151
West Indian Review, The, 82, 103
Westermann, D., 26, 73, 80, 89, 95, 143, 144
Weulersse, J., 28
Whitaker's Almanack, 42
Whitehead, A. N., 128
Williamson, J. A., 57
Wilson, President, 40
Wrong, M., 48
Wyndham, H. A., 10, 30, 52, 56, 67, 78, 83

GENERAL INDEX

Abuse not argument, 43
Abyssinia, 30, 51, 83
  and Italy, 30, 39, 51, 83
  inhabitants not Negro, 40, 82, 83
Achimota College, 89, 138
Africa, Chiefs in, 49, 139
  Christianity in, 26, 34, 35, 54
  difficulty of access, 127
  disease in, 129
  education in, 27
  for the Africans, 40
  land in, 50
  partition of, 148
  political agitation in, 44
  problem in, 15
  slavery in, 21, 26
  treaties with Chiefs in, 47, 50
  white control of, 25
African, effect of cinema on, 39
  in Great Britain, 17
Ainu, 33, 101
Akassa, 83
Alpine Race, 24
Amanzimtoti Institute, 57
America, colour of aborigines, 99
  discovery of, 20, 46
  slavery in, 22, 148
  white control of, 46 (see also United States)
American Revolution, cause of, 71
Amorites and Jews, 18
Anglo-Indian, use of word, 64
Anglo-Saxons, prejudice amongst, 29
Ankylostomiasis, see Hook-worm
Anopholes Mosquito, 13
Antigua, 63
Ape, relationship to, 98, 101
  use of word, 22, 68, 76
Arabs and miscegenation, 35, 121
  numerals derived from, 128
  prejudice amongst, 34
Argentine, 99
Art, Negro, 79, 82, 128, 144
Aryans, 19, 24, 77 (see also Nordic)
Asia, problem in, 15
Asiatics in South Africa, 56
  superior to Negroes, 77
Association of West African Merchants, 93
Australia, 46, 47, 101, 118
Aztec civilisation, 128

Baboons, 63
Bad manners, see Manners
Bahamas, 30, 57, 129, 144
Ballot, 57
Bantu, 34, 43, 59, 67, 70, 79
Barbados, 22, 30, 56
Barbarians and Roman Empire, 47
Beauty of different races, 112–14
Bell tolling, 63
Bengal, 130
Benin, 49, 79
Berlin Conference, 47
Bermuda, 56
Bible, The, 47
"Black Caribs," 35
Black colour, associations with, 114–15
"Black Peril," 42
Black Races, 42, 97 (see also Negro)
Black Star Steamship Line, 41
"Blameless Ethiopians," 137
Blood groups, 97
Boers, see Dutch
Boy Scouts in South Africa, 62
Brahmins, prejudice amongst, 33
Brain of Negro, 86, 101–6
  of Women, 102
Brazil, 78, 114, 124, 135, 148
British colonies, 9, 25, 48, 141
  Columbia, 145
  Empire, loyalty of Negroes, 9, 71
  Empire, problem in, 16
  Honduras, 12, 35, 39
  land policy, 46
  law, 10, 94
  officials, 10
  prejudice amongst, 29
  West Africa, see West Africa
  West Indies, see West Indies
Brown Races, 42, 97

California, 35, 131, 145, 146
Canaan, Curse of, 19, 21
Canada, 43, 47, 99
Cannibals, 83, 111
Cardiff, 31, 146
Caribs, 35
Carnegie Corporation, 73
Carthaginians, 81
Cassava, 132
Caste abolished by Islam, 35
  analogy with United States, 20

156

GENERAL INDEX

Caste in India, 19, 20, 32, 33
  in Peru, 18
Catholics, 26, 47, 150
Caucasians, 42, 97, 98, 113
Central America, 120, 128
Ceylon, malaria in, 130
Chartered Company (Niger), 47
Chiefs, leadership of, 49, 139
Children, Negro, 103-4
  of inter-racial marriage, 119-21
  without prejudice, 110
China, 33, 37, 64
"Chinaman," use of word, 64
Chinese and miscegenation, 118
  discrimination against, 61
  in California, 61, 146
  in West Indies, 91
  nurses, 110
  prejudice amongst, 33
  ugliness, 112
  war, 33
"Chink," use of word, 64
Christ claimed as a Nordic, 76
Christianity and discrimination, 18, 34, 42, 47, 67, 75
  and land tenure, 47
  and lynchings, 54
  and slave trade, 21
  in South Africa, 34, 55
  Nordic view of, 76
  spread by whites, 26, 50
  valued by Negroes, 50 (*see also* Missionaries, Religion)
Churches in Africa, 34
Cinchona Bark, 131
Cinema, effect of, 39
Civil War in United States, 125
Climate, affects colour, 98, 100
  and genius, 24
  changes in, 129
  effect on Negro, 32, 89, 129
  effect on whites, 32, 50, 129
  in Kenya, 51
  in West Africa, 50, 51
  of tropics, 51, 128, 129
Clubs, 71, 139
Codrington College, 22
Colonial Administration, 10, 45
Colonial Office, 48
Colour, a handicap, 114, 122
  adopted as criterion, 18, 148
  and race, 42, 97
  associations with, 114
  Bar Act, 57
  causes repulsion, 116
  dependent on climate, 98

Colour in New World, 99
  of early man, 98, 100
  of Negro, 97
  prejudice, *see* Prejudice
Coloured Man, use of term, 66
Communism and the Negro, 123-4
Concubinage, 117
Conference at Fort Hare, 58
Congo, 78
Constitution of Florida, 119
  of South Africa, 55
  of United States, 45
Coon, use of word, 63, 66
Co-operation, Negro lack of, 137
"Cornerstone Speech," 19, 52
Costa Rica, 120
Courtesy and civilisation, 150
Covenant of League of Nations, 40
Cranial capacity, *see* Brain
Creole, 35
Cromagnon Man, 98
Crown Colony Government, 30
Cuba, 148
Culture and colour, 150

Dago, use of word, 64
Dahomey, 49
Dakar, 34
Dampness of tropics, 32, 128, 129, 134
Danes in England, 147
Darky, use of word, 66
Declaration of Independence, 52
Delegoa Bay, 47
Detroit, 31
Devil assumed to be black, 115
Diet, *see* Food
Discrimination justified, 61, 75
Disease, 129
Druids, 147
Dutch, against miscegenation, 117
  in Japan, 33
  prejudice amongst, 18, 30, 55-9
  Reformed Church, 114

East Africa, *see* Kenya
East Indian, use of term, 64
East Indies, prejudice in, 30
Economic reason for prejudice, 145-7
Economic rivalry, 17, 31, 44, 72
Educated Negroes, 10-11, 29, 44, 94, 129, 137, 140, 143
Education desired, 27
  in Africa, 27
  of Negroes, 82, 105

157

Egypt and Negro culture, 81
  decline due to miscegenation, 121
  for the Egyptians, 40
Egyptians, 34, 40, 118
El Salvador, 120
Emancipation, 30
England, see Great Britain
English, see British
Environment, importance of, 75, 127, 134, 149
Eskimo, 102
Ethiopia, see Abyssinia
Ethiopian, "Blameless," 137
  can change his skin, 98
  colour of, 99
  woman and Moses, 19
Eugenics Society, 102
Eurasian, 64
European government in tropics, 47–51
  in South Africa, 56
  posts, 71, 95
  settlers in tropics, 51
  women, 28, 29
Ewe tribe, 48
Eyes of whites, 111, 113

Fairness desired by Hindus, 33
  desired by Negroes, 113
Fantees, 139
Fascists, 29
Fear of witchcraft, 95
Feringhi, 64
Films, see Cinema
Florida constitution, 119
Food, effect of different, 98
  in tropics, 132, 133
"Foreign Devils," 33
Fort Hare Conference, 58
Franchise for Negroes, 56
French, 47
  colonial administration, 10, 49
  officials, 10
  prejudice amongst, 29, 30

Gaiour, 64
Gentile and Jew, 33, 150
Gentleman, use of word, 65
Germany, 29, 39, 108
God and the Nordics, 76
  assumed to be white, 115
Gold Coast, 21, 31, 48, 71, 93, 131, 140
Great Britain, prejudice in, 17, 70, 146
  Romans in, 147
"Great Race," 24, 75
Great War, see War
Greeks, 18, 130

Grievances of Negroes, 44
Grondwet, 55
Guatemala, 120
Guiana, 78

Hair of different races, 97, 98, 101
  straightening, 113
Hairy Ainu, 33, 101
Haiti, 43, 78, 83
Half-caste, see Mulatto
Ham, curse of, 19, 21
Harlem, 36, 40
Hastings, Battle of, 17
Hatred for whites, 44, 62, 141, 142
Heaven, segregation in, 114
Hebrews, see Jews
Help, use of word, 64
Heredity, 23, 75, 148
Hindus, 19, 20, 33, 91, 118
Hittites and Jews, 18
Honduras, 12, 35, 39, 120
Hook-worm, 130–2
Hotel, coloured persons excluded, 61, 70, 71
Hottentots, 76
House of Assembly, 30, 56
House of Commons, 90
Humidity, see Dampness
Humour of Negro, 143

Illegitimacy, 121
Illinois, 52
"Immorality" Act, 51
Inconsistency of arguments, 125
India, caste in, 19, 20, 33
  malaria in, 130
  use of words "native," etc., in, 61, 64
Indian (Red), see Red Indian
Indians against miscegenation, 116, 118
  as nurses, 110
  despise Egyptians, 34
  disliked by Arabs, 34
  in Great Britain, 17
  in South Africa, 70
  not all the same class, 60
  prejudice amongst, 33, 34
Indirect Administration, 11, 49
Inferiority complex, 39, 43, 64, 95, 140
Ingratitude of Negro, 26, 27
Insect-borne diseases, 129
Insults to Negroes, 17, 44, 45, 60–8
Intellect, see Brain of Negro
Intelligence tests, 87–9
Interbreeding, see Miscegenation
International law and primitives, 46
Ireland, law against miscegenation, 119

GENERAL INDEX

Islam, *see* Muslims
Israelites, *see* Jews
Italians and Abyssinia, 30, 39, 40, 51, 82
 prejudice amongst, 29
Italy, 83, 130

Jamaica, 41, 87
 prejudice in, 30, 72, 101, 123
Jamboree of Boy Scouts, 62
Janissaries, 35
Japan and Peace Treaty, 40
 and United States, 40
Japanese, discrimination against, 35, 61, 146
 prejudice amongst, 33
 revulsion from whites, 111, 113
 Russian war, 38
 sympathy for Abyssinia, 40
Jealousy of Negro, 95, 137, 139
Jebusites and Jews, 18
Jekri Tribe, 36
Jersey City, 40
Jew and other races, 18, 33, 36, 140, 150
 Christ said not to be a, 76
 Nordic attitude to, 76
 prejudice amongst, 18, 33
 religion derived from, 128
"Jim Crow" cars, 61, 62
Journalism, Negro, 43, 141-3

Kenya, Brain of natives of, 101-3
 lands, 46, 51
 problem in, 25
Kru tribe, 92

Labour Party and colonies, 25
 and prejudice, 57, 146
Lagos, 36, 71, 82
Lagos Dining Club, 31
Land tenure, 46, 50, 90
Laws against miscegenation, 20, 30, 52, 119
Lawyers, Negro, 94
Laziness of Negro, 89-90
"Lazy Man's Disease," 131
League of Coloured Peoples, 36, 63, 65, 151
 of Nations, 40
Legal discrimination, 44, 45, 51, 52, 59, 61
Liberia, 48, 52, 64, 84, 85, 92
Libya, 99
Liquor in Africa, 21
Living, standard of, 145
Loyalty, 9, 71, 144
Lynching, 53-5, 125, 135

Makerere, 48
Malaria, 130, 131
Malaya, Chiefs of, 49
Malayan race, numbers of, 42
Manchester, 150
Manners of Negroes, 37, 43, 63, 141, 144
Manners of whites, 44, 60, 72, 141, 149
Marriage, restrictions on, 20, 52, 117, 119
 (*see also* Miscegenation)
Maryland and miscegenation, 119
Matabele, 49, 125
Maya civilisation, 128
Mean Whites, *see* Poor Whites
Mediterranean race, 24, 98
Melanesians, 113
Mental effect of climate, 32
Mentality, primitive, 26
Mestizo, 22
Mexico, 21, 47
Miasma, 131
Mineral deficiency, 133
Mines and Works Act, 57
Miscegenation, 22, 23, 67
 causes deterioration, 35, 81, 119, 121, 122
 disliked by all, 116
 legal sanctions against, 20, 30, 51, 119
Missionaries, prejudice amongst, 12, 34, 35
Missions, support of, 26 (*see also* Christianity and Religion)
Missouri, 52
Mixed marriages unsuccessful, 119, 120
Mongolians, 42, 97, 98, 118
Monogamy and social energy, 133
Monrovia, 48
Moors, 133
Mosquitoes, 127, 129, 130
"Mr." and "Mrs.," omission of, 66
Muhammadans, *see* Muslims
Mulattoes, 22, 119-25
 superior to Negroes, 123-5
Music and the Negro, 135, 144
Muslims and Hindus, 33
 and caste, 35
 decline due to miscegenation, 122
 discrimination amongst, 35
Muslims in the Empire, 9
Mustee, 22

N (capital N for Negro), 67
National Association for advancement of Coloured Peoples, 41
Nationalism, 15, 20
Native Administration, 11, 49
 bureaucrats, 49

159

Native courts, 71
use of word, 60, 64
Neanderthal Man, 102, 106
Negress, use of word, 66
"Negro Anthology" reviewed, 123
Negro, achievements claimed, 81, 82
  affected by climate, 32, 89, 129
  aggressive manner of, 96
  alien in United States, 69
  and Islam, 42
  and polygamy, 133
  art, 79, 82, 128, 144
  at Olympic Games, 69
  attitude to miscegenation, 116
  backward, 86
  bad master, 49
  beauty, 112–14
  bitterness, 41
  boastful, 96
  boisterous, 63
  bombastic, 95
  bored with routine, 90
  boxers, 86, 101–6
  brain, 90
  capable of improvement, 149
  carelessness of, 31
  cautious, 38
  childlike, 87
  children, 103–4
  civilisation, claim to, 81
  claims to achievement, 81–2
  classes of, 63
  colleges, 124
  colour of, 97
  communism and the, 123–4
  contempt for the whites, 37
  crossing with, *see* Miscegenation
  dancing, 126
  desire for fairness, 113–14
  diet of the, 130–2
  different classes of, 63
  dirty, 112
  discontent, 38, 43
  discrimination, 35–7, 123–4
  dishonest, 91–4
  distrusts his leaders, 41, 137–9
  doctors, 94
  dress of, 95
  drinking, 92
  early description of, 21
  economically helpless, 135
  educated, *see* Educated Negro
  education, 82, 105
  effect of weaning on, 134
  failings, 21, 90–92
  faithful, 144

Negro fatalism, 27
  good-natured, 135
  governments, 83–5
  grievances, 44, 60
  hair of, 97, 98
  hatred of whites, see Hatred
  his own enemy, 139
  honesty needed, 151
  humour of, 143
  imitative, 143
  improvident, 90, 92
  imprudent, 43, 141
  inefficient, 90
  in Egypt, 81
  in "European Posts," 71, 95
  inferiority complex, 39, 43, 64, 95, 140
  inferiority of, 12, 77–8
  in South Africa, 70
  instability, 91
  insults to, 17, 44, 60–3, 68
  in United States, 11, 53, 67–9, 84, 87, 89, 141
  in West Indies, 82, 92
  irresponsible, 92–3
  jealous of one another, 95, 137, 139
  journalism, 43, 141–3
  judges, 94
  kindness, 135
  lack of achievement, 77–82, 134
  lack of character, 92
  lack of continuity, 90
  lack of co-operation, 137
  lack of forethought, 91
  lack of moral courage, 93
  lack of opportunity, 127
  lack of self-respect, 91
  lawyers, 94
  lazy, 89–90
  leaders, 15, 43, 139
  leaders criticised, 41, 137–9
  like talking, 96
  long enslaved, 38
  loud talking of, 96
  love of justice, 135
  loyalty, 9, 71, 144
  lying, 91
  magistrates, 94
  manners, 37, 43, 63, 141, 144
  memory, 89
  musical, 135, 144
  newspapers, 43, 72, 141–43
  noisy, 112
  not all alike, 63
  not blameless, 137
  not contented, 38, 43
  not inherently inferior, 12, 127, 149

GENERAL INDEX

Negro novels, 141
number of race, 42
nurses, 62, 70, 110
obsessed on colour, 140–1
officials, 49
on vehicles, 61, 70
original habitat of, 127
over-sensitive, 61
patient, 135
poetry, 141
politically helpless, 135
polygamous, 133
poverty of, 59, 133
prejudices of, 35–7
progressing, 82
puberty of, 103–5
qualities of, 143–4
race-consciousness, 38
race, numbers of, 42
religious, 144
resents criticism, 44
resents White attitude, 60
retrograde, 83
revulsion from Whites, 111
said to be an ape, 22, 68, 76
said to be different species, 22
said to be not human, 22
sculpture, 144
seamen, 31
secretive, 38
seldom appointed Judge, 94
seldom black, 97
servants, 61, 69, 93, 104, 135, 144
sexuality, 91, 104–5, 125, 126
shiftlessness, 91
slavery, effect of, 26, 67, 78, 91, 121, 135
social disadvantages of, 60
soldiers, 135, 144
spelt with small "n," 67
stationary, 83
students, 94
superstitious, 26, 27, 91, 95
suspicious, 12, 13, 61, 94, 141
sympathetic to wrongdoers, 93–4
truculence, 49
ugliness, 112
undependable, 90
ungrateful, 26, 27
unstable, 90
untidy, 112
use of word, 66
vanity, 135 (*see also* African)
work slipshod, 90
Negrophile, 13
Negrophobia, 13, 145

Neurasthenia, 129
"New Brain," 101
Newspapers, Negro, 43, 72, 141–43
New York, 39
Nicaragua, 120
Niger Company, 47
Nigeria, 11, 12, 31, 47, 50, 70, 83, 123
Nigger-lover, 43
Nigger Minstrels, 65
Nigger, use of word, 65, 69, 76
Nile, 127
Nilotic civilisation, 81
Nordic attitude to religion, 75, 114
  Christ said to be a, 76
  School, 9, 24, 37, 77, 78, 100, 108
  theory, 17, 75–7, 83, 114
Normans and English, 17, 147
Northern Nigeria Lands Committee, 50
Nose, differences in, 100, 110, 113
Nurses, training of, 70
Nutrition, 132, 134

Obeah, 95
Octoroon, 22
Olympic Games, 69
"Open" Voting, 56

"Pale-face," 33
Paludrine, 131
Panama Canal, 90
Panama Indians, 33
Pan-Arabia, 40
Pan-Islam, 42
Paris, Negroes in, 30
"Passing," 20, 22, 114, 122
Pathfinders in South Africa, 62
Pax Britannica, 49
Peace Conference, 40, 52
People of colour, use of term, 66
Persians, 34
Peru, 17, 19, 21, 47, 128
Phaeton, myth of, 99
Phelps-Stokes Commission, 138
Phoenicians, prejudice amongst, 18
Physical beauty, 112–14
  repulsion, 116
Pigment, *see* Colour
Piltdown Man, 106
Political Darwinism, 77
  Discrimination, 61
Political leaders in Colonies, 44
Polygamy, 133
Poor Whites, 57, 72, 73, 145, 146
Portuguese, 47, 49
  decline due to miscegenation, 121
  in West Indies, 91
  prejudice amongst, 29

Poverty of Negroes, 59, 133
Prejudice always existed, 17, 20, 147
  among ancient peoples, 18
  among Europeans, 29
  among Negroes, 35, 36
  among women, 28, 29
  among working class, 146
  and sex, 110
  exists, 15
  greater in lower classes, 72
  increased by segregation, 62
  increasing, 15, 16, 20
  instinctive, 145
  not among children, 110
  not inevitable, 149
  really economic, 20, 146
  said to be recent, 18
  universal, 32–6
  varies among races, 29, 30
Press, Negro, 43, 141–3
Prestige, 31
Primitive mentality, 26
  peoples, rule of, 9
Problem insoluble, 149
  urgent, 15
Propaganda, 40
Protestants, 47, 150
Puberty, effect of, 103–5
Purity of White race, 148

Quadroon, 22
Quinine, 131
Quintroon, 22

Race consciousness, 38
  number of each, 42
  prejudice, *see* Prejudice
Races from common stock, 98
  in South Africa, 56
Racial repulsion, 109, 110, 115
  riots, 31, 44
  war, 41
Railways, Negroes on, 61, 70
Rainfall in tropics, 133
Rape and lynching, 54
Red Indians, 33, 38, 78, 99, 119
Red Race, numbers of, 42, 97
Religion and caste, 20
  and the Negro, 44
  colour prejudice in, 18, 34, 114, 124
  in Africa, 34
  more important than colour, 18 (*see also* Christianity and Missionaries)
Restaurants, coloured persons excluded, 61
Rhine Army of Occupation, 39

Rhodesia, 125
"Rising Tide of Colour," 17, 31
Roman Catholics, 26, 47, 150
  civilisation, 21, 47, 128
  Empire, overthrown, 130
  Empire, prejudice in, 18, 147
Royal Niger Company, 47
Russo-Japanese War, 38

Sahara desert, 82, 99, 127
Saint Vincent, 35
Salisbury (Southern Rhodesia), 63
Salvador, 120
Sambo, 22
Savannah, Georgia, 19
Saxons in England, 147
Schools for Negroes, 61
Science unable to prove difference, 100
"Scottsboro" case, 53
Seamen, coloured, 31
Secretary of State for the Colonies, 90
Secret ballot, 57
Segregation, 55, 62–71
  in Heaven, 114
Self-determination, 40
Self-government, 48
Semites, numbers of, 42
Semitic origin of alphabet, 128
Servant, Negro, 61, 69, 93, 104, 135, 144
  use of word, 64
Sexual apprehension, 116, 125
  intercourse, *see* Miscegenation
  prejudice, 110, 117
Sexual and mineral deficiency, 133
  and social energy, 133
  of Negroes, 91, 104, 125, 126
Shaking hands, 66
Shine, use of word, 66
Shoes, uses of, 132
Sierra Leone, 36
Skin bleaching, 113
Skulls, 86, 100, 104, 106
Slavery, 49, 72
Slavery and sex, 68, 117, 119
  effect of, 26, 67, 78, 91, 121, 135
  in Africa, 18, 25
  in United States, 52, 53, 78, 135
  in West Indies, 51, 135, 148
  justified, 19, 148
Slave Trade, 18, 24, 148
Sleeping Sickness, 129
Smell of different races, 111
Social equality, 11, 150
  segregation, 45
Socialists, 25, 146
Society for Propagation of Gospel, 22

GENERAL INDEX

Sokoto, 47
Soldiers, Negro, 35, 144
Song of Solomon, 19
South Africa, absence of lynching, 55
and miscegenation, 117, 119
Boy Scouts, 62
Churches in, 34
constitution of, 55
Labour Party in, 146
land in, 46, 51
legal discrimination in, 44, 51
"Passing" in, 122
Poor Whites in, 73
prejudice in, 12, 16, 30, 55-9, 70, 108, 124
Press, 58
problem in, 25
races of, 56
treatment of coloured people in, 66, 70 (*see also* Bantu)
South African Republic, 55
South Carolina, 55
Southern Rhodesia, 63
Southern States of America and miscegenation, 119
Negroes in, 89
treatment of Negroes, 43, 73
Spaniards in America, 17, 47
prejudice amongst, 29
Sphinx, 81
Spices, 132
Spirits, *see* Liquor
Standard of living, 145
Stegomyia mosquito, 129
Sterility of Mulattoes, 22
Street-cars, Negroes on, 61
Student Christian Association, 58
Stupidity caused by dampness, 129
Superstition of Negroes, 26, 27, 91, 95
"Survival of the Fittest," 23, 77
Swaraj, 40
Swimming baths, coloured persons in, 70
Syria, 40, 91

Terceron, 22
Teutons, prejudice amongst, 29
Togoland, 48
Trade spirits, *see* Liquor
Unions, prejudice in, 57
Trains, Negroes on, 61, 70
Trams, Negroes on, 61, 70
"Treason to the Race," 44, 94
Treaties with chiefs, 47, 50
Tribal jealousy, 95
Trinidad, 90, 142
Troops in colonies, 48

Tropical Africa, 127
neurasthenia, 129
Tropics, dampness in, 32, 128, 129, 134
diseases in, 129-32
food in, 132-3
Whites in, 51
Trusteeship Council, 48
Trypanosomiasis, 129
Tsetse fly, 127, 129
Turks, 34, 35, 64
Tuskegee Institute, 34, 63, 69

Uganda, 129
Umayyad Caliphate, 34
"Uncle Tom," 43
Under-nourishment, 132-3
United Nations, 48
United States and caste, 20
and Japan, 40, 146
and miscegenation, 119
Army, mentality in, 87
civil war in, 125
constitution, 45, 59
Labour Unions, 146
legal discrimination, 45, 55, 61
lynching in, 53-5
malaria in, 130-1
Mulattoes in, 123
Negro leaders in, 15, 41
Negro Press in, 141
Negroes at puberty, 105
Negroes in, 11, 53, 67-9, 84, 87, 89, 141
"Passing" in, 122
prejudice in, 12, 17, 36, 73, 123, 146
problem, economic, in, 146
proposal to deport Negroes from, 68
racial riots in, 31, 44
slavery in, 53, 135
Supreme Court, 52
sympathy for Abyssinia in, 40 (*see also* America)
Universal Negro Improvement Association, 41

Vanity of Negro, 135
Varna, 19
Versailles Treaty, 41
Victoria Nyanza, 129
Vitamins, 160
Votes, *see* Franchise and Ballot

Waiting rooms for Negroes, 61
War, 1914-18, 39, 40
"Watch tower" speech, 56
Weaning of children, 134

West Africa, 9, 30, 44, 46, 49, 71, 72, 79, 90, 91, 121
  loyalty of, 9, 71
  sympathy for Abyssinia in, 40
  White control in, 46, 48
West Indies and Christianity, 26
  and miscegenation, 118
  and slave trade, 21
  Chinese in, 91
  discrimination amongst Negroes, 35, 123
  Indians in, 38, 91
  loyalty of, 9
  Mulattoes in, 123–5
  Negroes in, 82, 92
  newspapers in, 142
  Obeah in, 95
  "Passing" in, 122
  political agitation in, 44
  Portuguese in, 91
  prejudice in, 30, 72, 123
  slavery in, 21, 51
  Spaniards in, 47
  sympathy for Abyssinia, 40
  use of words "Native" and "Negro," 64, 66
White colour, associations with, 114, 115
White culture desired, 143
White House, Negroes at, 69
White Indians of Panama, 33
"White Man's Burden," 25
"White Man's Nigger," 43, 94
White Race, achievements of, 21, 25
  affected by tropics, 51
  and drink, 112

White Race and miscegenation, 116
  beauty of, 112
  borrowed from other races, 128
  claim to superiority, 75
  conscience of, 38, 148
  contempt for Negro, 21
  eyes of, 111, 113
  indigestible, 111
  in tropics, 51
  manners of, 44, 45, 60, 72, 73, 149
  numbers of, 42
  outnumbered, 42
  purity of, 45
  ugliness of, 111
White troops in colonies, 48
White women and cinema, 39
  and prejudice, 28, 29
Witchcraft, 95
Women, beauty of, 113
  brains of, 102
  Negro, 66, 67
  votes of, 56
  White, 28, 29, 39
Women's Enfranchisement Act, 57
"Wop," use of word, 64

Yams, 132
Yellow fever, 129
"Yellow Peril," 42
Yellow races, 42, 97
Yoruba, 36, 100

Zimbawe, 79
Zulu, 49, 76